Fiction is obliged to stick to possibilities. Truth isn't.

—MARK TWAIN

Antæus

EDITED BY

DANIEL HALPERN

TANGIER/LONDON/NEW YORK

NO. 63, AUTUMN, 1989

Publisher

DRUE HEINZ

Founding Editor

PAUL BOWLES

Managing Editor

LEE ANN CHEARNEYI

Production Manager

BRUCE SHERWIN

Advertising Manager

LEE SMITH

Contributing Editors

ANDREAS BROWN   STANLEY KUNITZ

JOHN FOWLES   W. S. MERWIN

DONALD HALL   EDOUARD RODITI

JOHN HAWKES   MARK STRAND

Antæus *is published semiannually by The Ecco Press, 26 West 17th Street, New York, N.Y. 10011. Distributed by W. W. Norton & Company, Inc., 500 Fifth Avenue, New York, N.Y. 10110, Ingram Periodicals, 347 Reedwood Drive, Nashville, TN 37217, and B. DeBoer, Inc., 113 East Centre St., Nutley, N.J. 07110. Distributed in England & Europe by W. W. Norton & Company, Inc.*

Contributions and Communications: Antæus
American address: 26 West 17th Street, New York, N.Y. 10011
European address: 42A Hay's Mews, London, W1, England
Four-issue Subscriptions: $30.00. Back issues available—write for a complete listing.

Books from The Ecco Press are available to *Antæus* subscribers at a 10% discount. Please write for a catalogue: The Ecco Press, 26 West 17th Street, New York, N.Y. 10011.

ISSN 0003-5319
Printed by Haddon Craftsmen, Inc.
ISBN 0-88001-226-9
Library of Congress Card Number: 70-612646
Copyright © 1989 by Antæus, *New York, N.Y.*

Cover Painting:
A Girl and Her Duenna *by Bartolome Esteban Murillo, c. 1670.*
By permission of the National Gallery of Art, Washington.
Widener Collection.

*Publication of this magazine has been made possible in part by a grant
from the National Endowment for the Arts.*

Logo: Ahmed Yacoubi

CONTENTS

ESSAYS

JOHN BARTH

"Still Farther South:"
Some Notes on Poe's Pym

In 1838, at the age of thirty, Edgar Allan Poe published his first and only novel: *The Narrative of Arthur Gordon Pym of Nantucket*. Its teenage hero, with a little help from a friend, stows away on a ship outbound from that island and undergoes the adventures summarized in Poe's subtitle:

> COMPRISING THE DETAILS OF A MUTINY AND ATROCIOUS BUTCHERY ON BOARD THE AMERICAN BRIG GRAMPUS, ON HER WAY TO THE SOUTH SEAS, IN THE MONTH OF JUNE, 1827. WITH AN ACCOUNT OF THE RECAPTURE OF THE VESSEL BY THE SURVIVERS [sic]; THEIR SHIPWRECK AND SUBSEQUENT HORRIBLE SUFFERINGS FROM FAMINE; THEIR DELIVERANCE BY MEANS OF THE BRITISH SCHOONER JANE GUY; THE BRIEF CRUISE OF THIS LATTER VESSEL IN THE ANTARCTIC OCEAN; HER CAPTURE, AND THE MASSACRE OF HER CREW AMONG A GROUP OF ISLANDS IN THE EIGHTY-FOURTH PARALLEL OF SOUTHERN LATITUDE; TOGETHER WITH THE INCREDIBLE ADVENTURES AND DISCOVERIES STILL FARTHER SOUTH TO WHICH THAT DISTRESSING CALAMITY GAVE RISE.

Like many a tall tale before and since, *Pym* presents itself as a sober, factual account of an increasingly fantastic voyage, in this instance culminating in the hero's imminent disappearance (in the final sentence of his first-person narrative) into a watery abyss at the South Pole. In a straight-faced preface dated some ten years later ("New York, July, 1838"), "Pym" informs us that "Mr. Poe" has lately published, with his consent, two early installments of his adventures *as fiction*, and that he wishes now to set the record straight; he does not, however, explain how he got from the polar abyss to Richmond (where he claims to have met Poe) and New York. In a similarly straight-faced appendix to the narrative, an anonymous "editor" mentions, also without explanation, "the late sudden and distressing death of Mr. Pym"—immediately after his composing the preface, evidently—and regrets that "the few remaining chapters which were to have completed his narration . . . have been

irrecoverably lost through the accident by which he perished himself."
He informs us further that "the gentleman whose name is mentioned in
the preface"—that is, Mr. Poe—has expressed "his disbelief in the entire
truth of the latter portions of [Pym's] narration."

In short, the fiction that the fiction is factual includes its dismissal,
by its factual author, as fiction.

Such ontological mirror-tricks, a stock in trade of contemporary
"metafiction," did not sit well with *Pym*'s nineteenth- and early twentieth-century readers. "Imaginative bankruptcy," Robert Louis Stevenson said of the novel's ending—acknowledging however that at least Poe
"cheats us with gusto." Henry James, no fan of Poe's in any case,
declared that *Pym*'s "climax fails . . . because it stops short, and stops
short for want of connexions. There *are* no connexions." Others dis-
missed the novel as a hoax, meant to fool unsuspecting readers into
thinking it a factual account of South-Polar misadventure. Poe himself,
having written and published the novel quickly between editorial jobs
in Richmond and Philadelphia, apparently had second thoughts about
its merits.

In our time, however, *The Narrative of Arthur Gordon Pym of Nantucket* has enjoyed considerable and sophisticated critical attention:
enough so that in honor of the sesquicentennial of its publication, Poe
scholars from around the country convened on foggy Nantucket Island
in May 1988 for a three-day conference on that novel, sponsored by The
Pennsylvania State University. What follows is adapted from my remarks to that conference, which I was invited to address not as a high-
tech Pymster but simply as one novelist sizing up another.

My late acquaintance Italo Calvino was once commissioned by the
publishing house of Ricci in Milan to write a short novel involving the
Tarot cards, to accompany a facsimile edition of a medieval Tarot deck
fully annotated by a scholarly tarotologist. Calvino told me that his first
artistic decision in this instance was to purge his imagination altogether
of the cards' traditional significances; to look at those famous icons as
if he knew nothing whatever about them, like an intelligent visitor from
an alien culture. The happy result was his novel *The Castle of Crossed
Destinies*, on the facing pages of Ricci's beautiful volume *I Tarocchi*.

That is the spirit in which (on this conference's commission) I have
lately taken another look at Edgar Poe's only novel, *The Narrative of
Arthur Gordon Pym of Nantucket*. The task of purging my imagination of
150 years of critical commentary on that novel—beginning, I suppose,

with Poe's own remark that it is "a silly book"—was made immeasurably easier for me by the circumstance that I have read virtually none of that commentary. Indeed, though the author died where I live, and though I feel certain other connections with him as well, I happen not even to have read his first and last voyage upon the bounding main of the novel until maybe ten years ago, when I had conceived and was in the early gestation of my own half-dozenth novel: one called *Sabbatical: A Romance*.

The story of Poe's *Pym* drifts in and out of that novel like a bit of saltwater flotsam on the brackish tides of Chesapeake Bay. The time of its present action is the last weeks of spring, 1980. Susan Rachel Allan Seckler, a young professor of classical American literature on sabbatical leave (to finish a study of Poe's *Pym*), and her husband, Fenwick Scott Key Turner—an ex-CIA agent turned exposeur and aspiring novelist—have just returned to the Chesapeake from a nine-month sailing cruise to the Caribbean in their 33⅓-foot cutter. In the course of this sabbatical adventure they have confronted but not yet successfully dealt with various big-ticket problems and questions in their recent past and their present—including the question whether to beget children at this possibly late hour of the world. Their sailboat's name, *Pokey*, is among other things an amalgam of the surnames of one each of the couple's real or putative ancestors: in Fenwick's case, Francis Scott Key, of whom Fenn is a lineal descendant; in Susan's case, Edgar Allan Etc., an obviously more problematical genealogy.

Susan Seckler is alleged to be descended from Edgar Poe, but she can't account for the allegation since Poe had no known children, as neither will she. Similarly, the narrative that she shares the lead in can be said to be a maverick, recycled descendant of *The Narrative of Arthur Gordon Pym*, at least in a few respects—and I can't really account for that, either, except to say that like many another American writer, no doubt, I think of Poe as among my literary forebears, for better and worse: not my great-grandfather, but a brilliant though erratic great-uncle, maybe. There have been in my literal genealogy a couple of sharp-tongued maiden aunts, more or less dotty, in whom (as in all the fish in one's gene-pool) I have seen alternative, in this case cautionary, versions of myself. When I contemplate the famous face of my fellow Baltimorean, my Great-Uncle Edgar, I never fail to be struck by the certain familiar looniness in it: that flakey-Romantic strain most uneasy-making to me not in his overtly gothic fictive preoccupations—live burial, putrefaction, sibling crypto-incest, and the rest—but rather in his more apparently calm and reasoned productions. Hugh Kenner has remarked that nothing looks more Victorian than a Victorian pagoda, for example; just so, I think I hear my great-uncle's half-hysteria most clearly when he's trying to keep it out of his voice: in his reasoned refutation of Maelzel's chess-playing automaton, for example, or his prescient explanation (in *Eureka*) of why the night sky happens to be dark instead of ablaze with the aggregate luminosity of stars, whose number is infinite and one of which must therefore occupy absolutely every line of sight from Earth. If (like Fenwick Scott Key Turner in the novel *Sabbatical*) I myself feel more affinity for Henry Fielding's and Laurence Sterne's eighteenth century than for Susan's and Poe's "self-tormented, half-hysterical" nineteenth, there is in that feeling an element of prophylaxis, or exorcism. Susan no less than Fenn *c'est moi*, in this regard; I feel honored that the venerable house of Putnam's, which published *Eureka* (though not *Pym*), was also the publisher of *Sabbatical: A Romance*.

As for *Pym, Pym, Pym, Pym, Pym, Pym, Pym:* God knows it is, if not "a silly book," a very odd duck of a novel, as impossible in its way as Melville's *The Confidence Man* (though mercifully shorter) and as likely to be overvalued, I fear, by ingenious readers for its real or projected ingenuities in the teeth of its patent tiresomeness, its gothic preposterosities, and its dramaturgical shortcomings. And yet . . . and yet, by gosh and by golly, the thing works, sort of—especially the opening paragraphs of chapter one and the closing paragraphs of the magical last chapter (twenty-five, in which the hero goes down the drain), if the nonspecialist reader has, with young Pym, survived the twenty-three chapters between. Captain Edgar manages after all to skipper his maiden (and final) novel out of some fairly shaky heavy-weather realism, down through gothic doldrums into latitudes of rather more plausible irrealism, and finally "STILL FARTHER SOUTH" (as Poe's subtitle advertises in boldface caps) into a realm where I too have done some narrative navigation: a realm whose resistless current I recognize and, reading *Pym, give* myself over to at last, whether or not I have ever attained it in my own novelistic expeditions.

Speaking not as an expert critic or scholar but as a fairly seasoned fellow novelist and, by the way, a not-inexperienced amateur sailor, I report that I find *The Narrative of Arthur Gordon Pym* sometimes less credible in its more realistic stretches and more so in its less. I won't comment here on its metafictive narrative frame, which Susan Seckler and many other contemporary critics have spoken much to. What most impresses me about the opening paragraphs of the story proper [in which sixteen-year-old Pym and a school chum go night-sailing and are run down by a homeward-bound Nantucket whaler] is the tone of the camaraderie of the two boys' escapade in Pym's little sloop *Ariel* that October night in 1825. Young Augustus Barnard's drunken post-party oath— "that he would not go to sleep for any Arthur Pym in Christendom, when there was such a glorious breeze from the southwest"—and young Pym's counterboast that he too is "tired of lying in bed like a dog, and quite as ready for any fun or frolic as any Augustus Barnard in Nantucket"—these and the other details of their setting out I find as refreshing as a breeze out of the English eighteenth century: out of a scapegrace-*roman* by Fielding or Smollett, say. I don't recall anything elsewhere in Poe, certainly not in *Pym*, quite as appealing and convincing in this line. God forgive me, I myself have undertaken such reckless, not-quite-sober late-night sails in years gone by (it's always a southwesterly that promotes them), and Poe has got it right: the little sloop chafing against the dock-piles, the boys' underestimation of the wind and overestimation of their abilities after Substance Abuse, the fast-sobering scariness, for Pym anyhow, of the night-sea out there, from which one is lucky to return intact. The author even supplies, somewhat belatedly, the bright moon normally required, along with a glorious southerly, to inspire such lunacies. Yo, Poe!

Already by the fifth paragraph, however, I'm having trouble, as are the young night-sailors. In keeping with his temporarily realist mode, Poe describes *Ariel* in some detail as a *sloop*, under whose unreefed mainsail and jib the boys have set out. But when an accidental downwind gybe in paragraph five "carrie[s] away the mast short off by the board" (that is to say, the apparently unstayed mast breaks off just above deck level and is lost over the side along with the boom, the gaff, and the mainsail), Arthur and his passed-out buddy roar along downwind "under the jib only," without Poe's troubling to tell us from what—on a single-masted boat that is now a no-masted boat—that jib is flying.

Okay: Sometimes even good Homer nods, and in a novel whose principal characters zonk out as often and completely as do those in *Pym*, it would be a miracle if the author didn't blink from time to time— particularly in the realistic passages of his voyage, which have about them the clenched-jawed metonymity of a driver determined to stay awake on a featureless stretch of interstate. I certainly find this lapse more acceptable as a simple lapse than as a deliberate challenge to the "merely proairetic reader," as one recent critic has called the likes of us low-tech Pymophiles.

In the same spirit, I don't fret overmuch at my question marks in the margins of *Pym*'s jury-rigged chronology, such as the narrator's declaration in his preface of July 1838 that he returned to the United States "a few months ago" from "the South Seas and elsewhere" and met Poe in Richmond, etc., when his return would seem to have to have been closer to two *years* ago to jibe with the publication of the story's first installments in *The Southern Literary Messenger* in January and February 1837—dates that "Pym" verifies. Never mind, while one is at it, that the most meticulous reconstruction of the schooner *Jane Guy*'s movements in chapters fourteen and fifteen, in the neighborhood of Christmas Harbor, won't quite add up (Try it; you'll hate it: The schooner first arrives there on October 18, 1827, and her crew explores the neighborhood in the schooner's boats "for about three weeks." Then on November 12 she sets out in search of the Aurora Islands and "in fifteen days" [i.e., on November 27] passes Tristan da Cunha en route, but manages nevertheless to reach the reported area of the Auroras a whole week *before* that, on November 20). Let it go: Who among us novelists has not had such gaffes pointed out by sharp-eyed readers? The important thing about *Jane Guy*'s log is that it picks Pym up from the drifting hulk of the brig *Grampus* on August 7 somewhere off Brazil's Cabo de San Rocas—about 7° S. latitude by my calculations, of which more presently—and delivers him on the winter solstice (summer solstice down there) to the sixtieth parallel of latitude and Capt. Guy's decision on that portentous date to push on Still Farther South.

I wouldn't even have mentioned *Ariel*'s mastless jib (which has also been noted by Professors Burton Pollin and Herbert F. Smith) if not that it foreshadows my first more serious crisis of belief, just as the dismasting itself foreshadows the sloop's being run down in the dark by the whaleship *Penguin*. Three paragraphs later, after Pym revives from the first of his many, many losses of consciousness, we learn that the crewmen of the *Penguin*, having risked their lives valiantly to look for survivors, had turned back in the ship's jolly-boat. The whaler rolls in the heavy seas, and along with First Mate Henderson we see our hapless and unconscious young hero . . . *bolted through the neck?* Yup: bolted through the neck (and through the collar of his jacket) to the vessel's coppered bottom, alternately buried at sea and resurrected, like a fun-house corpse, as the ship rolls.

I know: The shot symbolizes A, B, and C and foreshadows D, E, and F later on in the movie. But I groan all the same at its sensational implausibility: the first of many such groans to come from this "proairetic reader." *Bolted through the neck,* and so securely that all that slow-rolling and dunking in a gale of wind don't dislodge him! Yet he neither drowns nor requires so much as a suture for his wound! The *end* of chapter one charmingly wears its portentiousness up its sleeve rather than on it—I mean the boys' coming down to breakfast next morning at Mr. Barnard's as if their night-sea adventure had not happened, and getting away with it—but I am not deceived by Poe's winning observation that "Schoolboys . . . can accomplish wonders of deception." I know now that it's to be the *Rocky Horror Picture Show* after all; I sigh and settle in with my popcorn, and take not a word of the story straight thereafter, not even the mesmerizing last chapter. So you scared those hard-case *Grampus* mutineers out of their wits by making like a zombie? Sure you did. And later on you saw a boat-load of deadies under full sail with sea gulls chewing on the crew, and later yet you cannibalized your shipmate Parker, and after that your dead pal Augustus's leg came apart in your hands like a . . . oh, like that rotten ham from chapter two, let's say, and you could hear the sharks chomping him up from a *whole mile away*, and on the island of Tsalal (where both the natives and the sea birds cry "*Tekeli-li!*") you were reburied alive and reresurrected for the fifth time out of six in twenty-five chapters? Right, right.

The documents of the days of sail are rich in actual such horrors, which in our time the Vietnamese boat people could doubtless match. In Poe's hands, alas, they almost invariably turn, not into "challenges to the proairetic code," but into genre effects. And for all Pym's elaborate subsequent logging of his psychological weather, as a credible, palpable novelistic character he goes down with the *Ariel* in chapter one and never resurfaces. Even in proto-metafiction, that's a casualty to be regretted.

Yet through even the barfiest of ghoul-flicks the deep myths sometimes speak, more or less, and through the tellings of a canny and intuitive though erratic genius like Poe they may speak strongly, however much or little their "medium" (in the spiritualist sense) might be conscious of them. Autodidact Edgar was unpredictably knowledgeable as well as plenty smart; the paradigmatic image of him in Dominick Argento's opera *The Voyage of Edgar Allan Poe* is surely not the whole story, though it seems a fair piece of it: I mean the tenor zapped flat onstage by his *daimon* after every second aria, the vessel of his rational consciousness overwhelmed. As I tour Great-Uncle Edgar's floating gothic fun-house, my own authorial consciousness respectfully notes that the shipwright managed some admirable and not so obvious formal touches along with the more conspicuous gee-whizzers; and something "still farther south" in my sensibility rides on the undercurrent of myth, stronger and stronger as we descend the parallels of south latitude. Umberto Eco reports that the last words of his friend Italo Calvino were, "*I paralleli! I paralleli!*": It's a better exit line for a writer than Poe's "Reynolds! Reynolds!" and regarding certain of *Pym's paralleli* I shall speak next as the author not of *Sabbatical: A Romance* but of certain earlier fictions inspired by the Wandering Hero myth: the Ur-Myth, which my imagination once upon a time became possessed by after critics pointed out to me that my imagination was possessed by it.

Inasmuch as every literary person nowadays knows at least the outlines of that myth, I don't doubt that Poe's commentators in our time have long since noted its parallels in *Pym*. The *Ariel* episode prefigures it in miniature, even down to the time-zapping and the returned hero's appearing as if nothing remarkable had happened, as if he'd never been away—in short, as if he were not who he is, the man who has come through. The voyage proper (serial voyages, rather, in serial vessels) incorporates literally or figuratively most of the cyclical myth's classic features: in its first quadrant, the reputable ancestry, with a particular role for the maternal grandfather and a mother so royal-virginal in this case that she's not even mentioned; the undetailed childhood in "another country" (New Bedford, where Pym is sent to school—by his maternal grandfather); the nocturnal summons to adventure; the sidekicks and helpers, tokens and talismans; in its second quadrant, the threshold crossings, the initiatory ordeals, disguises, contests, riddles, trips-out-of-time, incremental divestitures and subterranean (or submarine) weekends, all culminating in mysterious, even mystical passage from the Twilight Zone to a *coincidentia oppositorum* at the Axis Mundi: the transcension of categories; the "oxymoronic fusion" of dark illumination, winter and summer, et and cetera. And from there, from the edge of the South Polar Abyss itself (a place as spookily, equivocally white as the icy center of Dante's Inferno leading to the white-rose peak of Paradiso, or the Whiteness of the Whale and for that matter the white white room on the far side of time in Arthur Clarke's *2001*), our hero is cycled *still farther south* into the Quadrants of Return and Death. . . .

To which *I* shall return after nodding Yes to my fellow skipper's

large-scale calendrics and making a point about his structural navigation, so to speak. I mean in the former instance that rhythm of equinox
and solstice, for example, a common feature of such myths. I confess to
having done that sort of calendar-diddling myself in more novels than
one, even before I understood why. Ditto Poe's scheduling the death of
Pym's "first-stage" helper, Augustus, not only on the first day of his
eponymous month but at the formal center of the novel: chapter thirteen
of the twenty-seven narrative divisions, with thirteen units before it (the
prologue plus twelve chapters) and thirteen after (twelve chapters plus
the epilogue). Indeed, it's very nearly at the center of the center: Augustus dies at 12 noon on day nine (August 1) of the fifteen journalized days
comprising that central chapter, adrift in the hulk of the *Grampus*. The
very center of the center would be day eight of the fifteen (July 31), and
if nothing special is noted in Pym's log of that pivotal day, it's because
the desperate survivors are in no position to know at the time what Pym
could have calculated in retrospect but didn't, quite, though I daresay
his author did: that it will have been on that day that our hero drifted
across the equator into the southern hemisphere of the novel.

The necessary numbers are all given in chapter fourteen: The survivors were rescued by the *Jane Guy* on August 7 "off Cape St. Roque"
in longitude 31° W.: that is to say, comfortably off the nose of Brazil,
which extends from Cabo de San Rocas (at latitude 5° south) nearly 200
miles down to Recife (at latitude 8° south), its eastmost tip being at
about the seventh parallel. Given the instruments of the time, the
schooner's positions are approximate indeed, the longitude more so than
the latitude, since sextants back then were more reliable than chronome-
ters. Even so, young Pym reckons after the fact that *Grampus* must have
drifted south *"not less than twenty-five degrees!"* (italics and exclamation
mark his; distance 1,500 nautical miles; probability nil, since in fact the
prevailing ocean currents in those latitudes set inexorably west instead
of south—but never mind). Conveniently for us armchair navigators,
that drifting began on July 14: twenty-five days in all, which comes
neatly to 1° (sixty nautical miles) per day. That's a 2.5-knot current,
almost a Gulf Stream in reverse, and though it does not exist in fact (until
you get well *below* the nose of Brazil), we know where it's going. As for
where it's coming from, if we dead-reckon from a rescue at latitude 7°
S. and plot backward (which is how both novelists and navigators often
do their plotting), we'll find *Grampus* to have been at latitude 20° N.
back there on Bastille Day (i.e., just under the Tropic of Cancer) and

smack on the equator of the globe smack at the equator of the story. Another symbolic threshold crossed: one with its own initiatory traditions, as sailors and cruise-ship passengers know.

Way to go, Poe. If *that's* how his imagination works, and it seems to be, then I know where *he's* coming from enough to take a mildly curious look at where Pym, his coeval stand-in with the lookalike name, happens to be on—oh, his author's nineteenth birthday, for example, January 19, 1828, when Poe was at a very low point between lives, having just been obliged to drop out of the University of Virginia for nonpayment of his gambling debts and being on the cusp of his life-changing blow-up with John Allan, his foster father. Sure enough, that's the fateful day on which Pym reaches Tsalal, as no doubt I'm the last kid on the block to note, on the cusp of the life-changing blow-up of the schooner *Jane Guy;* and two months later in the story Poe sends his counterpart south from the lowest point in the world on just about the date when he himself split north for Boston, where he first came from.

Enough of that; we all do it, or almost all. Pym goes so far south from the South Pole that he ends up in Richmond eight years later, collaborating with Poe on *The Narrative of Arthur Gordon Pym;* Poe goes so far north from Richmond that he ends up in Richmond eight years later, ready to collaborate with Pym etc.

Back to the myth, and then to the novel: The first half of the generic wandering hero's night-sea journey (or whatever) ritually fetches him to the heart of mystery. The second half, as I read it, fetches him from mystery to tragedy and then recycles him. What there is of this latter half-cycle in Poe's novel is in "Pym's" preface and, glancingly, "the editor's" afterword (both written of course by Poe himself). The wanderer returns "home" from the bright heart of darkness in the netherworld unrecognized or unrecognizable, bringing something precious with him. He manifests himself, routs the usurpers, and delivers his message or whatever, which, being ineffable, must always be more or less garbled in transmission. He reigns peacefully for a time (about eight years, says Lord Raglan in *The Hero*) and then leaves his city to meet his mysterious end. No one knows for sure where his grave is; several cities claim him as theirs; one day he may return.

On the vernal equinox of 1828, when he goes down the hole, Arthur Gordon Pym is still a very young man: nineteen years old, though he seems to have been initiated out of boyishness back there between the Tropic of Cancer and the equator (his senior shipmates Parker and Peters never refer to him as "the kid"). By my calculations, the median age for these things is 33⅓; like his author, Pym's precocious. Eight blank years later he pops up in Richmond, and in the ninth and tenth years he endeavors to truthify his message, which has been cordially usurped and betrayed as fiction by "Mr. Poe"; when he dies in July '38 immediately after writing his preface, in circumstances even more equivocal than those of his author's death eleven years later, he's still only in his thirtieth year to heaven, a threshold more poetical than mythical. In the epilogue, at second or third hand, his creator disclaims the factuality of the bottom line of his creature's account, and the vertiginous paradox of that passing disclaimer at once betrays and affirms the ontological status of Arthur Gordon Pym and of the narrative: They are factual in the fiction but in fact fictional; what truth is in them is the truth of myth.

Yet despite *"i paralleli,"* every professional intuition tells me that Poe's novel is *not* a systematic and pointed reorchestration of the myth of the wandering hero. There are about as many and significant disanalogies as analogies (including the compass directions, which are all wrong), and lots of missing pieces. Some of those are supplied by Pym's sidekicks (it's Dirk Peters who makes the Odysseus-like inland trek—to Illinois—at the voyage's end), and several more can be supplied from the author's biography—Poe's late-adolescent setting out for his "true" home, the shrines to his memory in several cities, etc.—but surely that's cheating. More important, the *sense* of the great myth is absent from *The Narrative of Arthur Gordon Pym,* as it is not from the stories of Odysseus, Aeneas, Oedipus, Perseus, Jesus, and even Paul Morel of D. H. Lawrence's *Sons and Lovers.* Poe's novel rides on the myth the way the *Grampus* and then the canoe ride on that current, but it is not a rendition of the myth, nor is it sensibly about the myth. Beyond the metafictive paradoxes of its framing text, which I find to be of real though not unlimited interest, and beyond, in the story proper, the sundry contaminations of reality by irreality (as Borges puts it) and vice-versa, I think I don't after all know quite *what* the presenting sense of Poe's novel is: I mean its situational premise, its thematic center, and its moral-dramatical bottom line, apart from its symbolical razzle-dazzle and any encrypted messages about its author.

The problem is that Pym, and therefore his narrative, has no main-spring. As we say in fiction-writing workshops, his story is all "vehicle" and no "ground situation"; his actions, consequently (on the several occasions when he *takes* action rather than passively enduring what befalls him), seem to this reader meaningless, dramaturgically speaking, however resonant they may be from our experience of myth and of initiation novels. Moreover, as I have said, after that fine opening of the *Ariel* episode he is scarcely apprehensible as a character. To compare Pym and company with Billy Budd and company or Roderick Random and company or even Odysseus or Sindbad and company is to be reminded how little gift Poe had for the "realistic" aspects of characterization, even as we find them in fantastical mythographers like Dante and Scheherazade. And this defect is more conspicuous in a pseudorealistic narrative like *Pym* than in the flat-out gothics of *A Cask of Amontillado* or *The Fall of the House of Usher*. Indeed, I think I know Fortunato and Roderick Usher better than I know Dirk Peters and Arthur Gordon Pym. Poe's gifts, like Borges's, simply lie elsewhere.

In short, I confess to sharing the reservations of Henry James and Robert Louis Stevenson concerning our subject. The way I'd put it is that the young hero of *Pym* is altogether without the moral-dramatic voltage required of protagonists in particular, and desirable even in metafiction if it is not to become mere metaphysics. Pym is not a dramatic character but rather the simulacrum of a dramatic character, and Poe's novel ought to be regarded as some sort of simulacrum of a novel: not a counterfeit but an isomorph; not a hoax but a mimicry. *Pym* echoes the *Bildungsroman* and the Ur-Myth and mimes the contours of dramatic action the way a praying mantis mimes a green twig but is not a green twig. I am less than confident that Poe understood the difference (and his own motives) as clearly as the mantis may be said to understand them; novels were truly not his métier. I believe, however, that the reader who approaches *Pym* as if it were a bona fide novel, like the fly who approaches the mantis thinking that *lean* plus *green* plus *stationary* equals *twig*, is in for difficulties—less consequential ones, I trust.

I trust too that the scholars gathered here in conference on the island where Pym's voyage began, on the sesquicentennial of Poe's curious novel about it, are of all readers the least likely to make so innocent an approach. I have to hope, on the other hand, that in distinguishing the mantis from the twig, they don't mistake it for an eagle or a bird of paradise. Who ever heard one of those cry *"Tekeli-li!"*?

RICK BASS

Notes from Yaak

I'd been in the mountains before; I'd gone to a college built on the side of a mountain, Utah State University, and had never been so happy—not at being young, or being in college, or being free, but happy just at being on the landscape, moving across such a strange, wonderful land—I'd grown up in Texas, and worked, after college, for several years in Mississippi—and my girlfriend, Elizabeth, and I, liked very much the way the woods out west smelled at night, and when we first woke up, whenever we went camping there—out west—which was often. In the horrible, heated summer of 1987, we started out driving toward southern New Mexico, wanting to find the ideal "artist's retreat"—a place where Elizabeth could do her painting; where I could write (separate studios, of course, because we both like to work in the morning); a place near running water; a place with trees, a place with privacy—a place of ultimate wildness, with the first and last yardstick of privacy—a place where you could walk around naked, if you wanted to—which we did—and a place with a barn and stables, and a field, for keeping horses, because Elizabeth loved to ride—and if there was an indoor swimming pool, and maybe some tennis courts on the premises, and a little garden, well, that would be all right, too.

Because we were so damn poor—defiantly poor, wondrously poor—not owing anyone anything, and in the best of health—we were looking for a place to rent, rather than purchase, though the thought had crossed our mind that maybe we could buy an acre of land somewhere (at the end of a gravel road, near running water, with trees . . .) and *build* on it—understand that sharpening a pencil is a great mechanical adventure for either of us, we're a little artsy, I'm sorry to say, but no matter, such was our fever, the heart's desire, to get out west, to live our lives there—it felt as if too much time had already gone by, we were both twenty-nine—and so we began looking. It didn't matter what state: we just wanted it to be in the west.

In Whitefish, Montana, Elizabeth had a feeling—one of those premonition things. We went in to see a realtor on the little main street.

The realtor—a slow day, a slow town, and a nice man, Ross Haffner—was delighted with our plight, our search, and he began telling us about a wild, magical valley that was even farther north and west than Whitefish—up on the Canadian line, and over near Idaho. Ross said the valley was named Yaak, and that it wasn't really a town—there were no electricity, no phones, no paved roads—but that a handful of people lived there year-round, sprinkled back in the woods and along the Yaak River. Ross said it was very hard to get to, that you needed four-wheel drive, which we had, and that he had a property there. It was the end of the world, said Ross: beautiful, but just too hard to get to.

Without phones, the only way to get in touch with the ranch was by mail or by short-wave radio, and even then, getting through that way was chancy (by radio); windy days in the spring were almost impossible. There was a small propane generator in the root cellar, to provide brief, sputtering electricity—for the electric typewriter, or a little record music in the evenings—and there were some twelve-volt deep-cycle RV batteries in a shed (charged and recharged each time the generator ran); those batteries provided the all-important reading light, along with propane lanterns, at night.

We left Whitefish and drove three and a half hours, not seeing anyone or anything—house, truck, car, or person—in the last hour and a half except moose, deer, elk and grouse, all of which ran across the road in great numbers. There were white daisies lining the one-lane dirt road we followed, and the farther we drove without seeing cabins or signs of human life—deeper and deeper into the last and largest spot of unroaded green area on our highway map—the more and more heartsick we became that we were poor.

When we came down off the summit and into the little blue valley—nothing but a mercantile and a saloon, one building on either side of the street, and a slow winding river working through the valley (a cow moose and calf standing in the river, behind the mercantile)—and still no sign of life, no people (it was as if they had all been massacred, I thought happily), we knew immediately that this was where we wanted to live, where we had always wanted to live.

We had never felt such magic.

*   *   *

A few uneventful, good days. We got four loads of wood yesterday—about one cord. We've been having hard frosts, every night—25°, 26°; but shirt sleeves and barefooted again, in the day.

The dogs keep finding more bones. Things seem to die around here.

Things to do: clean chimney trap; clean chicken house, convert it to winter dog residence; shovel ashes out of fireplace, wood stoves; git wood.

Elizabeth's busying and straightening, tidying, washing, all of it: I try to stay out of the way.

Good things to know if you are a logger: wear high boots, of course, to protect your ankles against spike-limbs; but also wear high-cuffed pants, and open, around the cuffs, not unlike bellbottoms. You want them stopping up high—around the ankle—so when you are climbing around in a pile of slash, every little branch and limb doesn't run up in your cuffs and trap you—but you want them baggy, flaring, so that if a branch does run up your cuffs, it won't wedge in there and trip you; you can just step out of it.

Truman told me this, over beers a few nights ago, and I'd forgotten it, until yesterday, when I fell. Everyone's so helpful.

I introduced Elizabeth yesterday to the Horners. Hojo was talking about how wonderful winter can be; how it got down to eighty (wind-chill) below their first year up here; how on a cold, clear day, in the heart of winter, with no one around, you can look up and see the sky swirling and sparkling with flashing ice crystals, all above you, the whole sky, crystals falling out of blue air, even though there is no wind.

Check the antifreeze. A simple, stupid thing that someone from easy times, from the warm, simple growth of Mississippi, might easily forget.

Everyone back east wants me to send them pictures, but very few of them sound serious about wanting to visit. This is fine with me. I will send them pictures.

A few nights ago, while getting wood, I saw some grouse. They are big, muscular, quail-chicken birds—runners, scooters—and taste wonderful—I've had them in Utah before.

Haven't seen Tom and Nancy in a while, not since Elizabeth got in. I think about Nancy a good bit. I want to ask both of them questions all day long, all winter: about dream hoops, about crows, about trapping.

The consensus—unanimously so—is that this is going to be a fierce winter. Fuzzy deer, already, men's beards growing faster, old people feeling it in their bones, their hearts: the way the stars flash and glimmer at night, the way the trees stand dark against the sky. . . . Driving back from the Shame, late at night, I've been seeing snowshoe hares that have already turned completely white. They've staked their lives on the fact or feeling that it's going to be an early winter, and a hard one.

Great huge fat white rabbits, like magicians, rabbits the size of large cats, hiding out in the darkness of the woods, gambling, waiting for the snow that will save them.

All these thousands of years, tens of thousands—the foolish ones have long ago been weeded out, the willy-nilly, turn-white-for-no-reason rabbits; those that turned white when there really wasn't any snow coming, or those that turned white too early, had nowhere to hide, and were quickly consumed, easy, visible prey to everything—wolves, coyotes, hawks, owls, bobcats, lions, everything. . . .

And the hares that stayed brown, that did not feel the hard winter coming, and did not prepare for it . . . they got theirs, in the winter, by these same predators—easy, visible brown prey on the ocean of snow, the cruel purity and sameness of winter, the beauty of it.

So I figure these rabbits know. What a remarkable thing, to bet your life, each year, twice a year, actually—because they must know when to turn brown again—and this year, I have been seeing white rabbits coming out of hiding after the sun goes down, white rabbits hopping across the logging roads as I come down off of the mountain with a load of wood—trying, with the windows rolled down, to listen, and feel for myself, and to learn, rather than always having to be told. I think that I can learn. It is why I moved up here. It is why Elizabeth moved up here.

There are cars and trucks parked outside the Dirty Shame, when I go past—mostly trucks—and it looks warm and inviting, a glow in the night woods—but I've got my window rolled down, I can feel it, feel what I *should* be feeling. What it tells me is that I have gotten up here late, to this little valley, maybe too late: but once I'm home, unloading the wood from the truck, smelling the fresh cut of it, and feeling the silence of the woods all around me, what I feel, like the rabbits, is this: that surely, better late than never—and with a flashlight, then, after eleven o'clock, I go back out into the night again, driving past the Dirty Shame once more, and up onto the mountain, for more wood, trying to beat what, like everyone else up here, I now know, rather than think, is coming.

What I feel is that I had better not stop, that I have lost time to make up for.

Hard dreams, of the line-backed dun across the road, his face iced over with snow and sleet, his back to the wind, staring straight ahead, as if seeing something far out in front of him: as if watching, through a looking glass, spring, and its thaw, its greenness. Dreams of heavy axes, hitting frozen wood; of gloves, of steaming coffee from a thermos, of sitting inside the Dirty Shame, the whole valley—thirty or forty of us, trapped by a blizzard—cheering, at the football game on the little TV screen, cheering and making bets as to who will win.

What Edward Hoagland has called the courage of turtles; I can see it, now, the wisdom of rabbits. There is so much to learn, now. Everything I have learned so far has been wrong. I'm having to start all over. I want to find Nancy today and ask her one more time about those dream hoops: ask her again how they work, and if there are life hoops, as well, though already I know she will tell me that yes, there are.

It can be so wonderful, finding out you were wrong; that you are ignorant, that you know nothing, not squat.

You get to start over. It's like snow falling, that first time, each year. It doesn't make any sound, but it's the strongest force you know of.

Trees will crack and pop and split open, then, later on into the winter; things opening up, learning. Learning the way it really is.

All through the forest, they say, you can hear them, on those coldest of nights: cracking and popping like firecrackers, like cannons, like a parade: while rabbits, burrowed in the snow beneath them, sit quietly, warm and white, saved, having learned—having made the right bet.

* * *

7:10 A.M., black coffee, candlelight. Aspen popping in the wood stove. Down in the greenhouse, chill seeping through the cracks in the logs. I'm doing away with caffeine, away with Sweet 'N Low, Equal, all of it. It's true that I've loaded the thermos with honey, but hey, so hey, sue me. . . . So I'm a little woman, what do I care? I'd like to say that the coffee tastes better this way, but not so, not true. Nancy in the Shame was telling me about how she hurt her wrist skiing one year: and it wouldn't heal, it was all drawn up and forever cramping; and a guy told her to stop drinking coffee, and she did, and two days later the wrist was supple again, strong.

We writers are different, of course. We can abuse our bodies. In a way, it's our trade: as a logger risks the saw's blade, or a physician the eternal, final, crushing malpractice, so the writer goes around dipping into pain and sorrow, then climbing up into euphoria; looks around, then, as the story dictates, swan-dives, plunges, back into hell. I try to keep a pretty straight line myself, but as far as any other writer goes, if they want to abuse themselves, well, it is okay, with me anyway. I can forgive, and do forgive, anything and everything in *good* writers. If this sounds hypocritical, then I apologize, for I have not explained it clearly enough.

I had bad dreams and recurring headaches all night—dreaming of dying, murder, cancer, fires, traffic jams—I need a dream hoop.

The long flame of the candle. Elizabeth upstairs, still sleeping. I am going to write fiction, later this morning.

One candle per three pages. Pages come slowly, and the candle burns fast.

I don't want to cut my beard! I want to cut hay in the tall pastures with a scythe! I will live forever! This is the afterlife!

We've been drinking, celebrating, a bottle of champagne: We'd passed the five-cord mark, and there are still ten days left in September.

Elizabeth, baking bread. Warm sun through the window—cheap champagne, and an expensive chainsaw, and being twenty-nine; this is the last year we will ever be young. But we did it. We were young.

Waiting on the eagles to come to Glacier Park. Every year, they come. Big mountains. We can hold hands, and look at them.

She's baking with honey. I'm putting on weight. It's good weight. Been lifting those logs, swinging that ax.

Not much of this fey little peck-peck-tapping of typewriter keys, fey little writer. Always the writer's dilemma, and perhaps everyone's: You can write about living, or talk about it, think about it—or, if you are lucky, you can actually go out and do it. Say what you want about Hemingway, get mad and throw things at him, but no one will ever say he was not a great writer (which is *not* the same thing as saying he never wrote poorly), and no one will ever say he did not live a life. Forget whether you liked his stories, or even his writing, or even how he lived. You have to say that he wrote, and lived. It is no easy thing. In fact, it killed him.

And forget his fear, perhaps his antagonism (though I do not know if that was what it was or not). So what if his mother dressed him up as a girl—a man dressed like, in the words of Tom McGuane, "some horrid *nancy*." He flew into the sky, flew airplanes into the ground, did the lion and elephant thing, the beautiful women thing, ate well, drank well, wrote some great sentences, even some great stories and great books, caught some impressive fish, saw parts of the world we'll all die without having ever seen: and if I am going on and on about him too much, which I think I am, it is only jealousy, only anger at myself, for the days when I sleep a little too late, for the nights when I go to bed a little too early.

McGuane, over in the Beartooth-Absarokas, north of Yellowstone (grizzlies), has a big ranch, a beautiful wife, fantastic children, fine horses, and the best dogs you've ever seen (this side of Homer and Ann): and he rides cutting horses (was national champion, one year), brands his own cattle, has only recently given up Cuban cigars and red wine; he ropes cattle, sails (takes his family down to the coast, in the winter, though he's an elk hunter: what a kind man)—and he shoots, he fishes, he used to ride motorcycles. . . .

I guess what I mean is, there is all this *energy*.

Evening. Writing again; throwing wood into the stove. Little wrist-size burn-up pieces; they burn up almost as fast as you can look at them. Energy. Can't have too much wood. Makes the valley smell good. Of course there are only thirty of us in this valley. This is the proper number. The Dirty Thirty. Next March, this winter, I will be thirty. If everyone in the world burned as much wood as I am going to this winter, the planet would be obscured, one great wood-smoke cloud. Don't know what to think about that. We're all dirty. But we're all sweet!

I recycle my aluminum! I don't litter! I try to pee on the rocks, not on the soil, to keep from killing things with too much nitrogen!

Thinking now of how my father pronounces the word "moron," sometimes when aiming it at me—"Mo-Ron." It sounds good (except when addressed to me). Maybe I am a Mo-Ron for using wood for fuel, rather than the similarly priced propane. (Though I get my wood for free; the saw, the ax, the biceps, deltoids.)

We all have dirt in us. Wood is better than coal, not as good as gas.

No, that's hypocritical, rationalizing. Wood is bad, inefficient, dirty, and it smells good. It's fun to chop, and I like to watch the flames, watch the erratic, pulsing heat it gives, and I like the snaps and pops, and when I'm dead and gone, I'll be glad I used it.

Mo-Ron, children of the centuries after me will cry. But there will be jealousy, as well as anger, in their cries, and we are all the same, always have been, and there is wood lying all around, wood everywhere, and it is free, and I have a life to live. Me first, it feels like I am saying, it is my turn, and you may not even get yours.

I do not burn wood unless it is cold.

You should hear him say it. In traffic, or watching a baseball game, when the manager makes a bad move: "Mo-Ron." It's like a wave at sea, rolling high on the Mo and cresting, rolling, down into the curl and lick and wave of Ron, sliding into shore, soft, sibilant; the word of the nineties, I'm afraid, environmental mo-ron, mo-ron, mo-ron. . . .

I know I should be burning gas, not wood, I know I should. I'm sorry.

*　*　*

There's an owl that looks as if he stands four feet tall—we looked him up in the book, he's a Great Gray Owl—and he's living in our field, sitting on various fence posts, motionless, watching us, as we walk to and from the truck, the woodshed, anywhere—cocking his head sometimes, and leaping down into the tall grass, or into the hay around the barn, to grab mice, which he then flies around with—the mouse hanging from his beak like a limp rag, as he flies—before landing on another fence post, or a stump. People say they've been seeing him around the Fix Ranch forever. I count his misses, tallying them against his attempts, in his war on the mice, and he usually goes about nine-for-ten. It's a surprise, to see him miss.

One morning last week, as I wrote in the greenhouse, a coyote came trotting down out of the woods, and sat down at the edge of the woods, in a patch of sun, and just watched the road. The wind was ruffling her fur—and I have no idea why I believe she was a female, only that I do—and after a while, she got up and slunk out into the tall grass, and then began pouncing, chasing a mouse: trying to pin it with her paws, hopping, lunging—and finally, just when I was ready to believe she was hallucinating, that there was nothing down in that tall grass, she plunged her snout down into the grass and came up triumphant, with a still-wriggling, writhing mouse in her jaws.

Immediately—whether for play, or because the mouse bit her—and it almost seemed that it could have been the latter—she flipped the mouse high into the air, twenty feet or more, and then stood there like a person, on her hind legs, waiting for it to come down, and she caught it again. She did this several times.

She trotted back up to her spot at the edge of the woods, then, and lay down and ate the mouse, and then looked out at the empty gravel road, and at the field beyond that, for a while.

Things were going through her mind. You can't tell me that they were not. She just sat there in the sun, in the wind, with her fur ruffling, getting ready for winter.

This field is full of mice. They surround the barn, hiding in the hay, getting ready for winter.

Some of them will never see it. There are other forces out there, besides just winter.

But the coyotes and the owls—they too are responsible to the force of winter, to the brunt of its coming power. It exerts a competitive force, rather than a unifying force, on the whole forest. It is dynamic, rather than static.

You can sit there and watch the coyote catch the mice, and the owl catch the mice, long before winter comes—or even shortly before it comes—and know, even before you see the first falling flakes, that it is dynamic, that it *will* come, but that it will then also leave—that it will not last forever.

And that it is larger than mice, or owls, or coyotes, or even men and women—that it controls their actions, that it is the force of the world, and must be respected and feared, if not understood—but that it changes, shifts, weakens, dissolves—leaves, again, finally—while, with luck, mice, and coyotes, and people, stay.

Cloudy tonight, and a wind out of the north. My back's so sore, from cutting. Clouds blowing past the moon, no stars visible, dark clouds, blowing past. I took the dogs outside and when I came back inside Elizabeth asked how cold I thought it was.

"Cold," I said. It was about 10:30.

We sat there and thought about how much colder it was yet to become. It was a strange and scary feeling—knowing that it, the great cold, lay out there in the future, in the dark, a certainty.

The good old Falcon, the good old V-8: pulling tons of wood, gliding up and down the hills with it, through the mountains, along ridge tops looking down at the rivers, far below. O, Falcon!

Alice Horner was calling her husband Numb-Nuts today. I was on the phone to Texas, clearing up some things about a prospect my geology partner and I have going, an oil well, over in Alabama, and Alice was right next to the pay phone, and she bellowed it across the street to Hojo, her husband, who was standing outside the Dirty Shame, shooting the breeze with Truman: "Hey, *Numb*-Nuts! Come over here!"

"Wild country," I explained to my partner, an older gentleman. "A hard country."

And I pictured him telling it, later on, to top people in the Petroleum Club, at lunch: how there is a woman in the Yaak Valley who stands out in the middle of Main Street and shouts, "Hey, Numb-Nuts!" when she wants to get her husband's attention.

* * *

Saturday, October 10

Gleeful, it's so cold! I don't know what the temperature is—we can't pick up any radio stations—but it feels the coldest yet. I'm guessing about 15°. I had to hold the pen over the stove this morning to warm it so that the ink would start flowing; just a regular old cheap ballpoint (Larry Levis, a massively great poet, uses a black Parker). (I'd forgotten about that until just now. Anything Larry Levis says to do, about writing, I'd better do. And now I'm remembering Jim Harrison's advice: Black pen at night, gold pen in the day. Anything Harrison says . . . likewise.)

It was cold in the house. We fell asleep on the floor in front of the fireplace, warm, after the lemon grouse (fat and juicy, dripping) and dirty rice and homemade bread, baked potatoes, season's last salad—but this morning, it was not warm, and I fixed coffee on the propane stove, and held my hands above the tiny blue hissing spouting flame as the water heated; I didn't want to take them away, when the water started to roll. I wanted to stand there all day.

And then, coming out here, I ran, carrying the notebook and thermos. The ideal thing would be (like a man coming home from work at the end of a day, ready to see his wife) (or vice versa: I am a child of the fifties, the sixties, and so on)—the ideal thing would be for me to be running like I was running because I couldn't wait to get to my writing.

But it was just too cold to walk, was all.

The points of my cheeks, and the part of my nose that makes it be too big—these things were stinging hard, it was real winter.

The pond across the road was frozen, for the first time.

You could hear everything, if there had been anything to hear.

And the greenhouse was cold, but not so cold as outside. But now it is hot, stuffy hot, and the stove is stuffed with wood, packed tight, and I'm ready to give fiction another go, ever and again, always, this morning.

You old journal, you: You're just a physical substitute. You poor old thing. I get warmed up on you, and then when the room finally gets warm, I leave.

Chest and arms, face, warm; but below the bench I'm sitting on, a pool of icy air, cold drafts wrapping my ankles, my toes. Maybe I should write standing up, like Hemingway. Maybe I should at least sit in a high chair. There's a loft above the woodshed (it would be a fine place to write but I'd have to keep trooping down and then back up the little ladder whenever I needed to add wood to the stove, and also, mainly, there are asteroid-sized holes in the shingled roof above this section of loft, holes providing immediate access to the arctic sky—and so I stay down here on the first floor.

Maybe I should forget Hemingway, forget Levis and Harrison, and just sit closer to the stove, and forget everything. The line in *True Grit* (Charles Portis), where the bad guy (long ago forgotten) says to John Wayne (playing John Wayne), "I call that bold talk from a one-eyed fat man!"

Lots of bold talk, flying around here this morning. Time to put up or shut up—or however the saying goes.

Anyway, it's true.

Later in the afternoon. Double wood. I need double wood, I need to fill the greenhouse with it (I use ten chunks a morning, plus probably twenty kindling pieces—thirty pieces in all—thirty × October–November–December–January–February–March—and who knows what part of April, even into May, equals at least 5,400 pieces of wood).

This, for the selfishness of the greenhouse, and my brief writing time.

Thinking again, and probably forever, about what Tom Lyon, a nature-writing professor I had in Utah, said. It's been nine years, and still I can hear him saying it, still I find myself thinking about it, hearing him say it, once a week, sometimes only once every two weeks: "When you sit down to write, you should strive to make what you are writing be worth the life of the tree that was cut down to give you the paper on which you are writing."

Boy, I have come a long way. Have I ever fallen. I feel like the child preacher, star of the fourth grade Sunday School class, who, thirty years later, is the smut-king of Hollywood; I feel as if I'm selling dirty needles to child hooker junkies, and stealing organs from donor banks, to further my writing.

I've gone from being concerned with one thin sheet of paper, 8½ by 11 inches, to a frigging forest.

But I'm poor! I'm poorer!

Two sparks just banged emphatically, inside the stove, as if to say amen, amen: You can say that again, brother.

I'm not whining, though. I'm doing what I want—writing—and

I'm warm, and I had fat grouse and wine last night, and my back is holding up, I've got fifteen cords in (fifteen to twenty still to go), and I'm stronger than ever, no muscle injuries, no cuts, no chainsaw tragedies—I still want to get over to Glacier, before the park closes for winter—but first I have to get my wood in.

O, Falcon! While the Japanese are creeping about, punctuating their spells of *hibernation* with occasional flurries of lethargy, searching for a replacement transmission—for eleven days, now, they have not been able to find one; not in Denver, not in Seattle, not in the United States, not in Japan—while the Jap truck has been in the coma, the old Detroit V-8 has been pulling heavier, greater loads up and down the mountains, in the back seat alone.

Springs shot, frame scraping the pavement, sometimes—driving fifteen, twenty miles an hour, on the way home—wood lashed to the hood, to the roof, and the trunk bulging open as if a car bomb has gone off; the windows down, extra logs hanging out the windows—wood in the front seat, wood on the dash, wood in the glove box, wood in my lap—groaning, back and forth to Hensley Mountain, the little Falcon, never before called on to be even a *passenger* car, not in the last ten years, anyway—valiantly, she fills in, struggles on, knowing the severity of my predicament.

To take her on a vacation to Glacier might be asking too much: getting greedy, or getting lazy: it just has the wrong feel to it.

The old Falcon, getting dirtier by the day, getting holes poked in her upholstery, chainsaw oil stains on the seats, wood bark ankle-deep on her once-immaculate floorboards . . . but there is no other option. It's do or die, and she's doing.

Scab wood-getting. The Nissan is on strike, luxuriously so, while in the meantime, winter advances.

It's funny, at eleven o'clock in the morning, a bright day, to see the moon still so high in the west, pale, washed out, but still up there, over the western ridge, watching, not wanting to go away.

They say it's really cold, on the moon.

Midnight. Two cords of wood cut, carried up from the bottom of the hill, loaded into the Falcon, driven back home (four trips), unloaded, split, stacked, then back to Hensley for more. There's nothing that gets you as dirty as wood-cutting. I thought roughnecking was bad, but that was nothing.

Roughnecking is a tea party, ginger cakes and lemonade; roughnecking is washing your hands, and blowing your nose with a lace hanky, compared to wood-getting.

I go through a pair of leather gloves each day.

The steel teeth of the saw's chain need filing, sharpening, each night.

My clothes cannot come in the house. They are too soaked with oil, with sweat and gasoline, and caked with sawdust. It's in my beard, my hair, down under my shirt, it's all over me; and the dust, from this, the dryest year on record, is everywhere.

Like a swami, like something immortal, from another planet, perhaps—Mississippi—the Falcon glides through it all, sometimes obscured by the clouds of dust that are its own raising; like the Peanuts cartoon character Pigpen, the Falcon and I are still getting wood.

My knee is blown out and stiff from where I whacked it with a backswing of the maul today; bruised ligaments, I hope, rather than torn: I went down with a scream and stars in my eyes, twisting halfway around and falling on my back, coming to seconds later to see clouds, lying on my back and looking up at the sky like a dead actor, and there are blisters on my feet from trudging up and down the hills in my steel-toed boots and splinters from where wood has stabbed through the worn-out places in my gloves; but I'm going to hang in there with the Falcon, if I can.

And never mind my back, from bending over so much, sawing all day; and never mind the Falcon's transmission.

I'll bet we moved twenty tons of wood today.

Fingernails split. Whitefinger. And I have escaped the real injuries.

*   *   *

Damn I need a haircut. Test driving another Nissan today in Bonners Ferry, Idaho: I told the salesman I was a writer, and he looked at me and asked, What, science fiction? But it's true, I look like a nut, like a lunatic.

Saturday, October 31
It's a dark, slow morning. Purple clouds out over Libby, over the Kootenai. Not cold at all—I've got a fire going and am in the greenhouse—but I still wore a light sweatshirt, walking over here this morning. The window panes in the greenhouse look funny, this morning: clearer and thinner than usual, and also, everything *looks* still—that kind of stillness

that seems perfect, when you just stare out at it, hearing nothing, no sounds except for the ocean noises in your heart—but then, as you focus on an individual stem of late-season wheat, perhaps—you see that all is not entirely still, that there is a slight breeze along the ground, anyway, that the smaller grasses are moving, slightly—but only if you focus upon them. . . .

Everything else is still.

Rain, down there in Libby, forty miles away, turning to snow? The salesman in Spokane was a turd. Fortunately we didn't even have to shake hands.

Halloween in Yaak is this: strap on a pair of deer or elk antlers, go down to the Dirty Shame and drink a six-pack. No glitter, no make-up.

Ranier. Schmidt. Olympia. Bud. Strohs.

In 1983, it snowed on December 8.

In 1984, it snowed on October 27.

In 1985, it snowed on November 7.

In 1986, it snowed on October 31 (a foot and a half).

I would like to win the snow pool. I would like to buy a round for everyone at the saloon, and then firewood, with the remaining money. I did not get it all in. I monkeyed around, and went to Mississippi for a party, went to Alabama for an oil well I had going; I dallied around in Libby, some days, when I'd go in to make photocopies, and I jacked around and didn't buy a new truck soon enough. I've got a deer hunt in Texas coming up, with my family, and then another well to go to in Alabama again, and then a short story reading in New York: and I've got some wood in, a lot of wood—eighteen, maybe twenty cords—but I'm burning some of it every day, now, out here in the greenhouse, and in the kitchen stove, and I didn't get the thirty cords I wanted to have by this date.

Writers. Half-assed at everything, it seems, except, occasionally, their writing.

I'll go get another load today. Tricky, of course, because (once again—the days rushing past so fast)—it's a weekend, and I don't want to start the saw up in the woods, don't want to ruin the deer and elk hunting for others.

I know how I'd feel if I were up in the mountains, watching for deer, and heard a chainsaw start.

I'd wonder why he didn't get his wood in in July, in August, in September and October, as the larches were beginning to turn gold, and the leaves were blowing in the wind, tumbling across the roads.

Cottonwood leaves, yellow and knee-deep, up on either side of the road going up to Hensley. A lot of the trees are getting bare, now. This is sort of like a marriage. Something is coming on. I hope I can do this.

* * *

The egotism of the present; the innate (and *not* exclusive to Americans, as is always being so nastily impugned) irreverence for history, for the past: I'm watching the wind blow this morning, and listening to a far-off logging truck, that fierce growl as he hits the hills, and climbs the mountains—and I'm awed, a little frightened to be writing so close— five, six, seven hours away—to so many writers.

I mean, *living* writers. Montana, contemporary writers: great ones. Knowing beyond a shadow of a doubt that with this wind blowing this morning, with winter coming on, storm systems moving in from the Pacific, they are all probably writing, this morning. Richard Ford and Thomas McGuane and Ivan Doig, and over in Wyoming, Gretel Ehr- lich—William Kittredge in Missoula, James Welch, David Long in Kalispell—everyone *writing*, and the ones I haven't yet met or don't know, everyone writing probably pretty fast, because of this warm wet wind that is blowing this morning—the warmness of it, paradoxically, reminding them how little time there is before the big cold comes.

Trying to finish up little projects, before it hits.

It's an odd feeling, knowing they're out there, all within a day's drive: I could go back into the house, and get their books out, and open them up, and begin reading; or I could get in the truck, start it up, and drive over and knock on their doors, see their living, breathing faces.

In Mississippi, it was different. Faulkner was gone, the way God, or Jesus, is gone—there, still, but not really—not the way he *used* to be—and Hannah, when I was there, was still on the run, still moving around, dodging things—Alabama, Montana, even a little time in the East—(stove fire is too hot; just slipped off one of my sweaters)—and Eudora Welty was more like a grandmother to writers than a writer, truthfully, when I was there—before she'd written the wonderful *One Writer's Beginnings*—she was for me a great kind influence (whom I never met) whose presence, when seen in the grocery store, or outside in her front yard, reminded me that it was all right to write, that normal, decent folk could do it, too—that it was even an admirable, respectable thing to do, and not at all wicked—and that's an invaluable thing to have, that kind of confidence or reassurance—but for all of Mississippi's literary immortality, all of its *richness*, I was still free to feel wild, still free to live down on the farm in Mississippi and not know, or believe, that there was anyone else out there: that I was the only writer for a hundred miles.

I felt as if I had to tell the stories, or they wouldn't get told.

Barthelme, at the University of Southern Mississippi, was always gone—Houston, Florida, New York, etc.—and Richard Ford was summering in the Delta, but it was a quiet summering, busy, spent writing, and his stories were always about Montana, then . . . there were other novelists too, like Ellen Gilchrest and Ellen Douglas and Rebecca Hall, but a lot of them were using other names, or living in Arkansas and New York, in North Carolina and New York—Gloria Norris, too—and for all the talent, there was no one at that time squaring up and digging in and just living their lives out, in Mississippi—Walker Percy had long ago gone back to Louisiana, and Willie Morris had come back home, was in Oxford, but wasn't writing so much anymore; Larry Brown not yet having written anything, or published—and so it was the best of both worlds, and it was too easy, it was Easy Street, and it frightened me that I would grow weak, digging in like that and having things, rich things—wonderful stories, a wonderful culture—come to me, instead of me going out after them and hunting them down—and so I left.

Out of the skillet, and into the fire. Into a den of writers, a nest of writhing writers. Some mornings I have to think about them being out there, so that then I can forget them. It was the same way in Mississippi, at first.

For about five years, actually.

I was so awed by being in Miss Welty's city that I volunteered to be her yard boy. I passed out circulars in her neighborhood, volunteering my services at ridiculously low prices, picturing myself, I think, winding slow circles around her lawn with the mower, peering in her window and watching her as she wrote, each time I went past with the mower; watching, to see how she did it—but the closest I ever got was the corner house, three houses down, and I had to run out and buy a lawn mower, to do that man's lawn. . . . I never did a good job, for I was always looking up the street, or back over my shoulder, waiting for her to walk out and water her own lawn, or to back out of the driveway in her brown Olds Cutlass, and I didn't keep a close enough eye on the lawn, I scalped it, and buzzed it, and I was let go from my capacity. . . . But I would have done a good job on *her* yard, I would have done the best. . . .

Beth Henley took *Crimes of the Heart* to Los Angeles, and hasn't been back since; Tennessee Williams died, while I was living there, but he hadn't been back in a long time. Reynolds Price and Shelby Foote had moved out: I had almost the whole playground to myself.

It was so empty that now, with Ford, Welch, Crumley, McGuane, Kittredge, and the ghost and spirit and soul of Hugo living in Missoula, five hours away—that's a long way—I still feel crowded, here in the Yaak Valley.

That's how empty Mississippi was, then. That's how many stories were floating around, uncontested, so easy to find.

Slipping my last sweatshirt off, now; writing shirtless, in November. A strange country. The landlord assures me I will not be able to write straight through the winter, in here.

It's not a particular goal of mine, to do so. If it happens, it happens. I will have plenty of wood, just in case. I will try to.

Ten o'clock: an hour later. The wind has shifted direction 180°, and is now blowing even harder from the north than it was from the south. A fine mist is sleeting, and I step outside of the greenhouse to watch it, to feel it. When I go back inside, I am surprised at the woodshed's smokey smell, like a meathouse, and its warmth. The sleet is bouncing off of the old shingles, spitting against the glass.

I'm surprisingly calm. I don't know if this is it: but I've got all of my wood in. I'm about ready to get on with it, if this really is winter. I'm almost ready.

What a good sound the wind is making. What if this is the sound you hear, after you lie down and die? I am not ready for that, but I am ready for this. I will try anything once.

*　*　*

A cold front came down out of Alaska yesterday, dropping the temperature from twenty above to fifteen below in less than half an hour— branches and limbs blowing from the trees, everything tumbling past, and the wind biting, ripping—and it kept dropping, after dark, crackling cold stars, plunging, bottoming out around thirty-eight, thirty-nine below, and then the wind disappeared, and it's staying that cold—the air motionless, the way they said it would be, forty below at night, and warming up to ten or twelve below in the day. We are sleeping in front of the fireplace, around the clock, turning the pages of books clumsily with our gloved hands.

Forty below. We're a little frightened. We're at its mercy. We hope for mercy.

It's as if the brutal cold is looking for something, passing over, searching. I hope it doesn't find it here.

ROY BLOUNT, JR.

One Draft in Longhand

[I revise a great deal, with good reason. Many of the most informative things I have read, however, have been dashed off ill-advisedly. Late one night several years ago, in a time of marital strife, I wrote the following in one draft in longhand. It contains injustices, embarrassments, barbarisms, and probable lies. I can't fix these; every time I try to, the whole thing unravels.]

I grew up having to understand more than one world at once. Because—for several reasons.

One was my mother and my father. Indissolubly incompatible. So far as I could see. Two different worlds. My mother profoundly affective, my father prominently effective. More complicated than that (my father got his feelings hurt, my mother was tendentious) but as *stark* as that.

That's why I have so much trouble—that's *one* reason I have so much trouble—dealing with the notion of sexual equality. I am in favor of it, I crave the mesh of differences but also release from the wrench of them; but I know in my heart that men and women are different organisms.

I try to live as if they weren't. But I believe that they are. Apples and oranges. And I, an apple, tilt toward the oranges at least as much as toward the apples (that is to say, toward my mother at least as much as toward my father); but I know I am an apple—partly because I've applied myself to being one, but also because I have the deep feeling that I *should* apply myself to being one, and that feeling comes from biology, from givens: I take as a given that there are such things as givens (pun here on Robin Givens?), and one of the givens I have to work with is that I am a guy. Which means, okay, I have had a better chance to get in on certain things. (*What* things, though, that I actually have gotten in on? Fishing. Professionalism. The Army. Hey there, Male-Dominated Culture: thanks a lot.)

But it also means I am the oppressor. I don't want to be the oppressor. When did I ever personally oppress anybody? In any way that brought me any satisfaction or that either of us knew any way of getting around? What have I ever gained from sexist upperhandedness that I haven't had to pay so much for that I'd rather have done without it?

That's one way I live in two worlds: feeling put-upon and yet being cast as an oppressor. It seems to me that if I'm going to be considered an oppressor I ought to be able to get a kick out of oppressing. It's only fair. But I don't.

Because I want to do right. There's another two worlds: I was raised, by my indulgent mother, to gratify myself ("If it makes him happy, why not let him do it?" I can hear her saying, to whom?), and also *not to do wrong*, by my censorious father *and* mother. And my sense of license and my sense of urge-denying morality are both so strong that I can never—I can seldom, and never without irony—satisfy them both. Two different worlds.

Then too I was raised a white southerner, which is wrong. I had no more control over it than a black person has over being brought up oppressed; but there it was, I was raised an oppressor in that category too. And I realized it. I still have a high school diary in which I came to the conclusion that the separation of movie theaters into first-run and Colored was wrong. In college—although it was a southern college strong on tradition—I began to realize that my *heritage* was wrong.

It is no easy thing to accept that one's heritage is wrong. *And at the same time to hold onto the feeling that it is juicy*, in lots of ways. And of course as my education has continued relentlessly over the years I have had to accept that *American* culture, as a whole, oppresses the Third World if not the whole world. (I could have changed my mind on this during the eighties, as many other Americans have, but I haven't: I believe that the eighties gave self-esteem a bad name.)

So although I started out in journalism thinking of myself as ill-suited to it because I was shy, the truth was that I was if anything too suited to it: a hard-shell relativist. My greatest narrowness is that I don't understand why *everyone* isn't a relativist. I will be out drinking in the middle of the night with an admittedly violence-prone black person in a black after-hours club in a town where I don't live and I can be accepting his world hand over fist and all of a sudden I get to the point that I'm saying, loudly, "Speaking as a white person. . . ." And suddenly, it doesn't go. Nobody wants to hear me speak as a white person. And I was even, you know, a little tongue-in-cheek there, though perhaps not as tongue-in-cheek as usual—it seems to me that, even in such a context, I might be allowed a few words with a little lower irony quotient: *why must I live in irony always?*

[*Jesus. Do something about that. How about, "Irony is no picnic"?*]

Better irony than poverty. Better irony than chains. Better irony than fear. Irony is the price the honest oppressor pays.

I accept that analysis.

It's hard, though. How many honest unwilling oppressors are there, who I can pal around with, have consciousness-raising (or -lowering, whichever is apposite) sessions with, sit around telling honest-oppressor jokes (at our own expense) with?

And I'm not in a line of work in which being an oppressor is worth all that much. If I were a financier, fine. If I were a lawyer, fine. If I were an ad man, fine. But being a writer, a largely first-person writer . . . the terrible thing is that once you have enough irony to be an honest oppressor, you're not really an oppressor in any self-serving way anymore. That's what irony is: a substitute for self-service. When you realize that in your particular case self-service is immoral, you resort to irony.

But self-service *is* immoral. By definition. Isn't it? There again I'm in two different worlds. The Christian and the bourgeois. In Sunday School I learned to turn the other cheek and do unto others as I would have them do unto me and leave the ninety and nine to search for the one lost lamb, and in school (nature red in tooth and claw) and community (got to out-hustle the other guy) I learned different. And both lessons seemed hallowed. My mother seemed to represent the Christian and my father the commercial, but my mother fully (except in an insidious psychological unasserted way that was crucial) supported my father's commercialism (she had to depend on it, at any rate, it had brought them both up from want), and my father's commercialism insisted upon being part and parcel of Christianity. So there were two different worlds *within* each of the two different worlds I had to acknowledge as a child.

And there was the world of sensuality vis-à-vis the world of religion, complicated by the fact that the very hymns were sensual:

> I come to the garden alone,
> While the dew is still on the roses,
> And the voice I hear,
> Falling on my ear,
> The son of God disclo-o-ses;
> And . . . he walks with me,
> And he talks with me,
> And he tells me I am his own.
> And the joy we share

As we tarry there,
None other
Has ever
Known.

The girls I felt sensual with were religious. (I didn't know any irreligious girls.) I felt particularly sensual sitting next to them in church. Perhaps that sounds integrative. It wasn't. It wasn't *bad,* Lord knows. But it ironized my blood.

And so to bed.

[The truth is, though, that in the course of running the above through my word processor five or six times I have rewritten it quite a bit, and now I'm inclined to revise it some more and work it into a primarily nonautobiographical novel I'm writing, as it is beginning to sound like an essay by somebody else. I am less sniveling than this when I write an essay—but I promise you this is less sniveling than the original, which I wrote.

[Maybe the essayist's secret agenda is to put something down where he or she can see that he or she is sniveling/bloviating/blithering and can revise. ("You'd better change your tune, young man.") Of course that may not be the case if the essayist speaks for the truly wronged.

[I think I would have been good at being among the truly wronged and protesting it. (I don't mean protesting that I was among them, though that's something a person could get eloquent about: "Why me?" *I mean protesting the wrong.) But maybe not. Maybe if I were truly wronged I'd just be all beat down and not worth a shit—if I'm this sorry (even after several rewrites), white and male. "Why must I live in irony always?"* Jesus.

[But I will say this: Irony is no piece of cake.]

ANNIE DILLARD

Luke

It is a fault of infinity to be too small to find. It is a fault of eternity to be crowded out by time. Before our eyes we see an unbroken sheath of colors. We live over a bulk of things. We walk between a congeries of colored things that part before our steps to reveal more colored things. Above us hurtle more things, which fill the universe. There is no crack. Unbreakable seas lie flush on their beds. Under the Greenland icecap lies not so much as a bubble. Mountains and hills, lakes, deserts, forests, and plains fully occupy their continents. Where then is the gap through which eternity streams? In holes at the roots of forest cedars I find spiders and chips. I have rolled plenty of stones away, to no avail. Under the lily pads on the lake are flatworms and lake water. Materials wrap us seamlessly; time propels us ceaselessly. Muffled and bound we pitch forward from one filled hour to the next, from one filled landscape or house to the next. No rift between one note of the chorus and the next opens on infinity. No spear of eternity interposes itself between work and lunch.

And this is what we love: this human-scented skull, the sheen on the skin of a face, this exhilarating game, this crowded feast, these shifting mountains, the dense water and its piercing lights. It is our lives we love, our times, our generation, our pursuits. And are we called to forsake these vivid and palpable goods for an idea of which we experience not one trace? Am I to believe eternity outranks my child's finger?

The idea of infinity is that it is bigger, infinitely bigger, than our universe, which floats, held, upon it, as a leaf might float on a shoreless sea. The idea of eternity is that it bears time in its side like a hole. You believe it. Surely it is an idea suited for minds deranged by solitude, people who run gibbering from caves, who rave on mountaintops, who forgot to sleep and starved.

Let us rest the material view and consider, just consider, that the weft of materials admits of a very few, faint, unlikely gaps. People are, after all, still disappearing, still roping robes on themselves, still braving the work of prayer, insisting they hear something, even fighting and still dying for it. The impulse to a spiritual view persists, and the evidence of that view's power among historical forces and among contemporary ideas persists, and the claim of reasoning men and women that they know God from experience persists.

"A young atheist cannot be too careful of his reading," C. S. Lewis observed with amusement. Any book on any subject—a book by a writer the young atheist least suspects of apostasy—may abruptly and unabashedly reveal its author's theist conviction. It may quote the Bible—that fetish of Grandma's—as if it possessed real authority. The young atheist reels—is he crazy, or is everyone else?

This Bible, this ubiquitous, persistent black chunk of a best-seller, is a chink—often the only chink—through which winds howl. It is a singularity, a black hole into which our rich and multiple world strays and vanishes. We crack open its pages at our peril. Many educated, urbane, and flourishing experts in every aspect of business, culture, and science have felt pulled by this anachronistic, semibarbaric mass of antique laws and fabulous tales from far away; they entered its queer, strait gates and were lost. Eyes open, head high, in full possession of their critical minds, they obeyed the high, inaudible whistle, and let the gates close behind them.

Respectable parents who love their children leave this absolutely respectable book lying about, as a possible safeguard against, say, drugs; alas, it is the book that kidnaps the children, and hooks them.

> But he said unto Jesus, And who is my neighbor?
> And Jesus answering said, A certain man went down from Jerusalem to Jericho, and fell among thieves.
> And he said unto him, Who is my neighbor?
> But a certain Samaritan came where he was.
> And went to him, and bound up his wounds, and brought him to an inn, and took care of him.
> And he said unto him, Which now, thinkest thou, was neighbor unto him that fell among the thieves?
> And he said unto him, Who IS my neighbor?
> And Jesus answering said, A certain man went down from Jerusalem to Jericho, and fell among thieves.
> Who IS my neighbor?
> Then said Jesus unto him, Go, and do thou likewise.

This and similar fragments of Biblical language played in my mind like a record on which the needle has stuck, moved at the root of my tongue and sounded deep in my ears without surcease. Who IS my neighbor?

Every July for four years, my sister and I trotted off to Presbyterian church camp. It was cheap, wholesome, and nearby. There we were happy, loose with other children under pines. If our parents had known how pious and low-church this camp was, they would have yanked me. We memorized Bible chapters, sang rollicking hymns around the clock, held nightly devotions with extemporaneous prayers, and filed out of the woods to chapel twice on Sunday dressed in white shorts. The faith-filled theology there was only half a step out of a tent; you could still smell the sawdust.

I had a head for religious ideas. They were the first ideas I ever encountered. They made other ideas seem mean.

For what shall it profit a man, if he shall gain the whole world and lose his own soul? And lose his own soul? Know ye that the Lord he is God: It is he that hath made us, and not we ourselves; we are his people, and the sheep of his pasture. Arise, take up thy bed, and walk.

Who shall ascend into the hill of the Lord? or who shall stand in his holy place? He that hath clean hands, and a pure heart; who hath not lifted up his soul unto vanity, nor sworn deceitfully.

The earth is the Lord's, and the fulness thereof; the world, and they that dwell therein. The heavens declare the glory of God; and the firmament sheweth his handiwork. Verily I say unto you, that one of you shall betray me.

Every summer we memorized these things at camp. Every Sunday, at home in Pittsburgh, we heard these things in Sunday School. Every Thursday we studied these things, and memorized them, too (strictly as literature, they said), at our private school. I had miles of Bible in memory: some perforce, but most by hap, like the words to songs. There was no corner of my brain where you could not find, among the files of clothing labels and heaps of rocks and minerals, among the swarms of protozoans and shelves of novels, whole tapes and snarls and reels of Bible. I wrote poems in deliberate imitation of its sounds, those repeated feminine endings followed by thumps, or those long hard beats followed by softness. Selah.

The Bible's was an unlikely, movie-set world alongside our world. Light-shot and translucent in the pallid Sunday School watercolors on the walls, stormy and opaque in the dense and staggering texts they read us placidly, sweet-mouthed and earnest week after week, this world inter-leaved our waking world like dream.

I saw Jesus in watercolor, framed, on the walls. We Sunday School children sat in a circle, and said dimly with Samuel, "Here am I." Jesus was thin as a veil of tinted water; he was awash. Bearded men lay indolent about him in pastel robes, and shepherd boys, and hooded women with clear, round faces. Lake Gennesaret, the Sea of Galilee—it was all watercolor; I could see the paper through it. The southern sun, the Asian sun, bleached the color from thick village walls, from people's limbs and eyes. These pastel illustrations were as exotic, and as peculiar to children's sentimental educations, as watercolor depictions of lions and giraffes.

We studied the Gospel of Luke. In that world, people had time on their hands. Simon Peter, James, and John dropped their nets, and quit their two boats full of fresh fish: "And when they had brought their ships to land, they forsook all, and followed him." They had time to gather at the side of the lake and hear harsh words. They had time to stand for the sermon on the mount, and the sermon on the plain. A multitude followed Jesus and the twelve into a desert place belonging to the city of Bethsaida. The day wore away while Jesus spoke to them of the kingdom of God; then he had his disciples feed them—"about five thousand men"—with five loaves of bread and two fishes, which Jesus blessed and broke, looking up to heaven.

Luke's is the most reasoned, calm, plausible, and orderly Gospel. It does not claim divinity for Christ, but only a glorious messiahship. Jesus is the holy teacher who shows the way; he leads Israel and all the world back to a prayerful acknowledgment of the fatherhood of the one God. The coming of Jesus, attended by signs from heaven, does not interrupt the sacred history of Israel; it fulfills it. But Luke's Gospel is calm and plausible only compared to the swirling bewilderments of Mark and the intergalactic leapings of John. All of the Gospels are unprecedented, unequaled, singular texts. Coming at Luke from our world, we stagger and balk. Luke is a piece torn from wildness. It is a blur of power, violent in its theological and narrative heat, abrupt and inexplicable. It shatters and jolts. Its grand-scale, vivid, and shifting tableaux call all in doubt.

In a hurried passage, Jesus walks by Levi the tax collector and says, Follow me. That is all there is to that. He calms the storm on the lake from his skiff. He heals the centurion's servant from the road outside the town; he raises a widow's young son from his funeral bier. He drives demons into the Gedarene swine and over the cliff. He performs all with his marble calm, by his fiery power, which seems to derive from his very otherness, his emptiness as a channel to God. He moves among men who could not have been (as fishermen, but who nevertheless seem in contrast) panicky: "Master, master, we perish!" Jesus is tranquil in his dealings with maniacs, rich young men, synagogue leaders, Roman soldiers, weeping women, Pilate, Herod, and Satan himself in the desert. Resurrected (apparently as a matter of course), he is distant, enlarged, and calm, even subdued; he explicates scripture, walks from town to town, and puts up with the marveling disciples. These things are in Luke, which, of all the Gospels, most stresses and vivifies Christ's common humanity.

Long before any rumor of resurrection, the narrative is wild. Jesus dines with a pharisee. A slattern from the town walks in; she has heard that Jesus is in that house for dinner. In she walks with no comment at all, just as later a man with dropsy appears before Jesus at another house where he is eating. The woman stands behind him in tears; the men apparently ignore her. Her tears, which must have been copious, wet Jesus's feet. She bends over and wipes the wetness away with her hair. She kisses his feet, and anoints them with perfume from an alabaster flask.

After some time and conversation with the pharisee, Jesus says, "Seest thou this woman? . . . Thou gavest me no kiss: but this woman since the time I came in hath not ceased to kiss my feet. . . . Her sins, which are many, are forgiven; for she loved much." To the woman he says, "Thy faith hath saved thee; go in peace." (This is in Luke alone.)

The light is raking; the action is relentless. Once in a crushing crowd, Jesus is trying to make his way to Jairus's twelve-year-old daughter, who is dying. In the crowd, a woman with an unstoppable issue of blood touches the border of his robe. Jesus says, "Who touched me?" Peter and the other disciples point out, with exasperated sarcasm, that "the multitude throng thee and press thee, and sayest thou, Who touched me?" Jesus persists, "Somebody hath touched me: for I perceive that virtue is gone out of me." The woman confesses, and declares she was healed immediately; Jesus blesses her; a message comes from Jairus's house that the daughter has already died—"Trouble not the Master."

"Fear not," says Jesus; he enters the child's chamber with her parents and Peter, James, and John; says, "Maid, arise." She arises straightway, and he commands her parents to "give her meat." Then he calls the twelve together, gives them authority over devils and power to heal, and sends them out to teach and heal. When they come back he preaches to multitudes whom he feeds. He prays, teaches the disciples, heals, preaches to throngs, and holds forth in synagogues. And so on without surcease, event crowded on event. Even as he progresses to his own crucifixion, his saving work continues: in the garden where soldiers seize him, he heals with a touch the centurion's ear, which a disciple impetuously lopped off; hanging on his cross he blesses the pentinent thief, promising him a place in paradise "this very day."

Historians of every school agree—with varying enthusiasm—that this certain Jewish man lived, wandered in Galilee and Judaea, and preached a radically spiritual doctrine of prayer, poverty, forgiveness, and mercy for all under the fathership of God; he attracted a following, and was crucified by soldiers of the occupying Roman army. There is no reason to hate him, unless the idea of a God who knows, hears, and acts—an idea he proclaimed—is itself offensive.

In Luke, Jesus makes no claims to be the only son of God. Luke is a monotheist: Jesus is the Son of man, and the messiah, but Jesus is not God's only-begotten son, of one substance with the Father, who came down from heaven. Luke never suggests that Christ was begotten before all worlds, that he was very god of very god, that eternity interrupted time with his coming, or that faith in his divinity is the sole path to salvation. The substance of his teaching is his way; he taught God, not Christ. The people in Luke are a rogues' gallery of tax collectors, innkeepers, fallen women, shrewd bourgeois owners, thieves, pharisees, and assorted unclean gentiles. He saves them willy-nilly; they need not, and do not, utter creeds first.

Salvation in Luke, for the followers of Christ, consists in a life of prayer, repentance, and mercy; it is a life in the world with God. Faith in Christ's divinity has nothing to do with it. The cross as God's own sacrifice has nothing to do with it; the cross is Jesus's own sacrifice, freely and reluctantly chosen, and of supreme moment on that head. That Jesus was resurrected in flesh and blood means in Luke, I think, that he was indeed the messiah whom God had promised to lead the people— now all people—by his teaching and example, back to prayerful and spiritual obedience to God their father and creator.

Still, his teachings are as surprising as his life. Their requirements are harsh. Do not ask for your goods back from anyone who has taken them from you. Sell all that thou hast, and give it to the poor. Do not stop to perform a son's great duty, to bury a father. Divorce and remarriage is adultery. Forgive an enemy seven times in one day, without limit. Faith is not a gift but a plain duty. Take no thought for your life. Pray without ceasing. Unto everyone which hath shall be given; and from him that hath not, even that he hath shall be taken away.

The teachings that are not so harsh are even more radical, and harder to swallow.

> Consider the lilies how they grow: they toil not, they spin not; and yet I say unto you, that Solomon in all his glory was not arrayed like one of these.
>
> If then God so clothe the grass, which is to day in the field, and to morrow is cast into the oven; how much more will he clothe you, O ye of little faith? . . . your Father knoweth that you have need of these things.
>
> But rather seek ye the kingdom of God; and all these things shall be added unto you. Fear not, little flock.
>
> Ask, and it shall be given you; seek, and ye shall find; knock, and it shall be opened unto you.
>
> For every one that asketh receiveth; and he that seeketh findeth; and to him that knocketh it shall be opened.

"Fear not, little flock": this seems apt for those pious watercolor people so long ago, those blameless and endearing shepherds and fishermen, in colorful native garb, whose lives seem pure, because they are not our lives. They were rustics, silent and sunlit, outdoors, whom we sentimentalize and ignore. They are not in our world. They had some nascent sort of money, but not the kind to take seriously. They got their miracles, perhaps, but they died anyway, long ago, and so did their children. Salvation is obviously for them, and so is God, for they are, like the very young and the very old in our world, peripheral. Religion is for outcasts and victims; Jesus made that clear. Religion suits primitives. They have time to work up their touching faith in unverifiable promises, and they might as well, having bugger-all else.

Our lives are complex. There are many things we must consider before we go considering any lilies. There are many things we must fear. We are in charge; we are running things in a world we made; we are nobody's little flock.

In Luke, Christ's ministry enlarges in awfulness—from the sunny Galilean days of eating and drinking, preaching on lakesides, saying lovely things, choosing disciples, healing the sick, making the blind see, casting out demons, and raising the dead—enlarges in awfulness from this exuberant world, where all is possible and God displays his power and love, to the dark messianic journey that begins when Peter acknowledges him (Who do you think I am?) as the Christ, and culminates in the eerie night-long waiting at the lip of the vortex as Pilate and Herod pass Jesus back and forth and he defends himself not.

Jesus creates his role and succumbs to it. He understands his destiny only gradually, through much prayer; he decides on it, foretells it, and sets his face to meet it. On the long journey to Jerusalem, which occupies many chapters of Luke, he understands more and more. The narrative builds a long sober sense of crushing demand on Jesus the man, and the long sober sense of his gradual strengthening himself to see it, to cause it, and to endure it. (The account of his ministry's closure parallels the account of its beginning three years previously; Jesus very gradually, and through prayer, chooses, creates, and assumes his tremendous and transcendent role. He chooses his life, and he chooses his death.)

In that final long journey to Jerusalem, the austerity of Jesus deepens; his mystery and separateness magnify. The party is over. Pressure rises from crowds; pressure rises from the Jewish authorities.

His utterances become vatic and Greekish. Behold, we go up to Jerusalem, he tells his disciples. If anyone wishes to follow me, let him deny himself, take up his cross day after day, and so follow me. For the Son of man is coming into his glory. What awaits him is uncertain, unspecified, even unto the cross and upon it, but in the speeches of his last days, in this village and that, his awareness becomes stonily clearer. Privately, often, and urgently, he addresses his disciples in dire terms: When they call you before the magistrates, do not trouble yourself about what you are to say. I have a baptism to undergo. The days will come when ye shall desire to see one of the days of the Son of man, and ye shall not see it. "And they understood none of these things."

In a synagogue he addresses the pharisees who bring him a message from Herod ("that fox"): I must walk today, and tomorrow, and the day following: for it cannot be that a prophet perish out of Jerusalem. He adds an apostrophe: O Jerusalem, Jerusalem, which killest the prophets, and stonest them that are sent unto thee; how often would I have gathered thy children together, as a hen doth gather her brood under her wings, and ye would not!

And he does walk, that day, and the next day, and the day following, soberly, wittingly, and freely, going up to Jerusalem for the Passover in which he will not be passed over. There is little mingling with crowds, and only four healings, two of them provokingly on the Sabbath. His words are often harsh and angry. "Thou fool," he has God saying to a rich man. Ye hypocrites, he calls his disciples. In one of his stories, an outraged master says, "Depart from me, all ye workers of iniquity." I am come to send fire on the earth. But those mine enemies . . . bring hither, and slay them before me.

He enters the city on a colt, and is at once discovered driving the money changers out of the temple. Whosoever shall fall upon that stone shall be broken; but on whomsoever it shall fall, it will grind him to powder. As for the temple in which they stand, There shall not be one stone upon another. These be the days of vengeance.

The crowds around Jesus are so great in Jerusalem that the Roman authorities must take him at night, as he quits the garden. There he has prayed in an agony, Father, if thou be willing, remove this cup from me: nevertheless not my will, but thine, be done. Then he has prayed *more* earnestly, and his sweat fell down to the ground. Betrayed to the soldiers, he shuttles back and forth between Pilate and Herod all night; the cock crows; Peter denies him; and in the morning Pilate takes him—him supremely silent, magnificent, and vulnerable—before the chief priests and Jewish rulers, and before an unspecified crowd. They cry, Release unto us Barrabbas. And their voices and those of the chief priests prevail. As Roman soldiers lead Jesus away, "there followed him a great company of people." Where were they a minute ago, that they could not outshout the claque for Barrabbas?

In Luke alone, after Jesus on the cross commends his spirit to the hands of God, and dies, a Roman soldier is moved to say, "Certainly this was a righteous man." Luke alone recounts the incident on the road to Emmaus. Two disciples walking to Emmaus are talking about Jesus's crucifixion, which has occurred three days previously, when a stranger joins them and asks what they are talking about; the disciples, surprised, explain. The stranger interprets messianic prophesies in scripture for them, beginning with Moses, which seems to surprise them not at all. In the village, they invite the stranger in. When at table he takes the loaf, gives thanks, and breaks it, then their eyes are opened, they recognize him, and he vanishes.

Amazed, they walk all the way back to Jerusalem—another seven miles—that night, and tell the others. And while they are speaking, Jesus appears yet again. They are "terrified," but Jesus says, Why are ye troubled? And why do thoughts arise in your hearts? He shows them his wounded hands and feet, and they are full of joy and wondering, and very far from recognizing that, among other things, ordinary hospitality is called for—so Jesus has to ask, Have ye any meat? (They give him broiled fish and a piece of honeycomb.) Then the resurrected Jesus explains scriptural prophesies concerning the messiah's death and his resurrection on the third day; charges them to preach to all nations; leads them out as far as Bethany (two miles east); blesses them, and is carried up to heaven.

When I was a child, the adult members of Pittsburgh society adverted to the Bible unreasonably often. What arcana! Why did they spread this scandalous document before our eyes? If they had read, it, I thought, they would have hid it. They did not recognize the lively danger that we would, through repeated exposure, catch a dose of its virulent opposition to their world. Instead they bade us study great chunks of it, and think about those chunks, and commit them to memory, and ignore them. By dipping us children in the Bible so often, they hoped, I think, to give our lives a serious tint, and to provide us with quaintly magnificent snatches of prayer to produce as charms while we were, say, being mugged for our cash or jewels.

In Sunday School at the Shadyside Presbyterian Church, the handsome father of rascal Jack from dancing school, himself a vice-president of Jones & Laughlin Steel, whose wife was famous at the country club for her tan, held a birch pointer in his long fingers and shyly tapped the hanging paper map—shyly because he could see we were not listening. Who would listen to this? Why on Earth were we here? There in blue and yellow and green were Galilee, Samaria itself, and Judaea, he said— and I pretended to pay attention as a courtesy—the Sea of Galilee, the river Jordan, and the Dead Sea. I saw on the hanging map the coasts of Judaea by the far side of Jordan, on whose unimaginable shores the pastel Christ had maybe uttered such cruel, stiff, thrilling words: Sell all that thou hast.

The Gospel of Luke ends immediately and abruptly after the ascension outside Bethany, on that Easter Sunday when the disciples walked so much and kept receiving visitations from the risen Christ. The skies have scarcely closed around Christ's heels when the story concludes on the disciples: And they were continually in the temple, praising and blessing God. Amen.

What a pity, that so hard on the heels of Christ come the Christians. There is no breather. The disciples turn into the early Christians between one rushed verse and another. What a dismaying pity, that here come the Christians already, flawed to the core, full of wild ideas and hurried self-importance. They are already blocking, with linked arms, the howling gap in the weft of things that their man's coming and going tore.

For who can believe in the Christians? They are, we know by hindsight, suddenly not at all peripheral. They set out immediately to take over the world, and they pretty much did it. They converted emperors, raised armies, lined their pockets with real money, and did evil things large and small, in century after century including this one. They are smug and busy, just like us, and who could believe in them? They are not innocent, they are not shepherds and fishermen in rustic period costume, they are men and women just like us, in polyester. Who could believe salvation is for these rogues? That God is for these rogues? For they are just like us, and salvation's time is past.

Unless, of course—

Unless Christ's washing the disciples' feet, their dirty toes, means what it could, possibly, mean: that it is all right to be human. That God knows we are human, and full of evil, all of us, and we are his people anyway, and the sheep of his pasture.

Unless those colorful scamps and scalawags who populate Jesus's parables were just as evil as we are, and evil in the same lazy, cowardly, and scheming ways. Unless those pure disciples themselves and those watercolor women—who so disconcertingly turned into The Christians overnight—were complex and selfish humans also, who lived in the material world, and whose errors and evils were not pretty but ugly, and had real consequences. If they were just like us, then Christ's words to them are addressed to us, in full and merciful knowledge—and we are lost. There is no place to hide.

DENIS DONOGHUE

T. S. Eliot: The Communication of the Dead

I

Two lines from the last of T. S. Eliot's *Four Quartets*, "Little Gidding," are carved upon the headstone of his grave at East Coker:

> the communication
> Of the dead is tongued with fire beyond the language of the living.

What I propose to say this evening is a commentary on those lines. But I must approach them somewhat indirectly.

There is a passage in the first version of Yeats's *A Vision*, in which the poet is trying to find evidence in favor of his philosophy of history, and brooding for that reason upon certain artists whom he regarded with a mixture of admiration and dismay. The condition he found exemplified in Eliot, Pound, Joyce, and Pirandello was one in which the mind, recoiling from abstraction, turns upon itself. These writers, Yeats said, either "eliminate from metaphor the poet's phantasy and substitute a strangeness discovered by historical or contemporary research"; or they "break up the logical processes of thought by flooding them with associated ideas or words that seem to drift into the mind by chance." As in Pirandello's *Henry IV*, Eliot's *The Waste Land*, the early *Cantos* of Pound, and Joyce's *Ulysses*, the mind sets side by side "the *physical primary*—a lunatic among his keepers, a man fishing behind a gas works, the vulgarity of a single Dublin day prolonged through 700 pages—and the *spiritual primary*, delirium, the Fisher King, Ulysses' wandering." Yeats's explanation for these wild conjunctions was that myth and fact, "united until the exhaustion of the Renaissance, have now fallen so far apart that man understands for the first time the rigidity of fact, and calls up, by that very recognition, myth—the Mask—which now but gropes its way out of the mind's dark but will shortly pursue and terrify."*

*W. B. Yeats, A Vision (London: T. Werner Laurie, 1925, pp. 211–212).

In that passage, Yeats appears to mean that a fact is rigid when it presents itself as if by its own will, indifferent to the mind that witnesses it. I think he had in view the world according to realism and naturalism, in which the mind capitulates to whatever it happens to see. Myth, in turn, becomes monstrous when it is separated from every fact that would make it humanly available; monstrous, like the Furies, pursuing and terrifying their victim.

To prevent the separation of fact and myth, Yeats resorted to symbols; because a symbol is at once fact and the halo of value that surrounds it, it is an object in the world inseparable from its natural or ancestral associations. But in January 1925, when he wrote the paragraph I have quoted, he was in one of his recurrent apocalyptic moods; sensing that a great historical era was coming to an end, and troubling himself with visions of its successor, some rough beast slouching towards Bethlehem to be born. He had reason to fear that such a thing would ignore a poet's symbols and the desires they embodied.

I propose to start from Yeats's comment on *The Waste Land* and the separation of fact and myth, and to reach a point where Eliot, too, invokes the symbol in a spirit both like and unlike Yeats's. But I should say at once what I understand by a myth. I take it as a story always already told, a communication of the dead for the benefit of the living; a story recited over and over as a communal interpretation of life, and offered for the instruction and the cohesion of the community that receives it. It tells the members of a community what it is good for them to hear and to believe. The myth aims to be true, in the sense of universal, as we say of a story that it is true to life. It is designed to make sense of the human experience, and to protect the community that receives it from being enslaved to time and process. In that respect, a myth turns what has merely occurred into a narrative of repetitions, and its grammar becomes the continuous present tense: It gives point to anniversaries, recurrences, religious ceremonies, occasions on which people wish to assure themselves that they are members of a community. Like Yeats, we distinguish between a myth and a fiction. A fiction is a story that we do not claim to be true, but to be in some other way useful or diverting. We make such fictions, and we hold some of them in our minds, but we are not called upon to act on them or indeed to give them any special privilege. A myth, on the other hand, is, as Yeats said, "one of those statements our nature is compelled to make and employ as a truth though there cannot be sufficient evidence."* If a fact and a myth

*W. B. Yeats, Explorations *(London: Macmillan, 1962, p. 392).*

were to coincide, it would mean that the fact participated in the universal story, and embodied its truth. The myth would be, for its society, the one story and one story only worth the telling; the fact its incarnation. A myth does not merely report what happened, but what, having happened, is re-enacted as an archetype every time it is performed. When a fact lacks its myth, it is merely what it is, rigid as Yeats sees it. When a myth fails to find its proper communal embodiment, it seeks, and finds as in Fascism, a monstrous incarnation.

We can guess, I think, the attributes of *The Waste Land* that Yeats saw with whatever degree of dismay. He saw that its few intimations of happiness—the hyacinth girl, the "inexplicable splendour of Ionian white and gold" of Magnus Martyr—are uncanny because they are autonomous, they have no before or after, no story completes them. He saw, too, that while no single myth makes sense of the experiences that Eliot intuits in the poem, there are several myths from different cultures, and they imply several moral perspectives, each of them superior to the events it is called upon to judge. What each perspective lacks is completeness: One myth is succeeded by another. So the problem of authority is not resolved.

Eliot provided the theory of these several perspectives when he remarked, in his Harvard dissertation on F. H. Bradley, that "the life of a soul does not consist in the contemplation of one consistent world but in the painful task of unifying . . . incompatible ones, and passing, when possible, from two or more discordant viewpoints to a higher which shall somehow include and transmute them."* He repeated the theory, in effect, when he reviewed *Ulysses* in November 1923 and distinguished between the narrative method of fiction—which is the common procedure of realism—and the mythical method, which Joyce invented upon a hint, it appears, from Yeats's middle poems. By using Homer's *Odyssey* as the frame of *Ulysses;* by maintaining a continuous parallel between contemporaneity and antiquity; Joyce arrived at a method, as Eliot said, "a way of controlling, of ordering, of giving a shape and a significance to the immense panorama of futility and anarchy which is contemporary history." Eliot's way of reading *Ulysses* may or may not be useful: It is still contentious. I remark only that he found in the early chapters of *Ulysses*, as he read them between 1919 and 1921, hints toward the method he needed and, with Pound's editorial help, found for *The Waste Land.* The extent of the influence of *Ulysses* upon *The Waste Land* is still

*T. S. Eliot, Knowledge and Experience in the Philosophy of F. H. Bradley *(London: Faber and Faber, 1964, pp. 147–148).*

in mild dispute. The chief difference of form between the two works is that Joyce used the mythic perspective of one story, the *Odyssey*, while Eliot employed several provisional perspectives.

The moral bearing of these perspectives is clarified by Eliot's argument, in "Tradition and the Individual Talent," that writers should submit themselves to an historical myth, which he called Tradition; it was something far more valuable than any individual talent that addressed it. The self-discipline of a writer who is willing to surrender himself to tradition is "the historical sense." Tradition is the force that, when he became a Christian, Eliot chose to call Orthodoxy; the force not oneself to which a properly disposed mind submits. In *The Waste Land* the higher perspectives have mainly punitive intent; as Yeats and Pound recognized in thinking Eliot chiefly a satirist. Sometimes the judgment is imposed by voices that have every right to impose it; by the Buddha in "The Fire Sermon," by Ezekiel and then Dante in "The Burial of the Dead," by the divine voice of the *Upanishads* in "What the Thunder Said." But what we observe as the most formidable if also the most disturbingly repellent perspective is the one imposed by Tiresias, who foresees more than is good for him in the seduction of the bored typist, and foresuffers less than he might. In any event, Tiresias can only see the world as one alienated from it, he does not "give" or "sympathize," he does not participate in the suffering and transformation of "What the Thunder Said." When all is accounted, he merely enforces one of several discontinuous myths, charged with diminishing further the things he looks down upon.

In Eliot's early poems the main things looked down upon are instances of vanity, meaningless sexuality, the sundry masquerades that time resumes, and consciousness pathetically adrift from any valid purpose it might find for itself. But there are also things looked up to, including—in the "Preludes"—

> The notion of some infinitely gentle
> Infinitely suffering thing . . .

and the girl in "La Figlia che piange," "her hair over her arms and her arms full of flowers." These images are preserved from any punitive perspective, or they are held as if in parentheses, waiting for the redemptive perspective in which they will be completed.

It is a commonplace, but not one to be treated as commonplace, that in Pound and Wyndham Lewis and in the Yeats of "On the Boiler" and the last poems, the separated and deracinated myth found a dreadful form for itself: the rough beast turned out, at least for a few years, to be Hitler or Mussolini, the nearest likeness to an Italian Renaissance prince the twentieth century could produce as an exemplar of power and will. In Eliot, the myth took no contemporaneous form but the narrative form of Christ, his birth, death, and resurrection. Upon Eliot's conversion to the Anglican communion in 1927, he disposed his will to construe the facts of his experience in a Christian light. He submitted himself to a structure of belief that had as one of its great merits the fact that he had not invented it. Some readers regard his conversion as a scandal, and complain that for a whiff of incense a great poet abandoned them. There are readers, too, who think his conversion further proof, if proof beyond that of the early poems is required, of a pervasive debility beneath the surface of his work. My view is different. I believe that Eliot, far from being a man of little energy and will, knew himself to be a man of dangerously extreme passion; he put phrases together and somehow made poems of them in the desperate hope of keeping himself from falling apart. What he chiefly wanted, in writing poems, was the experience of exhaustion, of good riddance, that he found in releasing himself from certain intolerable feelings. As he moved toward the Christian communion, I think he felt the exhausting satisfaction of submitting violent and morbid imageries to the discipline of impersonal doctrines and dogmas. When he said, in "Tradition and the Individual Talent," that "poetry is not a turning loose of emotion, but an escape from emotion; it is not the expression of personality, but an escape from personality," he went on immediately to remark that "only those who have personality and emotions know what it means to want to escape from these things."*

In referring to Eliot's religious beliefs, one risks being impertinent. But his conversion has been the object of such intemperate comment from time to time that I think it worth making a single remark on the matter; that Eliot's right to be a Christian is as clear as anyone else's right not to. I do not understand why Eliot's becoming a Christian attracts more aggressive comment than any other poet's agnosticism. If it could be shown that his conversion resulted in the impoverishment of his poetry, that would be a different matter, but I don't see that any such consequence has been shown. There are readers who think *The Waste Land* Eliot's greatest poem, and the poetry of his Christian years a falling

---

*T. S. Eliot, Selected Essays (London: Faber and Faber, third edition, 1951, p. 21).

off from that achievement. But that, too, is a difficult case to make. A list of Eliot's most achieved poems that did not find places for "Marina," "Ash-Wednesday," and at least three of the four Quartets—I have doubts about "The Dry Salvages"—would be an eccentric show.

But it is reasonable to ask, within the context of Christianity, not: what precisely did Eliot believe and practice; but rather: what particular tradition, or traditions, within Christianity did he avow, since there is a certain latitude in that communion? The question is worth asking, because until we try to answer it we can't be sure where, in reading Eliot's later poems, the emphasis should fall.

Perhaps it is enough to say that in rejecting the Unitarianism in which he was brought up, Eliot moved toward the most stringent theology he could find. Within Christianity, two traditions, or two modes of emphasis, engaged him. One was Augustinian: it involved theological exactitudes extending from Augustine to Pascal. The other was the mystical tradition, which Eliot understood mainly from Evelyn Underhill's book on Mysticism—and it took the particular emphasis, for Eliot, of his reverence for the English medieval mystics and especially for Juliana of Norwich. In a crucial sense, he found enough scholasticism, enough Aristotle, enough Aquinas, in Dante's *Divine Comedy* and the *Vita Nuova* to reconcile every theological tradition he valued. These affiliations might with equal force have led Eliot into the Roman Catholic rather than the Anglican Church. He submitted to Canterbury rather than to Rome, I think, because he wanted to pay tribute to England, both the England in which he chose to live and the England of the early seventeenth century from which his ancestors set out to make a new life in America. He revered the English church of Lancelot Andrewes, Donne, Herbert, and Nicholas Ferrar. Besides, he did not regard the differences between Canterbury and Rome as at all comparable to those that distinguished Christianity from paganism.

I must try to be more specific. For Eliot, as for any Christian, the founding event of the Christian myth is the Incarnation, the birth of Christ as Son of God. The chief distinction of man, seen in the light of the Incarnation, is "to glorify God and enjoy Him for ever."* In that pilgrimage, the crucial force is faith, which takes precedence even over morals: religion "is not, and can never survive as, simply a code of morals." Morals are a consequence of one's faith, not a cause of it. Faith itself is never as secure as a believer would wish it to be, but doubt and

*T. S. Eliot, "Literature, Science, and Dogma": The Dial, LXXXII, March 3, 1927, p. 241.

uncertainty "are merely a variety of belief."* Genuine blasphemy, as in Baudelaire, depends upon the belief it affronts. Like any other Christian, but with unusually reiterated emphasis, Eliot believed in Original Sin, and he insisted that without a conviction of that categorical guilt, human life becomes trivial or brutal. In *After Strange Gods* he claimed that the diabolic element in modern literature was related to the disappearance of the idea of Original Sin: With its disappearance, and "with the disappearance of the idea of intense moral struggle, the human beings presented to us both in poetry and in prose fiction today . . . tend to become less and less real." It is, Eliot said, "in moments of moral and spiritual struggle depending upon spiritual sanctions, rather than in those 'bewildering minutes' in which we are all very much alike, that men and women come nearest to being real."* The bewildering minutes—a phrase Eliot found in *The Revenger's Tragedy*—are those in which, through lust or other violence, we lose ourselves.

Eliot's most emphatic statements on Original and particular sin are to be found in his essays on Dante, Pascal, and Baudelaire. In the essay on Baudelaire, he says that "in the middle nineteenth century, the age which (at its best) Goethe had prefigured, an age of bustle, programmes, platforms, scientific progress, humanitarianism and revolutions which improved nothing, an age of progressive degradation, Baudelaire perceived that what really matters is Sin and Redemption." To such a mind, "the recognition of the reality of Sin is a New Life; and the possibility of damnation is so immense a relief in a world of electoral reform, plebiscites, sex reform and dress reform, that damnation itself is an immediate form of salvation—of salvation from the ennui of modern life, because it at last gives some significance to living."*

It follows that Eliot insists on the letter of Christian doctrine that refers to Hell, Purgatory, Limbo, and Heaven, and construes its spirit in Augustinian terms. In Dante's *Inferno*, Eliot says, "the torment issues from the very nature of the damned themselves, expresses their essence; they writhe in the torment of their own perpetually perverted nature."* It is clear that Eliot regarded Hell, Purgatory, and Heaven as states of being, eternal conditions that, even on earth and in time, we could at least imagine. One could begin in this life to suffer the eternity of Hell. In a letter to Paul Elmer More, Eliot said:

*T. S. Eliot, "A Note on Poetry and Belief": The Enemy, I, January 1927, p. 15.
*T. S. Eliot, After Strange Gods (New York: Harcourt, Brace, 1934, pp. 45–46).
*Eliot, Selected Essays, p. 427.
*ibid., p. 255.

In this life one makes, now and then, important decisions; or at least allows circumstances to decide; and some of these decisions are such as have consequences for all the rest of our mortal life. Some people find themselves consequently in circumstances such that the whole of their mortal life must be a torment to them. And if there is no future life then Hell is, for such people, here and now.*

Eliot took the idea of Purgatory with corresponding gravity. He was shocked that Yeats, writing a play called *Purgatory*, did not recognize a purgatorial process. In the section of "Little Gidding" where Eliot refers to the refining fire by which the soul may be restored, he took the theology of Purgatory so seriously that he scolded his friend John Hayward for questioning the diction of the passage. In one of the drafts of that section, Eliot had the soul learning to swim in that fire, and when Hayward demurred over the swimming, Eliot reminded him that in Canto xxvi of the *Purgatorio* the people who talk to Dante "are represented as not wanting to waste time in conversation but wishing to dive back into the fire to accomplish their expiation."* Hayward should have remembered that Eliot put the relevant line into *The Waste Land*—"*Poi s'ascose nel foco che gli affina*"—and quoted it again in his major essay on Dante, remarking, "In purgatory the torment of flame is deliberately and consciously accepted by the penitent." The souls in Purgatory, Eliot said, suffer "because they wish to suffer, for purgation":

> And observe that they suffer more actively and keenly, being souls preparing for blessedness, than Virgil suffers in eternal limbo. In their suffering is hope, in the anaesthesia of Virgil is hopelessness; that is the difference.*

Blessedness, which Eliot usually called beatitude, is the soul's eternal gift, received from God, of His presence.

I risk a certain indelicacy in suggesting that Eliot's reflections on Hell, Purgatory, Limbo, and Heaven come with particular force from a man who felt himself suffer and prayed that his suffering would turn out to have been purgatorial and not meaningless. It is clear, in any case, that Eliot's early poems issue from an acutely personal context in which

*Quoted in B. A. Harries, "The Rare Contact": Theology, *March 1972.*
*Helen Gardner, The Composition of Four Quartets *(London: Faber and Faber, 1978, p. 196).*
*Eliot, Selected Essays, *pp. 256–257.*

the predominant emotions are those of guilt, self-disgust, and revulsion. A religious faith that offered to make sense of guilt and suffering, by extending the hope that these emotions could be turned to spiritual purpose, would have special provenance for such a soul.

The awkward side of this, we recognize, is the question of human relations in such a world. Eliot's satiric gift was propelled by what he regarded as inescapable cause. He felt that much of human life was indeed disgusting. In his Christian years he believed that his best recourse, in addition to daily prayer, was to regard human relations as provisional and ancillary to some relation beyond them. In his essay on Baudelaire he presents that poet "reaching out towards something which cannot be had in, but which may be had partly through, personal relations."

> Indeed, in much romantic poetry the sadness is due to the exploitation of the fact that no human relations are adequate to human desires, but also to the disbelief in any further object for human desires than that which, being human, fails to satisfy them. . . . Baudelaire has perceived that what distinguishes the relations of man and woman from the copulation of beasts is the knowledge of Good and Evil (of moral Good and Evil which are not natural Good and Bad or Puritan Right and Wrong).*

The force of this position in Eliot is as if to say: Love God, then you may do as you wish. Or: Act on the understanding that what we do must be either good or evil; we live in the choice—so far as we make it—between salvation and damnation.

But if we are afflicted with Original Sin, and if the blessedness of Heaven cannot be enjoyed in this life: What is the status of personal relations? In his essays, Eliot argued that we must be willing to postpone our demand upon happiness and enjoy it in the eternal company of God. In the essay on Dante he speaks of not expecting more from life than it can give, or more from human beings than they can offer; and of looking "to death for what life cannot give."* But sometimes in his poems, early and late, he allowed the reader to feel that intimations of beatitude occur and that one's experience of them is not necessarily a delusion.

But the question is complicated by the fact that in Eliot's poems

*ibid., *pp. 428–429.*
*ibid., *p. 275.*

an event and its significance rarely coincide: the fact and the myth are discontinuous. The meaning of an event becomes available only when it is recalled, or when it rushes back into one's mind, by grace of memory; or when it is reconsidered in relation to something else, on another level of being, by an act of hope. It is only by the force of a perspective other than the immediate or punctual one that an event takes on meaning. It follows that Eliot's poems—and indeed his plays and essays—are always displacing a conventional account of some event in favor of another one, from an apparently higher and more exacting perspective. The form of this displacement is given in the essay on Dante, where Eliot says that the *Vita Nuova* "can only be understood by accustoming ourselves to find meaning in final causes rather than in origins." He means to reflect severely, I think, upon Freudian psychoanalysis, Darwinian biology, and certain forms of historical research that are preoccupied with origins rather than ends. Similarly, Eliot displaces the common understanding of sexual love: the love of man and woman, he says, "(or for that matter of man and man) is only explained and made reasonable by the higher love, or else is simply the coupling of animals."*

Eliot's way of displacing the low dream in favor of the high dream, as he calls these practices in relation to Dante's poetry, is to commit himself first to the higher perspective, the higher dream, and to convey that by a myth, if he can find one adequate to the task; and then to let the ordinary human fact establish itself, if it can, in relation to the myth. In poems from "Marina" to "Little Gidding" he invokes spiritual reality first, the vision, the high dream of Christianity, and waits to discover whether it can also be embodied to any extent in flesh and blood. The paradigm of such an action is the meeting of Lear and Cordelia, in Act IV, scene vii, when Lear says to her, "You are a spirit, I know; when did you die?" The sequence begins with Lear's recognition of Cordelia as spirit: She must have died to one life before gaining a new life. The gradual, bewildered perception of her being at once spirit and body recovers Lear from his spiritual death.

But this order of precedence, in the structure of Eliot's interests, entailed grave moral risk. The priority of the pattern, the form "laid up in heaven," over the claims of any of its particles, led to a dangerous disjunction in him. One form of the danger was a moral instinct in favor of those few people whom he deemed capable of consciousness, as against the many whom he regarded as spiritually null. So far as biographical

*ibid., *p. 274.*

evidence is available, it strongly suggests that Eliot located his spirituality far above his mere deeds, and set a pattern in place before there was
any particular need of it. I cannot otherwise explain, and can't at all
explain away, his apparently heartless treatment of some people who
cared for him and devoted many years to that care. I am thinking of
Emily Hale, Mary Trevelyan, and John Hayward, people whose lives,
in one degree or another, Eliot appropriated; it was as if they had nothing
better to do with their lives than to sustain the pattern he prescribed for
himself. In the end it becomes difficult to exonerate Eliot entirely from
a charge of moral obtuseness; and the matter is not resolved by recourse
to his too-well-known distinction between "the man who suffers" and
"the mind which creates."

The necessary distinction, I am convinced, is between Eliot's prose
and his poetry. They served different motives. In his prose, as perhaps
in his personal life, the myth takes precedence over the fact, and imposes
stringent criteria in determining the facts to be recognized. Mikhail
Bakhtin and other critics have argued, though not with Eliot especially
in mind, that a myth exercises total hegemony over language, just as
language exercises hegemony over the perception and conceptualization
of reality. But the argument can be met, I think, or at least much of the
harm can be removed from it, by undertaking not to use the concept of
myth invidiously. Suppose we were to regard a particular myth as the
narrative basis of the moral principles by which members of the community to which the myth is addressed choose to live. Everyone wishes to
live a principled life, and to act upon particular principles, rather than
to be at the mercy of every fact he happens to come upon. A myth is
a story upon which, in a certain community, certain moral principles are
defined and maintained. In Eliot's prose, the myth determines the principles to be applied, and in turn the facts to be recognized. Failures in this
regard are then subjected to doctrines of sin and purgation: that one does
not always commit sin is ascribed to divine grace. But in Eliot's poetry,
experiences that are authenticated by being remembered, by emerging
irresistably from his past life or from a buried life of images, are never
disowned. The myth by which they will be tested is held at arm's length
until the experiences, the facts of the irrefutable case, are acknowledged.

The pattern of this acknowledgment, in the poetry, is one of emergence, and its most compelling paradigm is that of features gradually
forming themselves into a face. So in reading the poems, the misgivings
we feel about the polemical prose become far more honorably matters
of degree and emphasis as we act upon the elusive movements of tone

that establish themselves with extraordinary delicacy. The poems to offer in evidence of this emergence, with an implication of an achievement on Eliot's part at once poetic and moral, are "Marina" and "Little Gidding."

II

"Marina" begins with an epigraph from Seneca's *Hercules Furens*, Hercules's first words on coming to himself from the madness—imposed by Juno—in which he has killed his wife and children. He looks about, bewildered, and asks, "What is this place, this region, this shore": *Quis hic locus, quae regio, quae mundi plaga?* Eliot much admired this passage, and quoted it again in the essay "Seneca in Elizabethan Translation." The title of the poem is enough to recall the great Recognition Scene in Shakespeare's *Pericles* in which the lost daughter Marina is restored to her father. Her words to Pericles, and his to her, suffice to compel the recognition they precede. I will believe thee, Pericles says,

> And make my senses credit thy relation
> To points that seem impossible . . .

Like Lear, Pericles knows that she is a spirit: He has still to convince himself that she is also flesh and blood. "Have you a working pulse?" he asks her.

Some aspects of Eliot's "Marina" are clear enough. In the first lines the speaker awakes to the plenitude of restored images, and to a not-yet-secure relation they bear to his daughter. Since a soul must die to the old life before putting on a new one, the next lines record the process by which the old life, identified as Death, becomes unsubstantial. The emerging face does not present itself of a sudden, but as if intermittently, forming and fading as in a dream. Memory, bewilderment, intuitions of dissolving and emerging turn for the next lines on the building of ships. But the difficult lines come later:

> This form, this face, this life
> Living to live in a world of time beyond me; let me
> Resign my life for this life, my speech for that unspoken,
> The awakened, lips parted, the hope, the new ships.

It is a poem, clearly but not too clearly, about the new life we may be granted upon resigning the old one, leaving "the stye of contentment": the more lavishly granted for its realization in someone else, as here a daughter. William Empson once remarked of the poem that living "in a world of time beyond me" can scarcely be a description of heaven: "The daughter in the story at any rate was really alive and in the world, and he was glad to find her precisely because his stock would now live beyond him in a world of time." So the poem makes sense in an ordinary paternal reading: New ships are what one hopes for in this life, especially for one's children. The poem also makes sense as a poem about waking up to find yourself a Christian, not knowing quite what to make of it all. The notion of redeeming one's life by giving it away is available, too, in this world: The self-sacrifice may feel like death, but it may turn out to lead to a better life in the longer run. In any case the poem invites us to conceive of a state of beatitude, as the face forms and the father's desires are fulfilled. The movement from "O my daughter" at the beginning to "My daughter" at the end corresponds to the difference between a questioning invocation, coming to oneself in bewilderment, and at the end a decisive recognition, finding one's true life in the recognition of another's. It is Eliot's version of Pericles's saying to Marina:

> O, come hither,
> Thou that beget'st him that did thee beget.

But this giving and receiving of lives is marked, in Eliot's poem, not by a bold syntax moving from one achieved perception to the next, but by the tentative emergence of phrases, hauntingly intuited possibilities, divinations of a life for which one's ordinary experience gives little warrant.

The warrant is provided, in Eliot's later poems, by the ascetic and mystical traditions of Christianity. The ultimate perspective is death, identified with the possibility of new life in the enjoyment of God. Eliot conceives of that life on the analogy of the silence into which words, after speech, reach; or the form of a Chinese jar which moves perpetually in its stillness; or music

> heard so deeply
> That it is not heard at all, but you are the music
> While the music lasts.

Under any analogy, it is occult.

And for its being occult, Eliot has been much abused. In *The Living Principle* F. R. Leavis attacked him for trying to posit an end beyond the reach of our common experience: "the ultimate really real that Eliot seeks in *Four Quartets* is eternal reality, and that he can do little, directly, to characterize." Of course not: How could it be directly or even indirectly characterized? But the passage in the *Quartets* to which Leavis, in this regard, takes most severe exception is the fifth part of "Burnt Norton," where the use of such words as "form," "pattern," and "stillness" amounts, in Leavis's view, to a claim on Eliot's part to know what can't be known. But the passage in question, about the Chinese jar and the stillness of the violin, moves with entirely appropriate tentativeness from one glimpsed possibility to another, and a confession of the inadequacy of language properly brings the effort to an inconclusive if not entirely defeated end. What remains—what is indeed convincing—is the desire for a mode of life higher than the common one we practice: What the reader believes is the desire. No doctrine is insisted upon, unless it is the Aristotelian concept of God as the unmoved mover: that "the detail of the pattern is movement" is the only assertion made, and to that we can hardly take reasonable exception. It is through the movement of Eliot's lines, in this passage, that we gain at least some sense of a pattern that is beyond all movement, since it exists as a moral or metaphysical idea. No claim to the possession of such a state of being, absolute and unconditioned, is being made, so far as I understand the *Four Quartets*. But I can't see how we could decently deny to Eliot the desire represented in Dante by the movement from the *Inferno* through the *Purgatorio* to the *Paradiso*. It is in "Little Gidding" that such a desire is most acutely felt.

III

In May 1936 Eliot made a visit to Little Gidding, site of an Anglican community of about forty members, which Nicholas Ferrar and his family established in 1625: It is between Huntingdon and Oundle in Huntingdonshire. The community was of some historic significance: It sheltered King Charles I after his defeat at Naseby, it was ransacked by Cromwellian soldiers in the winter of 1646, it was destroyed by fire, the chapel was rebuilt in the eighteenth century and added to in the nineteenth. Five years after his visit, Eliot started drafting a poem of that name, the last of the Quartets, this one having not earth, air, or water, but fire as its element, appropriately, since its setting was the London of the War, German bombing raids, and the Battle of Britain. It is clear from the manuscripts that the governing theme of the poem was the return of the dead, a summoning of spirits from the past. The past in question was English history, and it culminated in Eliot's own struggles as a poet in the English language. Beyond those considerations, there was the Christian theme, the communion of saints, according to the Catholic catechism "the union that exists between the members of the true Church on earth with one another, with the saints in Heaven, and the suffering souls in Purgatory." Eliot's first scribbled notes for the poem include this program: "They vanish, the individuals, and our feeling for them sinks into the flame which refines. They emerge in another pattern @ recreated @ reconciled redeemed, having their meaning together not apart, in a union which is of beams from the central fire. . . . Invocation to the Holy Spirit."* In the final version, published on October 15, 1942, this note became the lines:

> And what the dead had no speech for, when living,
> They can tell you, being dead: the communication
> Of the dead is tongued with fire beyond the language of the living.

Here we have another "beyond," a further perspective upon the complacencies of communication.

The most admired passage in the poem is the most elaborate summoning of the dead, a familiar compound ghost. The immediate source is Dante's encounter with his dead master Brunetto Latini in Canto XV of the *Inferno*. There are also continuities between Eliot's early poems and this passage of "Little Gidding," notably the face of the compound ghost "still forming" and the recognition the spoken words precede. Indeed, the passage is Eliot's most achieved Recognition Scene. Gradually it emerges that the ghost is compounded of Yeats, Mallarmé, Swift, and perhaps one or more of Eliot's earlier selves. The dead master is encountered as if on a London street on the morning after an air raid. The words the master speaks come from the dead: From that perspective, there is no obstacle between life and death:

*Gardner, The Composition of Four Quartets, p. 157.

> But, as the passage now presents no hindrance
> To the spirit unappeased and peregrine
> Between two worlds become much like each other. . . .

The two worlds seem to be our own and Purgatory, much like each other because the world of war and fire is much like the purgatorial process. The word "peregrine" comes, as R. P. Blackmur noted in *Language as Gesture*, from Canto XIII of the *Purgatorio:*

> O frate mio, ciascuna è cittadina
> d'una vera città; ma tu vuo' dire
> che vivesse in Italia peregrina.   (xxx.96–8)

> O my brother, each one here is a citizen
> of a true city; but you mean
> one who lived in Italy while a pilgrim.

Peregrina means a foreigner, lacking the rights of a Roman citizen; or a pilgrim, not yet arrived at the place of pilgrimage. Dante has been asking the souls in Purgatory if there is any soul among them who is Italian. The reply, as C. S. Singleton has noted, marks "a striking change of outlook":

> These souls, being already elect and inside the gate of Purgatory proper now, have their conversation in Heaven and no longer indulge in those lingering attachments to the world of the living that were characteristic of souls in Antepurgatory, outside the gate, who were as pilgrims.*

So the spirit unappeased and peregrine between two worlds become much like each other is still in this world, still in London, but, with evidence of fire and death all around him, is ready to go through the fires of Purgatory. Bear in mind that Dante met Brunetto Latini in Hell, but the encounter in "Little Gidding" is with Eliot's literary masters, who can't decently be sent to Hell. So the first consequence of "peregrine" is to displace the meeting from Hell to Purgatory, and to interpret transition as the possibility of purgation and eventually of beatitude. The first sign of that progress is that the ghost finds "words I never thought

---

*The Divine Comedy, *translated, with a commentary, by Charles S. Singleton (Princeton: Princeton University Press, 1973, Vol. II, p. 278).*

to speak." The next is that what is shared by Eliot and the ghost is the common pursuit of true judgment, another achievement of perspective, a compound act of aftersight and foresight. What this perspective offers is a revision of standard axioms about growing wise by growing old:

> Let me disclose the gifts reserved for age
>   To set a crown upon your lifetime's effort.
>   First, the cold friction of expiring sense
> Without enchantment, offering no promise
>   But bitter tastelessness of shadow fruit
>   As body and soul begin to fall asunder.
> Second, the conscious impotence of rage
>   At human folly, and the laceration
>   Of laughter at what ceases to amuse.
> And last, the rending pain of re-enactment
>   Of all that you have done, and been; the shame
>   Of motives late revealed, and the awareness
> Of things ill done and done to others' harm
>   Which once you took for exercise of virtue.

It seems reasonable to take this passage as Eliot's redaction of many lives and experiences besides his own. I hear in it much of the Anglican morality of the early seventeenth century. The rage at human folly is Swift's, laceration being a word John Hayward suggested. The re-enactment of all that you have done and been is Yeats's, in *A Vision*, the last plays, and the poem "Vacillation." The things ill done that once you took for exercise of virtue strike close to home, and speak, I imagine, of Eliot's sense of his own actions, or of some of them. There is also, later on, the sense of the mug's game of having spent one's life as a poet, wrestling with words and meanings. Wallace Stevens reported that "Ariel was glad he had written his poems." Eliot was not so sure, in his own case. His doubt on that score was expressed by alluding to several writers as partial myths of the life of literature.

Of the several writers implied in "Little Gidding," Yeats seems to be the one most emphatically summoned. This is strange. For much of Eliot's early life as a poet, he did not take Yeats seriously: He was put off by the elder poet's dealings with magic and spooks, and he strongly criticized Yeats's attempt to make a religion for himself out of folklore, superstition, and table-rapping. Eliot regarded Yeats as a heretic, though not as dangerous as D. H. Lawrence in that respect. But he held back from appreciating Yeats for many years; until April 1916, if we may settle upon a date, when Ezra Pound brought Eliot to see a performance of *At the Hawk's Well* in London. Thereafter, Eliot knew that Yeats was a major poet, and he read the middle poems in a much more respectful light. But Yeats had to die before Eliot gave him full recognition as the greatest poet of his time, a tribute he paid in his memorial lecture in Dublin. In that lecture, praising Yeats as "pre-eminently the poet of middle age," Eliot quoted "The Spur":

> You think it horrible that lust and rage
> Should dance attendance upon my old age;
> They were not such a plague when I was young:
> What else have I to spur me into song?

On that poem, Eliot commented:

> These lines are very impressive and not very pleasant, and the senti-
> ment has recently been criticized by an English critic whom I gener-
> ally respect. But I think he misread them. I do not read them as a
> personal confession of a man who differed from other men, but of a
> man who was essentially the same as most other men; the only
> difference is in the greater clarity, honesty, and vigour. To what
> honest man, old enough, can these sentiments be entirely alien? they
> can be subdued and disciplined by religion, but who can say that
> they are dead? Only those to whom the maxim of La Rochefoucauld
> applies: "Quand les vices nous quittent, nous nous flattons de la
> créance que c'est nous qui les quittons." The tragedy of Yeats's
> epigram is all in the last line.*

The Yeats of "The Spur" is the poet who comes most powerfully into "Little Gidding." The perspective from which the ghost speaks is chiefly that of Yeats's last poems: "The Spur" was written in December 1936, a little more than two years before his death. It is especially appropriate, then, that in "Little Gidding" the hope of the purgatorial experience and of passing through it to eternal paradise is suggested in figurative terms common to Yeats and Dante:

> From wrong to wrong the exasperated spirit
> Proceeds, unless restored by that refining fire
> Where you must move in measure, like a dancer.

Eliot, Selected Essays, *pp. 257–258.*

The refining fire is a direct translation, as we have seen, from Dante. It is also an allusion to the spiritual fire of Yeats's "Sailing to Byzantium" and "Byzantium." In the third stanza of "Sailing to Byzantium" Yeats summons the "sages standing in God's holy fire" to be "the singing-masters of my soul." The passage in "Little Gidding" is Eliot's version of the same summoning, just as the words of the ghost are his judgment upon the condition of being "caught in that sensual music." The moving in measure like a dancer is pure Yeats, not only the poet of "Among School Children"—

> Labour is blossoming or dancing where
> The body is not bruised to pleasure soul

—but the dramatist of the Plays for Dancers. Measure or dance is movement according to the highest perspective of form.

The rest of the poem is inhabited by four interrelated concerns: memory, the past, love, and language. Each is adduced in the light of the end of all merely temporal things, death, and each shows an aspect different from the one disclosed by its common provenance.

Memory includes its voluntary and its involuntary characters. Why, Eliot wondered in *The Use of Poetry and the Use of Criticism*, out of all the experiences that one has had, do a certain few assert themselves, keep coming back: like his own experience, as a boy on summer vacation in Gloucester, peering through sea water in a rock pool and finding for the first time a sea anemone? Voluntary memory is the act of summoning the otherwise gone figures from his past, not in the hope of recovering them as they were but of finding one's apprehension of them becoming a new thing in the later light:

> See, now they vanish,
> The faces and places, with the self which, as it could, loved them,
> To become renewed, transfigured, in another pattern.

Here the process of revision, which corresponds to a Jamesian scruple, is conveyed through the elaborately suspended syntax, as if no noun could reach its verb, no past participle could be settled upon, until every possible alternative form of it has been considered.

But memory, in Eliot, is a morally complicated act. It was crucial to him, not because he needed to retain sensitive continuity with gone occasions but because he felt impelled to detach himself from the desire of them and maintain them in his vision. They could not make a claim upon him while he brooded upon their significance. Like certain mystics in this respect, he enriched his spirituality by detaching himself from every object that might claim his desire. There is a passage in Rilke's *The Notebooks of Malte Laurids Brigge* that might usefully be brought into Eliot's context:

> And still it is not yet enough to have memories. One must be able to forget them when they are many and one must have the great patience to wait until they come again. For it is not yet the memories themselves. Not till they have turned to blood within us, to glance and gesture, nameless and no longer to be distinguished from ourselves—not till then can it happen that in a most rare hour the first word of a verse arises in their midst and goes forth from them.

In Eliot's case, the memories no longer to be distinguished from himself must not bring with them any intimation of desire: they must minister to his vision, not to his appetitive zest:

> This is the use of memory:
> For liberation—not less of love but expanding
> Of love beyond desire, and so liberation
> From the future as well as the past.

The possibility of achieving love beyond desire has been well understood in the history of ethics, and especially in those ethical principles that are based upon aesthetics and aesthetic appreciation. It is a harder possibility when the object of love is a person. It is difficult, when human relations are concerned, to appeal to a perspective beyond desire: the appeal itself casts doubt upon the reality of the feelings engaged. What Eliot speaks of as liberation is hard to distinguish from indifference: Only the misgiving revealed in the poems keeps the distinction alive.

As for the past: it has been the subject of much rumination in "Burnt Norton." The third section of "Little Gidding" seems to disavow nostalgia: Let the dead bury their dead, it seems to say. Again the admonition is the same: Consider the end, the idea, the ideal form, of whatever claims your attention. In this passage Eliot distinguishes, among the dead, between the fortunate, those who have won, and the defeated, who in some sense have not—or not merely—lost. Walter Benjamin maintained, in his "Theses on the Philosophy of History," that history is always recited in favor of those who have won: There has never been a history of the defeated. But in the perspective of "Little Gidding"

> Whatever we inherit from the fortunate
> We have taken from the defeated
> What they had to leave us—a symbol:
> A symbol perfected in death.

This symbol differs from Yeats's, which is always in nature and the shared life even when he longed to find it or to project himself "out of nature." Eliot is unwilling to recognize a symbol as such until he has seen or imagined its force in the light of death; according to that vision, time is no longer mere *tempus*, one-thing-after-another, but *aevum*, time redeemed in the end and meanwhile lived in the light of that end.

And then there is language. In *The Waste Land* Eliot was much concerned with the question of authority in language; with the different sources and kinds and degrees of authority that sustain our words, or fail to sustain them. In "Little Gidding," released now from the familiar compound ghost, he speaks of language no longer in the apocalyptic or demotic terms of *The Waste Land* but by appeal to the idea of a decently composed sentence:

> And every phrase
> And sentence that is right (where every word is at home,
> Taking its place to support the others,
> The word neither diffident nor ostentatious,
> An easy commerce of the old and the new,
> The common word exact without vulgarity,
> The formal word precise but not pedantic,
> The complete consort dancing together)
> Every phrase and every sentence is an end and a beginning,
> Every poem an epitaph.

Every poem is an epitaph in the sense that it commemorates feelings otherwise formless if not defunct; and we recall that Wordsworth, another poet sensitive to memory and the decencies of our important occasions, wrote an essay upon epitaphs that is one of the finest considerations of the question: What should one say, given that occasions seem to call for something to be said?

And any action
Is a step to the block, to the fire, down the sea's throat
Or to an illegible stone: and that is where we start.
We die with the dying:
See, they depart, and we go with them.
We are born with the dead:
See they return, and bring us with them.

IV

"See, they return" is an allusion to a poem by Ezra Pound, the first words of a poem about the return of the gods: The gods, figures of an otherwise lost time, are seen returning, waveringly, but they are still unmistakably gods. I take Eliot's allusion to Pound's poem as indicating how we are to read this one, "Little Gidding": It, too, is a poem about the return, the survival, of the gods. There is a well-established history of this motif, to be consulted in Jean Seznec's *The Survival of the Pagan Gods: The Mythological Tradition and Its Place in Renaissance Humanism and Art* (1940, revised 1953). Modern variations on the theme are to be found in Heine's *The Gods in Exile* (1853), in Gautier's essay on Leonardo (1864), the chapter on Pico della Mirandola in Walter Pater's *The Renaissance* (1873) and Pater's "Apollo in Picardy" (1893). Heine describes, in the passage that Pater quotes in *The Renaissance*, how the gods of the older world, at the time of the definite triumph of Christianity, hid themselves among us here on earth under all sorts of disguises. That Apollo should be imagined turning up in Picardy is only one such mode of survival.

If we read "Little Gidding" as a poem about the survival of the gods, it is hardly necessary to say that Eliot's gods are not Pound's or Pater's or Gautier's or Heine's. He finds his supreme god according to the theology of the Christian Church, and therefore can freely summon as if they were lesser gods those men and women who were important to him in the respects he cared about; figures from his personal history, his family, the history of literature—mainly in English, French, and Dante's Italian. The allusion to Pound's poem is Eliot's way of paying tribute to one of his masters, and at the same time of separating himself from Pound in the considerations that mattered more. Pound took his gods where he found them, just as he took his myths opportunely if not opportunistically from Confucius, Ovid, Jefferson, and anyone else he admired. Remember that I have remembered, Pound said. It was far more important to Eliot that he believed, and that he subordinated every other consideration to that one. The communication of the dead is tongued with fire beyond the language of the living because the dead are now, as we are not yet, complete, perfected in death. "Tongued with fire"; an allusion, first and foremost, to the episode in the Acts of the Apostles when suddenly the apostles, gathered in a room, heard what sounded like a great wind from heaven, and something appeared to them that seemed like tongues of fire: These tongues separated and came to rest on the head of each of them. The shape of the flame, as in *Isaiah* 6, is associated with prophecy, the gift of tongues. A further explication is given in the last lines of "Little Gidding":

> And all shall be well and
> All manner of thing shall be well
> When the tongues of flame are in-folded
> Into the crowned knot of fire
> And the fire and the rose are one.

The immediate allusion is to the consolation offered in a vision to Lady Juliana; then to the passage in *The Dark Night of the Soul* in which St. John of the Cross says that love is like fire, which always rises up with the desire to be absorbed in the center of its sphere. A further reference is to the passage in the *Paradiso*, Canto XXXIII, where Dante sees the Divine vision as scattered leaves of the universe, ingathered now by love in one mass: substance and accidents and their relations—*sustanzia ed accidenti, e lor costume*—as though fused together, "so that what I speak of is one simple flame"—*che ciò ch' io dico è un semplice lume*.

At the end of "Little Gidding" Eliot has reconciled, more completely than anywhere else in his poetry, myth and fact; mitigating the abstraction of the one and the rigidity of the other. That he saw his poetic aim in these terms, one can hardly doubt; especially in view of the admiration he expressed in his essay on Dante for "the power of the master who could thus at every moment realize the inapprehensible in visual images." Referring to the lines in the *Paradiso* in which Neptune is imagined full of wonder at the passage of the Arno over his head, Eliot said that he did not know anywhere in poetry "more authentic sign of greatness than the power of association" that could introduce the river and the god of the waves into a presentation of the Divine vision.

V

There is no merit in dodging the fact that Eliot has again become a controversial poet. But the grounds of the dispute are not those on which readers of *Prufrock and Other Observations* and *The Waste Land* quarreled. I have no doubt that the poetry, as evidenced in "The Love Song of J. Alfred Prufrock," "Portrait of a Lady," "Gerontion," "La Figlia che piange," "Marina," "Ash-Wednesday," "Burnt Norton," "East Coker," and "Little Gidding," is the work of a major poet. I can't see how it could be thought to be anything less. But the current exacerbations, in Eliot's vicinity, touch the poetry hardly at all; they have to do with the image of Eliot as an authoritarian social critic, allegedly a sinister figure concealing himself behind an extraordinarily urbane style. There is much talk of Eliot's anti-Semitism, especially talk by critics who take pride in representing themselves as hating Christianity. Some readers are affronted that Eliot, even more successfully than Pound, appropriated Modernism, and established his version of a symbolist and modernist program as the only one worth pursuing. Most of this complaint issues from critics who advance the claims of an alternative authority, that of American pragmatism in the service of populism. But there is a far larger issue, arising from the question with which I began, the Yeatsian issue of fact and myth. The only reason for seeking a myth or accepting one is that you want to submit to a form of authority other than your own; either because you regard your own as frail or specious, or because you want to surrender your will to a force of greater explanatory power. Many readers who resent Eliot's conversion to Christianity claim that what they resent is his submission to any authority; it merely happened to be Christianity. They believe that after the Holocaust, no institution has the right to claim moral authority.

I am not, indeed, maintaining that poets since Yeats and Eliot have given up looking for a source of authority other than their own charisma. Charles Olson's *Maximus* poems are just as dependent as Yeats's upon a philosophy of history. Robert Duncan's poems turn toward myths just as resolutely as Eliot does, or the Joyce of *Ulysses* and *Finnegans Wake*. But most of the new poems one reads in magazines seem to trust in the power or the idiosyncrasy of their particular voices; they recite experiences, often local and domestic, and let the myths recede. Frost and Stevens, rather than Eliot or Yeats, are their masters: Frost, who got much from Emerson and more from Darwin but deemed the power of his individual will sufficient for any poetic purpose; Stevens, who wrote, in "Notes Toward a Supreme Fiction":

> Phoebus is dead, ephebe. But Phoebus was
> A name for something that never could be named.
> There was a project for the sun and is.
>
> There is a project for the sun. The sun
> Must bear no name, gold flourisher, but be
> In the difficulty of what it is to be.

Where Eliot named the project in Christian terms—Pentecostal fire, Ash-Wednesday, the Annunciation—Stevens retained the gods of an old world only as sites of a project that may or may not be pursued but must in any case live without the names. The pagan gods survive in Stevens hardly better than the Christian one, and only then because they make no demands of belief or practice. Much as I love "Notes Toward a Supreme Fiction," I have never been able to understand how Stevens's relation to the fictions that he declares upon his sole authority can be accounted belief.

Nor have I understood why it is necessary to choose, as here between Eliot and Stevens. I see no difficulty in acting upon the program that William Empson recommended—more in theory than in his subsequent practice, I must admit—in his *Milton's God*. "The central function of imaginative literature," he maintained, "is to make you realize that other people act on moral convictions different from your own."* I applaud the sentiment, and only wish it were taken more scrupulously. I assume that the "other people" include Christians, in which case we should not be hearing a prejudicial word against their beliefs, and Eliot should be recognized for the extraordinarily powerful poet he is.

*William Empson, Milton's God (London: Chatto and Windus, 1965, p. 261).

MICHAEL DORRIS

Life Stories

In most cultures, adulthood is equated with self-reliance and responsibility, yet often Americans do not achieve this status until we are in our late twenties or early thirties—virtually the entire average lifespan of a person in a traditional non-Western society. We tend to treat prolonged adolescence as a warm-up for real life, as a wobbly suspension bridge between childhood and legal maturity. Whereas a nineteenth-century Cheyenne or Lakota teenager was expected to alter self-conception in a split-second vision, we often meander through an analogous rite of passage for more than a decade—through high school, college, graduate school.

Though he had never before traveled alone outside his village, the Plains Indian male was expected at puberty to venture solo into the wilderness. There he had to fend for and sustain himself while avoiding the menace of unknown dangers, and there he had absolutely to remain until something happened that would transform him. Every human being, these tribes believed, was entitled to at least one moment of personal, enabling insight.

Anthropology proposes feasible psychological explanations for why this flash was eventually triggered: fear, fatigue, reliance on strange foods, the anguish of loneliness, stress, and the expectation of ultimate success all contributed to a state of receptivity. Every sense was quickened, alerted to perceive deep meaning, until at last the interpretation of an unusual event—a dream, a chance encounter, or an unexpected vista—reverberated with metaphor. Through this unique prism, abstractly preserved in a vivid memory or song, a boy caught foresight of both his adult persona and of his vocation, the two inextricably entwined.

Today the best approximations that many of us get to such a heady sense of eventuality come in the performance of our school vacation jobs. Summers are intermissions, and once we hit our teens it is during these breaks in our structured regimen that we initially taste the satisfaction of remuneration that is earned, not merely doled. Tasks defined as *work* are not only graded, they are compensated; they have a worth that is unarguable because it translates into hard currency. Wage labor—and in the beginning, this generally means a confining, repetitive chore for which we are quickly over-qualified—paradoxically brings a sense of blooming freedom. At the outset, the complaint to a peer that business supersedes fun is oddly liberating—no matter what drudgery requires your attention, it is by its very required nature serious and adult.

At least that's how it seemed to me. I come from a line of people hard hit by the Great Depression. My mother and her sisters went to work early in their teens—my mother operated a kind of calculator known as a comptometer while her sisters spent their days, respectively, at a peanut factory and at Western Union. My grandmother did piece-work sewing. Their efforts, and the Democratic Party, saw them through, and to this day they never look back without appreciation for their later solvency. They take nothing for granted. Accomplishments are celebrated, possessions are valuable, in direct proportion to the labor entailed to acquire them; anything easily won or bought on credit is suspect. When I was growing up we were far from wealthy, but what money we had was correlated to the hours some one of us had logged. My eagerness to contribute to, or at least not diminish, the coffer was countered by the arguments of those whose salaries kept me in school: My higher education was a sound group investment. The whole family was adamant that I have the opportunities they had missed and, no matter how much I objected, they stinted themselves to provide for me.

Summer jobs were therefore a relief, an opportunity to pull a share of the load. As soon as the days turned warm I began to peruse the classifieds, and when the spring semester was done, I was ready to punch a clock. It even felt right. Work in June, July, and August had an almost Biblical aspect: In the hot, canicular weather your brow sweated, just as God had ordained. Moreover, summer jobs had the luxury of being temporary. No matter how bizarre, how onerous, how off my supposed track, employment terminated with the falling leaves and I was back on neutral ground. So, during each annual three-month leave from secondary school and later from the university, I compiled an eclectic résumé: lawn cutter, hair sweeper in a barber shop, lifeguard, delivery boy, temporary mail carrier, file clerk, youth program coordinator on my Montana reservation, ballroom dance instructor, theater party promoter, night-shift hospital records keeper, human adding machine in a Paris bank, encyclopedia salesman, newspaper stringer, recreation bus manager, salmon fisherman.

The reasonable titles disguise the madness of some of these occupations. For instance, I seemed inevitably to be hired to trim the yards of the unconventional. One woman followed beside me, step by step, as I traversed her yard in ever tighter squares, and called my attention to each missed blade of grass. Another client never had the "change" to pay me, and so reimbursed my weekly pruning with an offering culled from his library. I could have done without the *Guide to Artificial Respiration* (1942) or the many well-worn copies of Reader's Digest Condensed Books, but sometimes the selection merited the wait. Like a rat lured repeatedly back to the danger of mild electric shock by the mystique of intermittent reenforcement, I kept mowing by day in hopes of turning pages all night.

The summer I was eighteen a possibility arose for a rotation at the post office, and I grabbed it. There was something casually sophisticated about work that required a uniform, about having a federal ranking, even if it was GS-1 (Temp/Sub), and it was flattering to be entrusted with a leather bag containing who knew what important correspondence. Every day I was assigned a new beat, usually in a rough neighborhood avoided whenever possible by regular carriers, and I proved quite capable of complicating what would normally be fairly routine missions. The low point came on the first of August when I diligently delivered four blocks' worth of welfare checks to the right numbers on the wrong streets. It is no fun to snatch unexpected wealth from the hands of those who have but moments previously opened their mailboxes and received a bonus.

After my first year of college, I lived with relatives on an Indian reservation in eastern Montana and filled the only post available: Coordinator of Tribal Youth Programs. I was seduced by the language of the announcement into assuming that there existed Youth Programs to be coordinated. In fact, the Youth consisted of a dozen bored, disgruntled kids—most of them my cousins—who had nothing better to do each day than to show up at what was euphemistically called "the gym" and hate whatever Program I had planned for them. The Youth ranged in age from fifteen to five and seemed to have as their sole common ambition the determination to smoke cigarettes. This put them at immediate and on-going odds with the Coordinator, who on his first day naively encouraged them to sing the "Doe, a deer, a female deer" song from *The Sound of Music*. They looked at me, that bleak morning, and I looked at them, each boy and girl equipped with a Pall Mall behind an ear, and we all knew it would be a long, struggle-charged battle. It was to be a contest of wills, the hearty and wholesome vs. prohibited vice. I stood for dodge ball, for collecting bugs in glass jars, for arts and crafts; they had pledged a preternatural allegiance to sloth. The odds were not in my favor and each waking dawn I experienced the lightheadedness of anticipated exhaustion, that thrill of giddy dissociation in which nothing seems real or of great significance. I went with the flow and learned to inhale.

The next summer, I decided to find work in an urban setting for a change, and was hired as a general office assistant in the Elsa Hoppenfeld Theatre Party Agency, located above Sardi's restaurant in New York City. The Agency consisted of Elsa Hoppenfeld herself, Rita Frank, her regular deputy, and me. Elsa was a gregarious Viennese woman who established contacts through personal charm, and she spent much of the time courting trade away from the building. Rita was therefore both my immediate supervisor and constant companion; she had the most incredible fingernails I had ever seen—long, carefully shaped pegs lacquered in cruel primary colors and hard as stone—and an attitude about her that could only be described as zeal.

The goal of a theater party agent is to sell blocks of tickets to imminent Broadway productions, and the likely buyers are charities, B'nai Briths, Hadassahs, and assorted other fund-raising organizations. We received commissions on volume, and so it was necessary to convince a prospect that a play—preferably an expensive musical—for which we had reserved the rights to seats would be a boffo smash hit.

The object of our greatest expectation that season was an extravaganza called *Chu Chem*, a saga that aspired to ride the coattails of *Fiddler on the Roof* into entertainment history. It starred the estimable Molly Picon and told the story of a family who had centuries ago gone from Israel to China during the disapora, yet had, despite isolation in an alien environment, retained orthodox culture and habits. The crux of the plot revolved around a man with several marriageable daughters and nary a kosher suitor within 5,000 miles. For three months Rita and I waxed eloquent in singing the show's praises. We sat in our little office, behind facing desks, and every noon while she redid her nails I ordered out from a deli that offered such exotic (to me) delicacies as fried egg sandwiches, lox and cream cheese, pastrami, *tongue*. I developed of necessity and habit a telephone voice laced with a distinctly Yiddish accent. It could have been a great career. However, come November, *Chu Chem* bombed. Its closing was such a financial catastrophe for all concerned that when the following January one Monsieur Dupont advertised on the Placement Board at my college, I decided to put an ocean between me and my former trusting clientele.

M. Dupont came to campus with the stated purpose of interviewing candidates for teller positions in a French bank. Successful applicants, required to be fluent in *français*, would be rewarded with three well-paid months and a rent-free apartment in Paris. I headed for the language lab and registered for an appointment.

The only French in the interview was *Bonjour, ça va?*, after which M. Dupont switched into English and described the wonderful deal on charter air flights that would be available to those who got the nod. Round-trip to Amsterdam, via Reykjavik, leaving the day after exams and returning in mid-September, no changes or substitutions. I signed up on the spot. I was to be a *banquier*, with *pied-à-terre* in Montparnasse!

Unfortunately, when I arrived with only $50 in travelers checks in my pocket—the flight had cleaned me out, but who needed money since my paycheck started right away—no one in Paris had ever heard of M. Dupont.

Alors.

I stood in the Gare du Nord and considered my options. There weren't any. I scanned a listing of Paris hotels and headed for the cheapest one: the Hotel Villedo, $10 a night. The place had an ambiance that I persuaded myself was antique, despite the red light above the sign. The only accommodation available was "the bridal suite," a steal at $20. The glass door to my room didn't lock and there was a rather continual floor show, but at some point I must have dozed off. When I awoke the church bells were ringing, the sky was pink, and I felt renewed. No little setback was going to spoil my adventure. I stood and stretched, then walked to a mirror that hung above the sink next to the bed. I leaned forward to punctuate my resolve with a confident look in the eye.

The sink disengaged and fell to the floor. Water gushed. In panic I rummaged through my open suitcase, stuffed two pair of underwear into the pipe to quell the flow, and before the dam broke, I was out the door. I barreled through the lobby of the first bank I passed, asked to see the director, and told the startled man my sad story. For some reason, whether from shock or pity, he hired me at $1.27 an hour to be a cross-checker of foreign currency transactions, and with two phone calls found me lodgings at a commercial school's dormitory.

From eight to five each weekday my duty was to sit in a windowless room with six impeccably dressed people, all of whom were totaling identical additions and subtractions. We were highly dignified with each other, very professional, no *tutoyer*ing. Monsieur Saint presided, but the formidable Mademoiselle was the true power; she oversaw each of our columns and shook her head sadly at my American-shaped numbers.

My legacy from that summer, however, was more than an enduring penchant for crossed 7s. After I had worked for six weeks, M. Saint asked me during a coffee break why I didn't follow the example of other foreign students he had known and depart the office at noon in order to spend the afternoon touring the sights of Paris with the *Alliance Française*.

"Because," I replied in my halting French, "that costs money. I depend upon my full salary the same as any of you." M. Saint nodded gravely and said no more, but then on the next Friday he presented me with a white envelope along with my check.

"Do not open this until you have left the Société Générale," he said ominously. I thought I was fired for the time I had mixed up krøners and guilders, and, once on the sidewalk, I steeled myself to read the worst. I felt the quiet panic of blankness.

"Dear Sir," I translated the perfectly formed script. "You are a person of value. It is not correct that you should be in our beautiful city and not see it. Therefore we have amassed a modest sum to pay the tuition for a two-week afternoon program for you at the *Alliance Française*. Your wages will not suffer, for it is your assignment to appear each morning in this bureau and reacquaint us with the places you have visited. We shall see them afresh through your eyes." The letter had thirty signatures, from the Director to the janitor, and stuffed inside the envelope was a sheaf of franc notes in various denominations.

I rushed back to the tiny office. M. Saint and Mademoiselle had waited, and accepted my gratitude with their usual controlled smiles and precise handshakes. But they had blown their Gallic cover, and for the next ten days and then through all the days until I went home in September, our branch was awash with sightseeing paraphernalia. Everyone had advice, favorite haunts, criticisms of the *Alliance's* choices or explanations. Paris passed through the bank's granite walls as sweetly as a June breeze through a window screen, and ever afterward the lilt of overheard French, a photograph of *Sacré Coeur* or the Louvre, even a monthly bank statement, recalls to me that best of all summers.

I didn't wind up in an occupation with any obvious connection to the careers I sampled during my school breaks, but I never altogether abandoned those brief professions either. They were jobs not so much to be held as to be weighed, absorbed, and incorporated, and, collectively, they carried me forward into adult life like overlapping stairs, unfolding a particular pattern at once haphazard and inevitable.

GERALD EARLY

Weight Watching: A Course in Women's Studies

Moreover when ye fast, be not, as the hypocrites, of a sad countenance: for they disfigure their faces, that they may appear unto men to fast. Verily I say unto you, they have their reward. But thou, when thou fastest, anoint thine head, and wash thy face. That thou appear not unto men to fast . . .
—MATTHEW 6:16–18

I know exactly how she feels; I see her strained face and hear her say that she is not hungry, that she does not need to eat. I know what she is undergoing.
—A CURED ANOREXIA NERVOSA PATIENT SPEAKING ABOUT ANOTHER SUFFERING FROM THE DISEASE, QUOTED IN DR. HILDE BRUCH'S *The Golden Cage*

During the starvation I put myself on a regimen that I felt was very unpleasant, but I endured it because I had imposed it upon myself.
—ANOREXIA NERVOSA PATIENT, QUOTED IN DR. HILDE BRUCH'S *The Golden Cage*

My wife, who has been a sometimes ardent, sometimes unfaithful member of Weight Watchers for the past several years, asked me just recently would I attend an open meeting, designed not only to entice new members but to allow "significant others" or "partners," as the terms go in these pansexual days, to understand the experience and struggle of losing weight. I looked up briefly from a book I was reading and replied, "Sure," not really thinking at the time that I was going to go. That is to say, it was a sort of put-off answer to a question one does not take seriously.

Surprisingly, when the Saturday morning of the open meeting came around, I went quite willing, docilely in fact. I was curious to know what people talked about at this sort of meeting. Several years ago my mother married a man who had been an alcoholic for a number of years. Those familiar with the drinker drinking can imagine how painful some of those years must have been. She has attended many of the meetings of an Alcoholic Anonymous affiliate, Al-Anon, designed for people who are related to alcoholics. As I considered Weight Watchers to be, and surely its founders must admit this, nothing more than a kind of parodic imitation of Alcoholics Anonymous—the encounter group way to end self-destructive habits through rehabilitative discourse, the psycho-therapeutic séance of shedding light into the dark night of the dark soul—I thought it might be, actually, quite important to go. I thought that in some mild way I might understand my mother's relationship with my stepfather if it were, in some harmless and amusing way, a cognate of some aspect of my relationship with my wife.

It is of course a peculiarly American optimism that evil is nothing more than a series of bad habits that can, through an exercise of self-control, be broken or at least made less compulsively excessive. I wanted to go because I had no understanding of people's bad habits and hence no patience with them. Ironically, it was because the emotional stakes were not nearly as large as they were with my mother and her life with an inveterate and awfully conspicuous consumer that I wanted to take my wife's concern about losing weight seriously.

No one would think my wife is fat or overweight from simply looking at her. One might think her to be bordering on a weight problem but not having arrived. Since the birth of our first child over nine years ago she has been struggling with her weight, up and down, but mostly a steady creep up until she was nearly forty pounds heavier than when we married. At one point I supervised a diet for her during which interval she lost about twenty or so pounds in about six weeks. She lost her period for one month as a result of the strenuous nature of the diet. The fact that strenuous dieting causes amenorrhea or what amounts to a kind of fictive pregnancy has been noted by physicians and scholars who have studied anorexia nervosa, a striking irony that shows how denial can signify a sort of fulfillment. My wife soon lost her periods for the next nine when it was discovered she was, indeed, pregnant again. Because she was pregnant, she lost the urge to diet. With a legitimate excuse to be freed from deprivation, she ate voraciously. She gained more weight than she should have. The birth did not produce the weight loss she hoped for.

Since that time, seven years ago, my wife has been trying to lose, quite unsuccessfully, the weight she gained during that pregnancy. She owns many clothes she cannot get herself into, she thinks she looks bad, she feels fat and ugly. She loves to read the comic strip "Cathy" whenever it deals with dieting. This is a typical kind of self-absorption that overweight people suffer from. Turns of self-pity and self-denouncement. It is not unlike a religious preoccupation with sin, with grace, with sanctification.

"How do you stay so thin?" she asks me, "What's your secret? You seem to eat anything you want."

Of course, I don't eat anything I want exactly. In fact, there are many times, especially during stressful periods, when I eat nothing at all for an entire day. We are dieting together now; she feels the only way she can stay on it is if I go on it as well. We eat all of our meals together. Because of that, I have eaten more food in recent weeks than I normally do; as a result, the diet is helping her to lose while I gain. The fact that I may gain a little weight makes her feel good, as if she is not, finally, some freak of nature.

When she saw magazine pictures of Walter Hudson, believed to be the world's heaviest person with a weight of over one thousand pounds, she was quite happy to know that she was not, at least, pathologically overweight. But this sort of thing seemed a long way 'round the mountain to achieve a bit of self-esteem. Her passion for eating would never make her a deranged glutton any more so than her passion for dieting would make her anorexic. But esteem comes a bit easier when she can compare herself with the overweight women who work around her. The problem here is that there are simply not enough of them.

She laughs at ads for weight reducing products like Dream-Away, a pill one can take before retiring to "melt off pounds the easy way." She knows the proper way to diet is by eating less and exercising more. Yet she dreams, as all compulsive eaters do, that something like Dream-Away really does work. The business of selling diets in this country has always been the business of selling illusions (everyone knows that, even the dieters themselves, but of course everyone's theme song in this country is "When I Grow Too Old to Dream"), reality being something that Americans generally have a hard time living with; but the business of selling to women, more so than to any of the rest of us, is the surrealism of posing desire as the Platonic perfection of yourself with a price tag. The real question for a woman as intelligent as my wife is not how to lose weight sanely but why eat foolishly in the first place. It is an especially intriguing one for one such as I who is not tempted by food and cannot understand people who are.

The meeting was just what I expected but was nonetheless startling—which means of course it was everything I hadn't really thought about wrapped in the rhetoric of everything I knew. It was quite crowded, close to one hundred people in a fair-size room in a bank building. There were only three men present, the rest were women which one expects because weight loss is an obsession with women in this culture and the weight loss industry, from pills to diet foods and drinks to exercise programs and health spas, from bottles of mineral water to self-motivation tapes, are all really directed to women, to make women feel insecure about their looks, their health, indeed, about the very phenomenon of being a woman, and thus, predictably, insecure about their sexuality, about their ability to capture men. Walking into a health food store or a diet salon and seeing row upon row of magical bottles containing elixirs of all sorts for dieting and health (for women are in a perpetual need of losing weight and taking vitamin supplements), as if being a woman, in the end, is a condition of which one must be cured, convinces one that bourgeois woman's culture truly is a culture of bottles.

Lois Banner, in her study, *American Beauty* (which should have been called *White American Beauty* since she does not, by her own admission, deal with blacks—who, after all, are American—but let's not quibble over such trivialities), talks about the nineteenth-century standards of feminine beauty: the thin, pale, steel-engraving girl; the voluptuous chorus line dancer and actress; the Gibson Girl; the flapper; each the dialectical supersession of the other. I suppose today we are caught between the athletic, fresh-looking Gibson girl (Heather Locklear and other Hollywood actresses who play romantic leads such as Cher, for instance, who does ads for Vic Tanny and whose body make-over was the subject of articles in women's magazines) and the super-thin steel-engraving type (virtually any model). But generally the desirable look is thin, hence the interest in dieting since most women cannot achieve the thinness of our feminine cultural icons without real persistence and effort. Of course no one cares if they do achieve thinness, only that they want to.

Certainly, no woman wants to look like the famous woman bodybuilder, Bev Francis, the "star" of the documentary *Pumping Iron II: The Women*, who has the physique of a man, because I think it frightens women in some way to think that they can, indeed, be as strong and muscular as a well-built man. For the average woman, where would the epistemology of womanhood be located if women can *look* like men. So, the current craze among women with working out is not really intended to assault, or even call into question, standard sexual roles. Florence Griffith-Joyner has proven that one can be a sexy athlete even in as sweaty a sport as sprinting.

As I walked in and saw the women, two popular culture remembrances sprang to mind: an old science-fiction film called *The Attack of the 50-Foot Woman* and an episode of an old television series, *Thriller*, called "A Wig for Miss Devore." The first is about how the mad, hysterical woman becomes a kind of outsized monstrosity, a deceptively remarkable look at the pathological narcissism which men believe is the root of woman's vanity. The second was a familiar theme in the 1950s and 1960s: An old woman finds a way of remaining young by wearing a magical wig; of course, she must kill her male suitors as part of this ritual which includes, incidentally, taking off the wig and revealing herself as a horrible hag (Devore must be a play on the word devour). That whole business is what some commentators have aptly called the woman as menopause monster, the woman willing to kill for her insane vanity and her sexuality. And it is, alas, their sexuality, their ability to approximate the look of whores—think of such currently popular women as Dolly Parton, Tammy Bakker, and Tina Turner, who look like better and paradoxically more lurid versions of the average street-walker—that make women interesting in this male-dominated society. And if they are not whores, they are nothing more than crows on a clothesline.

It is a major mystery to most men what makes women interesting to each other. Perhaps it is not a mystery, though. Perhaps what makes most women interesting to each other is exactly what makes them interesting to men. I have often been told that women wear make-up for other women and not for the benefit of men (I have been told that women dress for other women as well). This, I am sure, is true in the sense that men cannot and do not appreciate the aesthetics or artistry of feminine making-up, if one can assume that this totally contrived commercial invention by cosmetics companies is indeed an art (when one sees the exquisitely made-up, young women salesclerks at cosmetics counters in department stores dressed in white lab jackets as they commonly are these days, one is not sure if it is an art or a science, a craft or a technology). Yet I remember watching a documentary about pornographic films where a former actress in this genre said that make-up made every woman sexy and appealing. To be sure, in the scene where the actress was wearing make-up while filming, she did look a great deal more appealing, more beautiful in the way we have become accustomed to thinking women, particularly white women, in this instance, beautiful in this culture. Obviously, men respond to make-up, or one might say this make-believe, as well. For men, it seems so more much more alluring "to screw," so to speak, a made-up woman, which is why so many men want their wives or girlfriends to wear make-up to bed. In this regard, I find it striking how heavily made-up the contestants for the Miss America contest are, where the most prized value of the competing women is supposed to be their innocence. The made-up contestants look older than they really are (Miss America contestants are generally quite young; few are older than twenty-two or twenty-three; many as young as eighteen or nineteen); without make-up many would probably look no older than adolescents, so the make-up may serve a dual purpose: to give the women the "professional" look of the model and actress so that they will photograph better, and to give them a mature veneer so that their youth will not make us uncomfortable. Make-up may not quite mean making oneself a tart, as it did in the middle of the nineteenth century, but it has become a sign for a certain type of sexual suggestiveness, a deeply troubling woman's minstrel face or stage mask for the sexual come-on. But this is nothing new; too many feminists have said as much. Let's go on.

Most of the women at the Weight Watchers meeting were older, probably from their mid-thirties on. There were many who were in their fifties. There were very few young girls there, say, under the age of twenty-five or twenty. To be a man in such surroundings is a quite extraordinary experience. I cannot recall, offhand, being anywhere in recent years where I was outnumbered by so many women. And they were, by and large, a very ordinary-looking group of women, middle-class and lower-middle-class, mostly white, who were probably either housewives, receptionists, secretaries, schoolteachers, or low-level administrative bureaucrats of some sort. The sort of group where one expects to find, and usually does, an intense degree of mediocrity and philistinism which makes being middle-class the very dull and exasperating experience of unfulfillment that it is for most of us. But it was just this tempered boredom, this cloud of anesthetized frustration, that made being there of great interest for me, made me see the women as being deeply human—touching, wise, and foolish—and not simply as lust fixations or, even worst, nothing at all.

The meeting itself, which took awhile to start because all the members had to pay their dues and be weighed in, had all the combined characteristics of an encounter group session, a Dale Carnegie self-improvement class, a Sunday School confirmation complete with catechism, a high school varsity team meeting, and a religious service, a combination of elements that is, must be, uniquely American because only Americans can bring that much righteous and earnest determination to a project of such small virtue. The teacher, a woman, opens the class by asking how the weight loss went for members that week. People raise their hands and various responses are given: two pounds, three, four and a half, to which she gives appropriate words of encouragement like a proud parent working with a child on her mathematics. One man, the only one present who I think was really a member, responded that he lost ten pounds and that produced a hum and buzz of comments. The woman next to my wife and me said disdainfully, "Men always lose weight like that."

That seemed to be the consensus in the room: that the ease with which men lose weight or appear to lose it made them aliens in this enterprise. It was the *struggle* of losing weight that was the real subject of concern here and it was something, this struggle with an unwilling body, that was peculiarly and exclusively female: the struggle of having periods about which my wife complains bitterly ("You're so lucky to be a man and not have to go through this every month," she says to me); the struggle of giving birth and giving your body over to a child; of being addicted to sweet food and fashion model clothing; of having your body mutilated through breast cancer surgery or hysterectomies; of having to go through menopause. The life of a woman is her rite of passages with a very demonstrative body that, possessed by its biological imperatives and locked in the childish imaginations of men, seems to exist both beyond her will and to spite it, as a commandment and a punishment. One thinks of the edict of nuns: a life against nature; and the dieting practice of a young woman suffering from anorexia nervosa: "It's like forcing yourself to do something that doesn't come natural." It is, perhaps, how women understand not only their will, but will itself, as one's inner force against nature. And so in some sense women have defined the act of becoming themselves in many instances as being something which makes them cease to be women at all or at least cease being themselves. They enact quests to become invisible. But it is the great American heroine, Scarlett O'Hara, of Margaret Mitchell's *Gone With the Wind*, who gives polemical challenge to this when she says early on in that novel: "I'm tired of everlastingly being unnatural and never doing anything I want to do." "Why is it a girl has to be so silly to catch a husband?" Scarlett asks. Why is it, in so many respects, that a woman has to be silly so that we might know her to be a woman?

The teacher or leader, who was by turns a coach, a minister, an orchestrator, and a judge, built this week's lesson around jargon: She wrote words on the board such as "garmites," "telepression," and "retinus pigmentoastus," and had people try to guess their meaning. The fact that Weight Watchers would have their own discourse is not unusual and is indeed undoubtedly helpful to the women as it permits them to think of their experience as being special enough, and of their attempts at reforming their self-nurturing habits as profoundly critical enough to merit a language. There was talk of "red light foods" and "red light moments"—taboo foods and taboo periods of temptations in one's social activities—that made one think of the term "red light" in connection with prostitution and as a kind of stark symbol of taboo and woman in our culture. But naturally Weight Watchers does not believe in taboo foods, a member can eat anything; there is only the taboo moment of wanting the food that is so alluringly placed before you, like a seduction that holds unbearable consequences and unutterable gratification.

And obviously the real subject at these meetings is the meaning and ritual of woman's self-nurturing; for the religion offered here is not simply a new obsession with the body and the self but an attempt by these women to talk their way through to being able not to eat, in order to compensate for a starvation of another sort. For the eating does make up for other things, is a kind of make-believe in which the woman can escape other make-believes of a more sinister and demanding sort. To be fat affords one the pleasure of not having to worry about being thin—but only if one can live in peace with one's fatness. It is impossible for most women in America to be able to do that, tormented as they are by the illusion of beauty in the mass marketplace and by the guilt of the sin of gluttony. The women are here every week to have the sin of gluttony made a venial offense, to take comfort in knowing that, after all, one can be cured. In this secular age, it is the equivalent of being forgiven. Counselors now confer grace instead of priests. Ah, so perhaps coming to this Weight Watchers meeting is as close as I will ever get to witnessing the *culpa* of the convent when the nuns gather to proclaim each other's sins before the Mother Superior, the Living Rule. But more about nuns momentarily.

There is the usual self-reliance discourse here involving words such as "momentum" and "motivation" borrowed from the male worlds of business and sports but there is also the emphasis that eating within bounds, eating only your fair share, which is I think a particular moral preoccupation with women, is a way of life.

"There is no end," the teacher reminds them, "It isn't over when you have reached your ideal weight."

Indeed, for many of the members, the real struggle would only have begun at that point. After the conversion, one must fight the temptation of back-sliding. And there is an interesting emphasis on assertion. Many of the women, during the course of testifying at the meeting, spoke of how food is pressed upon them, how people around them expect them to eat, how their families push cake on them, how friends at parties insist on their eating. To say no to this is a very important step in the lives of these over-eating women; for the denial of self-nurturing gone neurotic is the first step for them to realize the bounds and limits of woman's nurturing ability in society itself.

Incentives for these women come from many sources but most particularly from the examples of famous, admired women: fat actresses and singers such as Dolly Parton, Oprah Winfrey, and Elizabeth Taylor lose weight and it becomes a celebrated event in American popular culture. But this brings to mind something else. Two of the most popular novels for women readers by women writers in twentieth-century America, both of which were made into highly acclaimed Hollywood films, are Margaret Mitchell's *Gone With the Wind* (1936) and Kathyrn Hulme's *The Nun's Story* (1956). It is quite enlightening to think how much the plots and themes of these two novels, which center largely on women characters, involve food and its consumption. For instance, in *Gone With the Wind*, the women eat tremendous amounts of food before dinner parties, a custom apparently, so that at the parties they eat very little and appear more delicate. As Scarlett's personal slave, Mammy, says: "Ah has tole you an' tole you dat you kin allus tell a lady by dat she eat lak a bird." Presumably Mammy's fat body and mammoth breasts are a sure indication that she is no lady. But of course the ladyhood business, in relation to food, is just a deception. It isn't that women do not eat; it is simply that they do not wish to be seen eating by men. But connections between women and eating abound in this novel: Mammy's concern for Scarlett's mother, Ellen, the good Catholic, because she does not eat enough; Scarlett's dreams of food during the difficult days of Reconstruction and her famous vow that she "will never be hungry again"; Melanie Wilkes, Scarlett's moral counterpoint, who is "too thin" and "too white" and who gives up her food but continues to overwork, exhibiting all the symptoms of someone suffering from anorexia nervosa, her small breasts and boyish figure slowly etherealized; Scarlett's days with Rhett Butler when she begins to eat huge meals with all the table manners of a child; and of course there is Scarlett's constant preoccupation with her eighteen-inch waistline.

Hulme's *The Nun's Story* is a thinly fictionalized biography of her friend, Marie Louise Habets, a Belgian nurse and a nun who asked to be released from her vows to join the Resistance underground during World War II. Here, too, food is everywhere. When Gabrielle, who will become Sister Luke, first enters the convent, the thoughts of the outside world that seduce her most are not about sex but about food; her last meal with her father, who opposes her entry into the convent, is his attempt to call "for all the temptings of life to speak to her where he had failed"; she grows particularly to dislike eating her meals on the hard wooden benches at the convent; one of her acts of penance required by her Superior is that she take a beggar's bowl and go from nun to nun during mealtime and beg a spoonful of soup from each; when her father visits her he invariably tells her how thin she is getting (indeed, the novel seems to be one long journey into thinness for Sister Luke); indeed, it was food that finally forces Sister Luke from the convent when, during the Belgian occupation, when everyone thought of food because there was so little of it, the convent-hospital where she is serving takes in the mistress of a German officer (who turns out to be a British spy) and in exchange for this the convent is sent a great deal of food. The mistress, a spoiled and irritating French collaborator, angers Sister Luke so that one day, during a phone conversation with the woman's lover, she responds to the woman's complaints about anal suppositories by saying customized ones are not manufactured in Belgium. The woman's lover is so amused by this that he sends a side of beef to the convent with Sister Luke's name on it. It is then that she makes her final request of the priest to be released of her vows, opening her last confession with him by saying, "I'm a food stamp, Father." I mention these books in passing only to show how much food is on the minds of women in this culture. So it is not surprising that ordinary women think of famous women by thinking about the ways these women handle food; food has become the essence of the struggle for selfhood for many of America's mythic and fictive women. In *The Nun's Story* and *Gone With the Wind* food is connected with the epistemology of religious devotion, with the carnal world, with capitalistic enterprise, with the sanctity of private property.

In short, food is the quiddity of woman's ambition in western bourgeois culture.

"Liz Taylor really looks good since she lost all that weight," my wife said to me about a year ago. "I think I might buy her book." She also told me she might buy her perfume, Elizabeth Taylor's Passion, which is apparently a line of toilet items. But when I was last standing and gazing at a department store beauty counter, I was so overwhelmed by the numberless rows of bottles of colognes, perfumes, talcs, nail polishes, lipsticks, eye shadows, mascaras, rouges, liquid soaps, make-up removers, astringents that I felt myself lost in a wonderland of bottles. I did not think it possible to find Elizabeth Taylor's Passion in a bottle. I never asked for it.

But why should my wife care about Liz Taylor at all and most strangely why should she care about something as absolutely trivial as Liz Taylor's weight. Yet Liz Taylor's weight struggle, inextricably bound up with her love life, seems to speak deeply to many women. Her struggle is their struggle, with food and with men. Her latest book, *Elizabeth Takes Off* (Taylor has written two other books and one hopes the world is found sufficiently unworthy so as not to merit a fourth), is, in some ways, the most perfectly wrought woman's autobiography imaginable. It is about food and dieting from beginning to end. As Richard Watson points out in his delightful *The Philosopher's Diet*, "The diet industry (philosophical analysis reveals) is part of the entertainment business. It belongs to the specialized branch that manufactures unnecessary things to do." So when the acting career goes fizz, why not write a dieter's autobiography? Simply shift from one form of entertainment to another—a relatively easy move for Taylor who, bless her heart, has never been under the conceited impression that she is an *artist*. Pictures of Taylor, both from stages in her career and from stages in her consumption of food, are side-by-side with recipes and exercise tips. Her book offers what will undoubtedly become an increasing popular genre with women: the autobiography and the advice column, the how-to book and the confession. It resembles nothing so much as some older boxing autobiographies such as Jack Dempsey's first, Jack Johnson's, and Archie Moore's first with their dieting and training tips, male athletes being among the only members of the male population who have been traditionally as interested in diet as women. (Incidentally, it must be remembered that the weight and dieting habits of some famous men have had a bigger impact in this culture than those of women: During his heyday Muhammad Ali's weight was the subject of almost daily conversation, and everyone knows that singer Mario Lanza dropped dead because of too many crash diets, just as everyone knows about the weight problems of Elvis Presley, the anorexic face of actor Peter O'Toole, the ups and downs of singer Luther Vandross, that Orson Welles's death was caused by overeating, that Marlon Brando's weight prevents him from acting these days but that Raymond Burr's does not.) Even more closely Taylor's mixture of forms resembles certain juvenile (didactic) biographies. Perhaps what we have with Taylor, in our subjective age, is the stridently anti-intellectual reinvention of Parson Weems. The symmetry and descriptive exactitude of the subtitle, *On Weight Gain, Weight Loss, Self-Image, and Self-Esteem*, isolates the proper subject of the book, the twin modes of the womanly self and the twin obsessions of consumption, eating and its renunciation. Although Taylor can frankly admit about her acting that she has "no techniques" and never took lessons, a confession that applies to her ability as a writer as well as to her expertise on the subject of weight loss and the psychological well-being of women, it is the sheer non-professionalism, anti-professionalism of Taylor's work that makes it endearing and appealing, its authority, as in fundamentalist faith, emerging from the heart (so Taylor's dieting is tied to the story of her marriages) and from experience (dieting tied to her career and her celebrity status). That unaffected naturalism seems both sincere and authentic, inspiring practical problem-solving. A few passages from the book may explain its popularity:

> Weight loss can provide an immediate boost to our self-esteem. And every woman knows it takes less effort to diet when she is happy.

> In my late forties, weight gain became a primary factor in my feelings of self-worth. And when I finally had the courage to do something about those added pounds, I was forced to acknowledge that loss of pride played a large role in the reasons I put on weight in the first place.

> One of the reasons I decided to write this book was that I was so disturbed by the hundreds of articles saying that my weight gain— and by implication other women's—was the result of outside forces I couldn't control. This simply isn't true. . . . During the time I took off all those pounds I learned a lot about self-image and self-respect— most of all that I was in control.

> You and only you can take charge of your self-image and weight loss.

> None of us really changes to please anyone except ourselves.

Even as a child, I insisted on determining my own fate.

I'm convinced the inner strength that rescued me from my destructive slide many years later was forged during those early studio years when I determined always to maintain control over my personal life regardless of studio demons.

The passages indicate that the book is really about the only subject of interest to women in American popular discourse, personal empowerment. High self-esteem signifies empowerment and dieting becomes the path to that holistic, unburdened selfhood. One of the most important passages in the book comes when Taylor discusses her conversion to Judaism in 1959. "It had absolutely nothing to do with my past marriage to Mike [Todd] or my upcoming marriage to Eddie Fisher, both of whom were Jewish. It was something *I* had wanted to do for a very long time" (emphasis mine). The idea of freely converting as an act of self-expression (most people assumed she converted to please her Jewish husbands) becomes of a piece with the will to diet and the ability to form one's own image. In essence, Taylor's book tells us that dieting is the womanly restatement of Arminianism in post-industrial western society. And since Arminianism has swept most of the Christian world, why shouldn't its promise that the kingdom of empowerment is within you sweep the bourgeois secular world as well? I understand why my wife wishes to read it. Black women, in particular, are suckers for tales with that moral.

But black women, burdened with the historical image of being the major feminine nurturers in our culture, have other models and sources in addition to the ones white women have: the regular feature in *Ebony* on some man or woman (mostly women) who has lost an incredible amount of weight; Aretha Franklin's constant, publicized battles with her weight; features such as the one in *Essence*, a black woman's fashion magazine, on Angela Davis's health routine; the images of the very slim figures of Whitney Houston and Anita Baker. But there is a greater ambivalence among black women about weight loss and exercise; several prominent black women such as Gladys Knight, Patti LaBelle, Janet Jackson, Kim Fields, Toni Morrison, and Jackee Harry are by no means thin. (There are black women athletes such as skater Debi Thomas, tennis player Zina Garrison, and track stars Jackie Joyner-Kersee and Florence Griffith-Joyner who surely possess goddess-like figures, but they are rarely, if ever, advertised as such. Probably Griffith-Joyner has received more attention in this way than any other black woman athlete, but her beauty has not been unquestioned. During the 1988 Summer Olympics Games, where both Griffith-Joyner and Joyner-Kersee won gold medals, Brazilian Joaquin Cruz was quoted as saying, "Florence looks like a man, and Jackie looks like a gorilla." White male sports writers responded indignantly, if somewhat patronizingly and with certain sexist assumptions. But the question is: Why was this obscure Brazilian quoted in American newspapers to begin with?) Moreover, one rarely sees black women jogging or doing aerobics while one watches through the window of some exercise spa. (I remember a few years back when Tina Turner's legs were being lionized, as it were, she remarked that she never exercised or worked out.) I suppose if the weight loss battle is, in part, tied to the business of sex and men, then the attitude of black women may have something to do with the common expression among black men that they "want a woman with a little meat on her bones." Blues singer Mississippi John Hurt once sang, "Woman, get your big leg offa mine," which may summarize a great deal. But as James Weldon Johnson pointed out many years ago, a point which still has a great deal of force, hardly anyone in this culture, black or white, has ever thought that black women were or could be beautiful. It has been said by scholars that one of the things that blacks taught whites about living during the days of slavery was how to slow down. When I see many of the white women running, jogging, and race walking in my neighborhood, looking distraught and impatient, I think that there might be a kind of beauty of motion that they could learn from their black sisters yet.

So, I wonder what my wife thinks of this: There was a white woman at the meeting who I suppose was in her fifties and who had lost a considerable amount of weight. In fact, she was quite thin, nearly anorexic. Her hair was dyed black, her face was heavily made-up, and she wore a sleeveless, low-cut leotard with leather pants (she had also some sort of fur, possibly mink, jacket) on a day when it must have been little more than ten or fifteen degrees outside. She was clearly one of those women who was trying to dredge up her lost youth. She wore the type of clothing she did because she was quite vain about her weight loss and her current figure. Looking at that woman made me think, oddly enough, of the first baby sitter my daughters had when we came to St. Louis, a quite overweight black woman who took care of children in the basement of her home. She was also a hairdresser on the side but, having few customers, would spend most of her time doing her own hair which, apparently, never ceased to fascinate her. She had a hot comb in her hair every day. Indeed, aside from food, hair seemed her most consuming passion. Her own daughter suffered from a disease that prevented hair growth, a source of great anguish for the mother. Many medications were tried. Whenever some small hair growth resulted, it was the cause of great celebration and a doing up of the daughter's hair in grand style. Perhaps the pencil-thin white woman and the heavy black woman were more alike and more in need of sharing their differences than anyone could imagine. I stood before *those* expressions of womanhood struck dumb with a kind of wonder. But my wife intensely disliked both women.

My wife told me Weight Watchers encourages members who have reached their goal weight to continue to come to meetings by making them life members and absolving them of having to pay dues. They are meant to serve as models for the other women who are struggling to reach the end. "It can be done and here are some who have done it." One has to find one's models where one can, I thought. But there are still some lessons that are too hard to be learned well that way. Or, put another way, when one considers what black women and white women can teach each other, when one considers the significance of these ordinary women sharing experiences in this way, the choice for women between eating and not eating is more fraught with a kind of feminist philosophy than many of us ever dreamt it was. Near the end of the meeting, when the teacher had whipped up more than a bit of enthusiasm and had her students shouting out what they needed to do to get through the next week of dieting, the resolve and strengthening that was required to resist the temptation of food, well, I must admit that that bit of womanly determination to be better women gave me a thrill.

MONROE ENGEL

Henry Green: Eros and Persistence

The case of a writer of great accomplishment who ceases to practice his calling while still apparently in full possession of his creative powers is tantalizing. E. M. Forster, for example, lived nearly half a century after the publication of *Passage to India* in 1924 without producing another novel. There are ways to think about Forster's career however that can mitigate regret. It seems entirely possible that he was, as his biographer P. N. Furbank suggests, "one of those who have 'only one novel to write,' " and that *Passage to India* was so full and telling a dramatization of his social vision that any novel that followed it would have been anticlimactic or redundant. And that he knew this. Fortunately too, he wasn't silent during these many succeeding years, but was able to turn successfully to other forms of writing to remain an influential presence in the world. The truncated career of Henry Green though—a lesser but nonetheless considerable novelist—offers no such comforts. In the couple of decades between the appearance of his last novel, *Doting*, in 1952, and his death in 1973, Green was effectively mute.

John Updike, in a tribute that is admiring, discerning, and graceful, acknowledges Green as the writer he would say had "taught [him] to write" if that didn't imply either that he *had* learned or that writing was "a business one learns." In spite of this disclaimer though, he says he "can launch [himself] upon this piece of homage and introduction only by falling into some sort of imitation of that liberatingly ingenious voice." Updike is predictably illuminating when he talks about the identifying characteristics of Green's fiction, and the lucid complexities of his brief essay also establish his earned right to offer an appreciation of this brilliant and sometimes elusive stylist. He hazards no guesses however about the silence in the last two decades of Green's life, which he is content to call a puzzle. That's respectful, but it also closes a door I'd choose to keep somewhat ajar, open at least to speculation. For thinking about what might have caused Green's ultimate silence is a way to think too about why he wrote a body of distinctive novels before he fell silent, about what was at stake for him in that repeated voluntary act. And a couple of Updike's perceptions about Green that strike me as at odds with each other, offer a useful approach to these related questions.

Updike attaches little value to what he calls the "pugnacious piety" with which Green denigrates the wealthy class to which he was born relative to the working class; but then having said that, he also notes without any suggestion that this might work against the judgment he's just made, that in his second novel, *Living*, Green "escaped into" the working class, "finding there a purpose and gaiety hitherto lacking from his life." That's an instructive understanding to which Updike doesn't attach the importance it may deserve. For in addition to purpose and gaiety, Green must have found in the working class what he represented in several of his novels as a very different, more life-sustaining eroticism than he encountered among men and women of his own class. That has to be an important discrimination for a writer most of whose novels can reasonably be called love stories.

Rereading is a destabilizing activity. When I read Green's novels again now, the distribution of their weight seems to have altered since I read them last. The view of life they project is far more traditional than it once seemed, and I'm aware of an unexpected, persistent, earnest sense of possibility that informs them even as they achieve their greatest ebullience in the years during and just after World War II. A hope for transformation, for a life that is other and better, is palpable in all but Green's late novels, where what is felt instead is the extinction of that hope. Love, and its relationship to work and class, figure critically in that hope. Eros was Green's subject, but it was also I think the force that energized his writing, kept him going. Following the related themes of class and love as they persist and develop in his novels suggests something about the mystery of his ultimate retreat into silence that isn't indicated by attending only to their continuing textual brilliance.

In *Pack My Bag* (1940), Green's mid-life autobiography, the hope for transformation is both explicit and achieved. The book ends with his discovery some time after leaving Oxford (where, he says, he "had been an idler") to learn a range of largely manual skills in a foundry in Birmingham owned by his father, a wealthy manufacturer, that though "being tired in the head was to be the brilliant fruit of my labours in the day to sour the evenings . . . there were advantages . . . I found the life satisfying and I had never before been satisfied . . . the life was happy." Though aware that some part of this happiness was probably attributable to the novelty of what he was doing, he was nonetheless confident of the value of work and of "the new standard which I had never met, that of costs and prices." His tempered, qualified recollection of what this time meant to him ends then (as does the book) with a remarkably unqualified avowal that what he had found "was life itself at last in loneliness certainly at first, but, in that long exchange of letters then beginning, and for the ten years now we have not had to write because we are man and wife, there was love."

The novels however, some preceding and some following *Pack My Bag*, describe a trajectory on themes of love and class—a need for, then discovered optimism about, but then also apparent loss of belief in some possibility more generous and life-sustaining than what passes for love in the novels in the moneyed world to which Green was born. I have no idea how much this curve does or does not reflect the immediate circumstances of Green's own life; but though the saving love imagined or enacted in the novels is individual, it has social implications, and sometimes suggests a basis for community of a kind Green can only have observed or imagined.

Green's early writing was determinedly literary. His first novel, *Blindness*, published in 1926 when he was only twenty-one, trumpets literary ambition, and its systematic shifts in point of view particularly lend it something of the character of a sequence of literary exercises. Demanding exercises however, and of formative importance for a writer the originality of whose most accomplished work depends consistently on constraint.

Blindness records the dissatisfaction of its protagonist John Haye, who loses his sight in the course of the story, with the trivialities of his effete well-to-do life, particularly at his school, Noat (presumably Eton, which Green attended and with which, as with Oxford too, he expresses very similar dissatisfaction in *Pack My Bag*). Hemmed in by pretentious inconsequence, at one point he remarks to a friend that "poor people are always much happier than rich people on the cinema." It's hard to know how much irony "on the cinema" introduces here when he also confesses a little later that "the cinema used to be the only way I had to see life." Everything in the novel that followed *Blindness*, however, *Living*, suggests conviction that poor people's lives, whether or not they are happy, are more genuine than are the lives of the rich. *Living* has to do chiefly with men employed in an iron foundry in Birmingham (presumably similar at least to the foundry in which Green went to work on leaving Oxford), and with a young woman, Lily Gates, who keeps house for three of these men: her widowed and worthless father Joe Gates, her timid but dependable suitor Jim Dale, and the patriarch Craigan whose house it is. Tempted by the possibility of some more romantic life, Lily gives up Dale for Bert Jones, a bolder suitor with whom she actually goes to the cinema. The household slides into disarray as this happens, but when Lily's elopement with Bert to his native Liverpool becomes a disaster and he deserts her, she returns to Birmingham and it is reconstituted. Craigan's continuing tenderness toward Lily, and Jim Dale's steadfastness, are presented as of greater value and more enduring than either romance or sex—about neither of which Lily discovers very much even with Bert.

Extreme contrast to Craigan's odd but endorsed working class household is afforded by the wealthy Dupret family who own the works in Birmingham and are figures of a kind that turns up regularly in Green's novels as representatives of his own class. Ned Dupret, the feckless son, falls in love repeatedly and sadly with pretty, whimsically named, and consistently undependable girls of his own class; and when his father is ailing and invalided, his mother, "though she had never been very fond of [her husband], was now thinking how very fond of him she was," and hires a "well known courtesan" to revive his interest in life when the pretty young nurses hired previously to do that have failed.

There are no factory workers in Green's later novels, but the major characters of *Party Going*, which follows *Living*, could all be members of Ned Dupret's circle. Ten years elapsed between the publication of *Living* and of *Party Going*, the end of which is inscribed "London, 1931–1938." That might seem a long time in progress for a rather slight novel, but the apparent slightness of *Party Going* is intentional and deceptive. Though constructed largely of somewhat tainted gossamer, it's a very strenuous achievement, and its narrative voice is continuously and arrestingly distinctive.

The story however is simple. A number of well-to-do young idlers off together to a house party in the south of France are delayed by deep fog in a London station and ultimately in the station hotel where they take rooms in order to avoid the moiling mob of less privileged travelers similarly delayed. ("This is what it is to be rich, he thought, if you are held up, if you have to wait then you can do it after a bath in your dressing gown.") The matter of the novel is chiefly banal conversation, flirtation, sexual maneuvering and sexual teasing. At one memorable point Amabel, the most flagrantly desirable of the young women, does take a bath, but leaves the bathroom door partially open to allow her to converse with one of the male guests so placed outside the door that he can hear but presumably not see her. It's unclear to the other guests that he cannot see her however, and the object of Amabel's careful arrangement is to excite the jealousy of her fickle lover Max, the wealthy host of the party—to win him away from one of the other young women guests in whom he is also interested. No direct authorial judgment is made on these activities, but the empty conversations and the erotic posturing are self-judging. There is also however dramatic judgment. An eccentric aunt of one of the guests, who has turned up to see her niece off, collapses after a visit to the bar. The immediate cause of her collapse is alcohol, but it seems possible that she's dying, and because that possibility constitutes an inadmissible threat to the party, her niece contrives to hide her away in a distant room in the hotel where she can have her cared for discreetly. This reminder of human mortality serves here for Green much as similar reminders do for Dickens (whose novels the patriarch Mr. Craigan in *Living* reads perpetually), to disclose the unreality of social existence.

Green's persistent engagement with the possibility of transformation lends poignancy to his depiction of the trivializing eroticism of the rich and idle. The love antics of his own class are his enduring subject, but he also recurrently creates working class characters capable of a more generous, more life-sustaining kind of love. Contrast to the sexual teasing and withholding ubiquitous in *Party Going* is provided by an incident in which the man-servant of one of the party guests, left to guard baggage in the mobbed station, sees a girl with "lovely blue eyes" at the other side of his pile of baggage, and asks her for a kiss.

> "I like your cheek," she said scornfully. "Here," she said, "if you want one," and crept around and kissed him on his mouth. Not believing his luck he put his arms around her and the porter said, "God bless me . . . God bless 'er little 'eart. . . . Come up out of the ground and gave him a great bloody kiss when he asked her."

A moment only, and nothing more is made of it. But in a novel in which judgments of human value can only be implicit, this slight episode earns attention because of its sharp contrast to what is otherwise happening. The contrast moreover is consonant with the judgmental associations of eros and class in both Green's earlier and his later novels.

Typically, the love that is accorded worth in Green's novels is in part compassionate. It implies an understanding of the pain and the limits of human existence. The casual kiss bestowed by the girl in the station has something of the quality of a glass of water given to a thirsty man. The most telling moments of tenderness in *Living* occur not between Lily and Bert, but in a scene just saved from the maudlin by being (perhaps incestuously) eroticized, in which old Craigan, whom Lily calls "granddad," sits by the bed into which she has collapsed on her return from her failed elopement. "Dear heart . . . don't grieve so," he says, and puts his hand over her eyes from which tears can flow only when his own tears have released them.

The world to which Green was born is the object of a lot of heady ambivalence both in his early novels and in his autobiography. Near the beginning of *Pack My Bag*, he reports his childhood fascination with his family's gardener Poole who "could never forgive my mother . . . [who] made him bowl mangel wurzels across one lawn for her to shoot at." He then adds however that he "adored" his mother, and describes listening to Poole's disparagement of her as his "first disloyalty": "it was as though someone were bringing out mean things about adoration to another full of his first love, what was said came as laughter in the face of creation and this and my love for my mother is what I first remember." The four novels Green wrote during and right after World War II— *Caught, Loving, Back,* and *Concluding*—are those on which any large claims for him must I think be founded, and *Caught* and *Loving* are also the novels in which this ambivalence is most strongly felt. Even here though, social hierarchy and moral hierarchy are pretty consistently in inverse order.

The war had a powerfully vivifying effect on Green's imagination. The threat to his world seems to have intensified his attachment to it, even to have caused a rediscovery of attachment to much that had previously felt devalued. *Caught* follows *Party Going* by four years, and the immediately apparent stylistic difference between them is the absence in the later novel of conspicuous innovation, such as absence of articles and decisive shifts in point of view. But *Caught* is also in complex service to an extraordinary time and set of historical circumstances. The story takes place in 1940, and a prefatory note declares it to be "about the Auxiliary Fire Service which saved London in her night blitzes."

In *Caught* too, and for the first time, Green creates a relatively intricate plot to bring into significant connection the lives of two men unlikely because of class difference to meet significantly except in time of war. Richard Roe, a well-to-do widower who (like Green) is deaf, joins the fire service as an Auxiliary (as did Green), where he receives instruction from a regular fireman named Pye. By unfortunate coincidence however, Pye's insane sister had once kidnapped Roe's son Christopher, presumably as a proxy for the child she has not had herself, and taken him to a room where Pye found and rescued him only after the boy was already in a state of terror. This unhappy event, which makes for continuing discomfort between Roe and Pye, serves also to bind them uncomfortably to each other. And these two very different men also have something psychically in common. The casual erotic adventures of wartime London weigh little for either of them against his most tenacious erotic memories. Roe falls recurrently under the spell of an imagined life with his dead wife whose "companionship" he "had taken . . . for granted" when she was alive, but whom now "he could not leave . . . alone when in an empty room, but stroked her wrists, pinched, kissed her eyes, nibbled her lips while, for her part, she smiled, joked, and took him up to bed at all hours of the day, and lay all night murmuring to him in empty memory." However melancholy, this is a relatively simple and even happy state of recalled life compared to Pye's obsessive memories of the first girl he'd made love to when he was a boy. Pye's is actually a double set of memories—of making love to a girl whose face he couldn't see in the dark, and then, later that same night, of watching his sister emerge out of the dark, returning home in the disheveled state of a defeated animal. The two memories inexorably take on causal connection. He comes to believe that his sister was the unidentified girl with whom he'd lain, and that this incestuous act was the cause of her derangement. The compassionate-erotic attachment to his sister that has evolved over the years from these joined memories leads Pye finally, by an intricate but persuasive set of associations, to an almost ritualized act, that destroys him. On a blacked-out street one night, goaded by his erotic memories and looking for a prostitute, he encounters instead a destitute boy who reminds him at once of Roe's son Christopher, and he takes the boy to the fire station where he feeds him and shelters him. However kindly, this is against regulations, and when it is discovered, Pye is suspected also of having molested the boy. The suspicion is unfounded, but imaginatively and psychologically, Pye's behavior does have murky associations. It's the sexual need incited by his thoughts about his sister that sends him into the streets; and there is strong similarity then between the way he shelters and sequesters the boy and the way his sister had kidnapped and sequestered Christopher. When the charge of moral turpitude brought against him coincides with the discovery of some relatively minor infractions of duty of which he is actually guilty, he feels disgraced and puts his head in a gas oven. He is found dead there by Roe who, "face to face" he says, pulls him out.

Green's view of the relationship of class to feeling, muted earlier in the novel, sounds strongly at the end. Having given his sister-in-law Dy a remarkable account of what the firemen had done during the first great raids on London, and gone on then to tell her what he knows about the events leading to Pye's suicide, Roe, stirred up, is appalled by her failure to respond in a way he considers appropriate to the compassion he has voiced for Pye, and to his pained sense of the injustice of the dead man's fate.

> "I can't help it," she said. "I shall always hate him and his beastly sister."
> This was too much for the state he was in. He let go. "God damn you," he shouted, releasing everything, "you get on my bloody nerves, all you bloody women with all your talk."

Stressing these thematic continuities, I of course scant the brilliance of the dialogue, sensual registration, and description that makes *Caught* so compelling. Roe's account of London under blitz, for example, is unequaled by any other account of this I know. But these virtues have been much remarked on, whereas the thematic elements that I think were probably crucial to Green's inventive energy, and an essential part of his personal stake in the act of invention, have been relatively ignored. His work diminishes in range and intensity, and he is then finally silent, as the interest invested in these thematic continuities is relinquished. I believe there's not just simultaneity, but causal connection as well, between these two lines of development.

Green's fiction is always artful, and after *Living*, he shows no interest again in simple verisimilitude. Nonetheless, the novels continue to press on experience, and some of the felt weight of that pressure depends on the value invested in a capacity for compassionate love that distinguishes to their advantage working people and servants who possess it from the wealthy who do not. By implication, that's an idea also about community. Green's view of his art however guarantees that these ideas will not have programmatic expression, and they may well not even have existed for him as ideas except as they animate character. But the variants of compassionate love developed in *Caught*—Pye's love for his sister, his misunderstood compassion for the stray boy, Roe's eventual commitment to Pye, the way Roe imagines his love for his dead wife and hers for him, even perhaps Pye's sister's abduction of Christopher—begin to be generalizing.

Compassionate love comes closest to communal realization though in *Loving*, the novel that follows *Caught*. Set in a wealthy household in rural Ireland during the war, it is an upstairs-downstairs story in which far more space and interest are accorded to the servants (mostly English) than to their masters about whom (as about the Duprets in *Living*) we learn only enough to make them effective contrast to the real principals. An adulterous affair upstairs between Mrs. Jack and Captain Davenport serves as foil to a couple of romances among the servants: between the beautiful maid Edith and the somewhat older and dyspeptic butler Raunce; and between the other, only less flagrantly comely maid Kate, Edith's friend and confidante, and the uncouth Irish lampman Paddy. For each of the maids, ordinary enough young women except for the luminous loveliness with which Green invests them, compassion for the men they are to marry is an integral component of the love that leads them to marriage. Mrs. Jack's more simply lustful doings with Captain Davenport however sexualize the entire household. The headiness of this is exacerbated too by the isolation of the household, in neutral Ireland, from England at war. The suffering imposed on the servants but not on their masters by this isolation—the concern of two of the servants particularly about distant parents—is presented with a moral earnestness unexpected in so brilliant a context. Green sets *Loving* though within formal boundary signs that suggest a fairy tale. "Once upon a day," the novel begins, and the last sentence is: "Over in England they were married and lived happily ever after."

Versions of compassionate love figure prominently also in the two other novels of Green's richest period, *Back* and *Concluding*. *Back* tells the story of Charley Summers who is repatriated from a German prisoner-of-war camp with a leg lost, and obsessed with a still greater loss, the death while he was gone of the married woman Rose whose lover he had been and whose son he may have fathered. In no other Green novel is an extreme artifice that doesn't distance employed quite so boldly and memorably. When we learn of Charley at the outset that he "had lost his leg in France for not noticing the gun beneath a rose," this is a first indication of his obsession with everything rosy—the name, the flower, the color. And Green's fictive world feeds this obsession abundantly. Soon after his return Charley meets and is drawn to a woman named Nancy whom he takes to be Rose resurrected, and who is indeed Rose's half-sister, her father's illegitimate daughter. When at the very end of the novel Nancy finally accepts Charley—she actually proposes marriage to him, realizing that despite his persistent muddled attention to her, he is incapable of proposing to her—she allows him to see her naked for the first time in the radiance of a lamp with a pink shade that

> seemed to spill a light of roses all over her in all their summer colours . . . but it was too much, for he burst into tears again, he buried his face in her side just below the ribs, and bawled like a child. "Rose," he called out, not knowing he did so, "Rose."
>
> "There," Nancy said, "there," pressed his head with her hands. His tears wetted her. The salt water ran down between her legs. And she knew what she had taken on. It was no more or less, really, than she had expected.

Again, honored love flourishes not despite but because of the beloved's disabilities and vulnerabilities, and the way they find place in a realistic view of the fragility of human existence. The class bias that has previously informed the depiction of compassionate love in Green's novels however—that it is a virtue of the working class unattainable by the wealthy—is modulated in *Back*. The chief characters in this novel all belong to a relatively undifferentiated middle-class. I can only speculate that Green may have been infected for a time with a kind of social optimism that was touchingly common in England during the war, and that this took some of the edge off his views of class difference.

I assume however that the distinction between the capacity for love attributed in these earlier novels to the wealthy and to the working class is drawn in the interest or hope of transformation, and if the absence of that dynamic of difference from *Back* can be taken as a hopeful sign, its continuing absence from the later novels cannot be. The version of state socialism enacted in Britain shortly after the war by the Labour Party all but instantly elicited from Green in *Concluding*, which followed *Back* in 1948, a vision of a dystopia set in a pervasively aberrant near future in which not just the economy but all aspects of personal life as well are subject to oppressive centralized control. Compassionate love as a basis for marriage has no discernible place in this straitened society, but the anarchic sexuality of the sequestered pubescent girls at the state boarding school that is its chief scene, figures as a last force of resistance to state control of private life in something of the way sexuality figures in *1984*, Orwell's otherwise very different version of the aberrational near future.

Green accords biology far more qualified honor in *Concluding* however than Orwell accords it in *1984*. The only human potential fully endorsed in *Concluding* is the nonsexual, compassionate, protective and patriarchal love of Mr. Rock—an old man who was formerly a distinguished scientist, and who survives as the exemplar of the best aspects of an earlier, better time—for his unstable granddaughter Elizabeth who has had a "breakdown at work." Vulnerable to the questionable mercies of the state she is now unfit to serve, Elizabeth's sexual needs do little for her but make her vulnerable as well to the uncertain loyalty of her lover Sebastian. His attachment to her is founded chiefly on his belief that Rock will be able to get the state to grant her assured possession of a house, something hard to come by in this starkly regulated society.

The poetic radiance that illuminates *Caught, Loving*, and *Back* recurrently, is found less frequently in *Concluding*. Green's imagination finds less to illuminate in a socially devalued world than it found in a war-time world the value of which was heightened by the possibility of its destruction. That distinctive light is all but extinguished then in Green's last two novels, *Nothing* (1950) and *Doting* (1952). Neither of these is of an interest comparable to that of each of the preceding several novels, but the difference can't be attributed to any diminution of Green's literary powers as such. The inventive skill he brings to the exhaustion of intentionally limited and essentially desolating possibilities in these final works is astonishing. James's achievement in *What Maisie Knew* could serve as a reasonable analogy if in either *Nothing* or *Doting* there was a Maisie to lend freshness to the otherwise pervasively sordid. No such contrasting figures exist however in a society Green pictures as motivated chiefly by enfeebled instinct. These two sadly comic novels return to the ambiance of *Party Going*, a version of the ambiance to which Green had readiest access. Now however the principals are no longer young, and though age has done little to change their interests or their characters, their flesh—and this is true of the young too when they appear as relatively minor characters—has lost all radiance. In *Party Going*, Amabel, however shallow or calculating she may be, is imagined in her bath by one of her admirers as pink with warmth and wrapped round with aromatic steam, "and her hands with rings still on her fingers were water-lilies done in rubies." In *Loving*, even Mrs. Jack, discovered in bed with the Captain, crosses "her lovely arms over the great brilliant upper part of her on which, wayward, were two dark upraised dry wounds". And when Albert gets the chance to hold Edith in his arms "for the first time" in a game of blind man's buff, and then to kiss her, he finds her head in this "short contact . . . in spite of being so short more brilliant more soft and warm perhaps than his thousand dreams." In *Back*, which follows *Loving*, the rosy aura of Nancy's nude body may be partly delusory, but it is nonetheless compelling. Female flesh in *Nothing* and *Doting* however is consistently, even formulaically, "fat" or "white" or both.

John Updike, as I mentioned at the start of this essay, finds that "the wit and poetry, the comedy and truth of [*Nothing* and *Doting*] show so little slackening of powers (though perhaps a more restricted channeling of them) that Green's lasting silence [following them] comes as a puzzle." Of course. But is it a puzzle to which Green's work offers no clues? Updike's claim for Green's neutrality as a creator and observer is I think excessive, and I take this as important to his finding so little falling-off in these last two novels. He writes, for example, that Green "never asks us to side with him against a character." Well, he may not ask us to do this, but he certainly causes us to do it, and apparently by intention. In an interview with Terry Southern published in the *Paris Review* in the summer of 1958, Green does say that "the author must keep completely out of the picture" if the fiction is to have "a life of its own"; but then he also says that the attitude toward the war of the English servants in *Loving* is "meant to torpedo the woman and her daughter-in-law, the employers." That's not neutrality, and here as elsewhere Green gives moral weight to those characters whose lives are conditioned by the exigencies of ordinary work, and who are capable as their social betters are not of what I've called compassionate love. If Updike sees such comparative weighings as aberrations rather than characteristic practice, that may account for his startling judgment that *Caught* is the "least enchanting of [Green's] novels."

The comic mode or modes of Green's novels, and their idiosyncratic brilliance, can easily disguise their earnestness. But the novels enforce a consistent moral judgment more evident when they are looked at collectively and chronologically than when taken singly, and that judgment is remarkably traditional. Green is not the first middle-class or upper-class English novelist in whose fictive world the working class poor are seen as more generous and more loving than their social and financial betters. And his ability to imagine and represent an alternative to the world he knew best seems to have been essential to the richest workings of his creative powers. When this alternative falls away, he finds nothing to take its place as a standard of the desirable, an energizing idea of another and better life. In *Nothing* and *Doting*, I detect some authorial admiration, even some limited relish, for the persistent scheming and contrivances by which his aging and jaded rakes of both sexes cling to the excitements of erotic life even when they are little more than vestigial. But the limited vitality available to them from this source isn't a basis for large hope.

Green belongs most nearly I think to a period of the English novel's development that had peaked shortly before he produced his major work. He is a less innovative stylist than Virginia Woolf and his moral earnestness never achieves the radical force of E. M. Forster's, but invoking those names suggests without denigration the identifying characteristics of his accomplishment, its formal daring and its commitment to amelioration of the human condition. Not immediately very much like either Woolf or Forster, Green was nonetheless close to them in spirit of literary ambition—the how and to what end that keeps the enterprise going—and the abrupt conclusion of his writing career suggests that he may have seen himself as a terminal figure in a lost quest.

ALMA GUILLERMOPRIETO

Samba

SAMBA: *A musical composition based on a two-by-four beat.*

SAMBA: *Dance(s) the samba (second and third person singular present of the verb sambar).*

SAMBA: *A gathering that takes place specifically to dance the samba.*

When I first arrived in Rio de Janeiro several years ago, I rented an apartment in Ipanema, a pleasant middle-class district, and along with the refrigerator and the bed and a couple of chests of drawers I inherited a maid: a stocky, very black woman in her fifties whom my landlady insisted she loved as one of the family. Nieta was nice, the landlady then warned me, but she had a tendency to steal little things, and it was important that as a foreigner I start off by imposing my authority, otherwise Nieta would, as maids do, start to get "uppity" on me. My secretary issued the same warning, and so did almost everyone else I met at the time. "Don't let her take advantage of you or you're in for trouble," they said urgently, as if the entire Brazilian social order were at stake. I liked Nieta enormously, but I was on the lookout for insubordination.

"*Ciao!*" she would say in the mornings, sending me off to work with a smile, one hand on hip, the other waving gracefully in a pose learned from television. In my own country, Mexico, maids were not supposed to be so casual or say sophisticated things like "*Ciao.*" Was this a sign of uppitiness? She had been trained to stand whenever she was in her employer's presence, but I had not been trained to provide a television for the tiny room off the kitchen where she lived. Consequently, when I came in late and found her watching television in the study she would stand up and I would sit down and we would watch television together. I encouraged her to sit, but I worried. Was I asking for trouble?

Despite the awkwardness of the situation, I enjoyed watching television with her: She was hip, in the way Cariocas—the people of Rio de Janeiro—are, and she had excellent information on the singers who appeared on the screen: which ones were fakes, which ones had spoiled their talent by going commercial, which were involved with the underworld. She filled me in on the background of the prime-time soap opera. The one then playing was set in nineteenth-century Brazil, and Nieta didn't think much of one of the actresses. "That woman has no originality, her body isn't expressive," she commented. And another night, as we watched the heroine being waited on by her favorite house slave: "Whites adore soap operas set in the old times. They really love to look at the slaves."

The first time we went to the market together I asked her why she was calling the elevator at the back of the hall. She rode down with me in the front elevator. We did this a second time, and then the third time she refused, saying a neighbor had seen us and complained to the doorman. "We're not supposed to ride the front elevator," she said then, for the first time, and I was too confused to ask her if the "we" referred to blacks or maids. In theory, Rio de Janeiro city codes prohibit servants, delivery people, and tenants in bathing suits from using the front elevators. In practice, the regulation ends up discriminating mostly against blacks.

Nieta went home on weekends and invariably came back edgy. Sometimes her problems had to do with the complicated lives of her two adult daughters, but more often it was a question of money. Refrigerator door off the hinge. Rains caving in one of the two rooms in her house. She lived about two hours away by bus, and when I suggested that she (that is, I) might prefer day work only, it was clear she had no appetite for the daily commute or the unrelieved contact with her own misery. Instead she said that some weekend she would like to invite me out to her neighborhood for a meal at home. But before I could make the trip—only a few weeks after she had begun working for me—I became convinced that she *was* stealing things like sugar and helping herself liberally to my makeup and perfume, and the loose change. I agonized over the unfairness of her situation: Perhaps the level of stealing she indulged in was normal and expected from underpaid servants in Brazil. Perhaps the sugar bowl and the small-change drawer were producing evidence of nothing but my own paranoia, fueled by a landlady's slander. Perhaps I had taken at face value a warning that she had intended not against Nieta but against the entire black race, meaning, "You've got to watch these people; they're unreliable." Perhaps it wasn't Nieta's fault that I couldn't trust her. But I couldn't, and I fired her.

I missed her very much after she wished me "everything good" at the kitchen door and waved *"Ciao!"* for the last time. For one thing, she was the only person who had—or could invent—answers for the growing pool of questions in my mind. The odd situation of blacks in Rio provoked my curiosity much more forcefully than the free-wheeling culture of beer and chatter common to white Cariocas of my income level, but I realized only after Nieta left that she was my single contact with the culture of a race that constitutes nearly half the Brazilian population. The new maid, a shy white woman from the Minas Gerais countryside who had converted to evangelism, certainly could not provide the answers Nieta could have come up with. Why aren't there any black waiters? Where can I find black music? Who is the black woman with blue eyes and a metal gag whose plaster image appears in all the religious-supplies stores? Just what, exactly, is a samba school? Why is it that at sunset, when the beaches in Ipanema are emptying, black women will sometimes approach the waves and toss white flowers into the foam?

The heat bloomed in December as the carnival season kicked into gear. Nearly helpless with sun and glare, I avoided Rio's brilliant sidewalks and glittering beaches, panting in dark corners and waiting out the inverted southern summer. Nevertheless, certain rhythms, an unmistakable urgency in the air got through to me. Although there were still three months left to the carnival celebrations that would close down Rio for nearly a week in March, the momentum was already building. The groups of men who normally gathered for coffee or beer in front of the tiny grocery stores that dot Rio were now adding a percussion backup to their usual excited conversation. They beat a drum, clapped their hands in counterpoint, and toyed with a stray verse of song before letting the rhythm die out again. There was a faster, more imposing beat to the sambas on the radio. I made tentative inquiries: Carnival? Boring. Vulgar. Noisy, some people said, and recommended that I leave town for that horrible weekend. Samba schools? Tacky, some said. Highly original, said others, and volunteered that the "schools" were in reality organizations that compete on carnival weekend with floats and songs and extravagant costumes, each group dressed entirely in its official colors. But was it true that carnival was something that happened principally in the slums? Why? There were shrugs, raised eyebrows. Who knows. Opium of the people. Blacks are like that. We Brazilians are like that. You know: On the day of the coup, back in 1964, people were happy because it meant they had the day off and could go to the beach. I recalled the way Nieta's gestures became expansive when she mentioned carnival. Opium, yes, probably. But surely it was fun? In March, I ended up with a ticket for the first of two all-night samba school parades.

In the official parade grounds—the Sambadrome—I thought the silence eerie until I realized it was in fact a solid wall of sound, a percussive din that did not sound like music and advanced gradually toward the spectators on an elaborate loudspeaker system set up on either side of the central "avenue," or parade space. At the head of the noise was a gigantic waggling lion's head that floated down the avenue and overtook us, giving way to dazzling hordes in red and gold. A marmalade-thick river of people swept past; outlandish dancers in feathers and capes, ball gowns and G-strings, hundreds of drummers, thousands of leaping princes singing at the top of their lungs. Drowning in red and gold, I struggled to focus. In the ocean of feathers and banners faces emerged: brown, white, pink, tan, olive. Young black men bopping in sweat-drenched suits; old women in cascades of flounces whirling ecstatically; middle-aged men and women with paunches and eyeglasses bouncing happily in their headdresses and bikinis. How much money did they make? How much had their costumes cost? Why, in Brazil's pervasively segregated society, had all the colors decided to mix? Four Styrofoam elephants trundled past on golden platforms, followed by gigantic Balinese dancers in red and gold. There were acrobatic dancers with tambourines; more spinning old women; a flag-bearing couple, who should have been paralyzed by the weight of their glittering costumes, twirling and curtsying instead through a dance that looked like a samba-minuet. Nothing was familiar or logical, and I was reduced to the most simple questions. How could that large woman over there in the sequined bikini be so unconcerned about her cellulite? Why was everyone singing a song about the Mexican chicle tree, and who had come up with this idea? Why were a spectacularly beautiful woman dressed only in a few feathers and a little boy in a formal suit pretending to have sex with each other for the audience's benefit, and why was everyone involved so cheerful? Were all these people from the slums? And if they were, how could they look so happy when their lives were so awful?

It was well after dawn when I left the crowd of ever more enthusiastic spectators, as the seventh samba school was about to begin its slow progress. Beyond the Sambadrome were the squalid last alleyways of a moribund red-light district, and beyond that the favelas—the slums, perched on their outcrops of rock. Back home, the Ipanema universe of orderly tree-lined streets and air-conditioned buildings seemed remote and barren when compared to the favelas I knew only from Nieta's descriptions, now suddenly come alive in my mind as the magical enclaves where carnival could be imagined and then made flesh. The peopled hills were everywhere—there was one only three blocks from my apartment building—and I spent months staring at the jumble of shacks pitched so artlessly across the steep slopes, imagining the hot, crazy life within. But it was a long time before I could find an excuse to get close.

* * *

I went to a North Zone favela for my first visit to a samba school. It was springtime in Brazil, when the weather in Rio is loveliest: washed clear of rains, the sky turns a cool and peaceful blue. The nights too are soothing, spattered with clean bright stars and edged with promise. Spring signals the beginning of the carnival season, which starts up in September with nightlong rehearsals designed to set the festive sap running for the real event. Year-round planning for the parade also shifts into full gear with weekly meetings at which samba school directorates define their strategies and assign tasks.

The taxi crossed the tunnel under Corcovado hill, which links Ipanema and Copacabana to the North Zone; skimmed past the massive shadow of Maracanã Stadium and the concrete wastelands of the state university; and stopped at the edge of a favela that chunnels precipitously from one particularly tall hill right down to the pavement itself. This was Mangueira.

The directors of the First Station of Mangueira Recreational Association and Samba School were holding one of their weekly planning meetings, chaired by the school president, Carlos Dória. With the other school directors—mostly black, mostly middle-aged to old—Dória discussed the coming parade, which was to commemorate the hundredth anniversary of the decree that abolished slavery, signed by the Brazilian Crown in 1888.

Like the other schools, Mangueira had already begun its samba harvest—a process of winnowing out competing sambas composed around the official parade theme, until one is selected to be sung in the Sambadrome by the school's five thousand members. There was general enthusiasm for the theme, and agreement that the competing sambas offered a rich crop, but some members of the directorate were unsatisfied with the costumes and the floats: They were too frilly, and they did not convey enough about the present situation of blacks in Brazil or about their past hardships.

I hung around the edges of the meeting and at the end spoke briefly with Dória, a burly man in his mid-forties with a paunch, thick gold jewelry, a moustache, and an unfriendly air. I told him I was a reporter and said I would like to follow Mangueira through its process of making carnival. Roughly, he told me I was wasting my time. I was persistent, but he was mean; he was a member of the state military police, and the hostility in his manner was both professional and frightening.

After we had reached an impasse, a young woman listening to our conversation interceded and took me aside. Nilsemar was very pretty, with the modest, precise gestures of a skillful nurse. She had been sitting at the directorate table with other women to whom she now introduced me: her grandmother, Dona Zica, widow of Cartola, one of the founders and outstanding composers of the Mangueira samba school; her friend Marilia, a white sociologist; Dona Neuma, daughter of a founder of Mangueira and an all-time sambista; and Neuma's daughter, Guezinha. The women were as friendly as Dória was brusque. They listened to my questions and invited me to attend the harvest dance the following Saturday. "Don't worry," Nilsemar said softly, when I said Dória might not approve of my presence. "He's gruff, but we'll convince him to let you see what you want to see."

* * *

The turnstiles were green, the rest of the façade glaring pink. A man in a pink T-shirt waved me through the turnstile of Mangueira's Palacio do Samba into the bright pink and green space beyond. It was shortly before midnight, and the harvest was not scheduled to start until one. The huge central dance space was empty and only a few of the red folding tables around it were occupied. A man in a pink and green crocheted muscle shirt, another in a pink felt hat, women in pink shirts and green dresses leaned casually against the green and pink walls. Banners hanging from the metal roof structure advertised the support of Xerox and Ypiranga Paints for the Mangueira cause. Ypiranga's contribution was evident: Other than the metal tables emblazoned with the Coca-Cola logo, not an inch of space was painted any other color than the two Mangueira favorites.

At the opposite end of the central area a few children were scrambling onto a green platform twelve feet high. When they reached the top, others handed them sticks, drums as tall as they, smaller metal objects that jangled. Soon the platform was full: some twenty small boys and their director, a wiry young white man in a Hawaiian shirt. It was 11:58. The boys, skinny and solemn-faced, fidgeted, fiddled, adjusted their shoulder straps, their shirts, their faded baggy shorts, and hit the drums. The sound wave began.

It was what one tied to the railroad tracks might hear as a train hurtles immediately overhead: a vast, rolling, marching, overpowering wave of sound set up by the *surdos de marcação*–bass drums about two feet in diameter in charge of carrying the underlying beat. Gradually a ripple set in, laid over the basic rhythm by smaller drums. Then the *cuica:* a subversive, humorous squeak, dirty and enticing, produced by rubbing a stick inserted into the middle of a drumskin. The *cuica* is like an itch, and the only way to scratch it is to dance. Already, people were wiggling in place to the beat, not yet dancing, building up the rhythm inside their bodies, waiting for some releasing command of the drums. Gradually, as the children drummed on with all the solemnity of a funeral band, husky morose men climbed the platform, hoisted their instruments, and joined in. There were more *surdos*, another *cuica*, a clackety metal *agogô*, a tambourine, and something that looked like a Christmas tree and sounded like a shiver—the *chocalho*.

For long minutes the wave rolled over us, a formal presentation of the *bateria*, the rhythm section that forms a school's core. Without a *bateria*, no school can parade, no school can exist. These percussionists are recognized as the hardest-working members of the samba world. While everyone else is having a good time, they are raising bloody welts on their shoulders from the drums' heavy straps, tearing the calloused skin on their hands with their ceaseless beating and rubbing of the metal instruments. Others enter and leave rehearsals as they wish; the drummers anchor a samba from the beginning. They are a paradoxical aristocracy, sweat-drenched princes who are among the poorest members of the school. By inheritance and tradition, most of the *bateria* make their living as day laborers in the Rio dockyards. They never smile.

The *bateria* director brought his arms down sharply. With a final shudder and slam the wave came to a halt. The samba harvest was open.

The *quadra*—or samba building—had filled up quickly. About five hundred people were now milling about, lining up for beer, occupying the tables or marking off private spaces for themselves along the edges of the *quadra* by setting their beer bottles in the center of where they intended to dance. There were groups of middle-aged women out for a night on the town, and whole families sitting at tables crowded with beer, soda pop and, here and there, sandwiches brought from home. A birthday party was in progress at one end of the *quadra*. Lounging at the opposite end were a handful of young men in slouchy felt hats, long T-shirts, Bermudas, and hightops. I spotted Guezinha and the sociologist, Marilia, at one of the front-row tables, and then, as I stood in line for a soft drink, Carlos Dória. I smiled in greeting and he turned away. Shortly afterward, he left.

The dance space itself remained empty, separated from the tables by metal parade barriers. Eventually two older men strolled into the inviolate space, slowly and with authority. One was short, stocky, heavily moustached and slightly stooped. He wore an assortment of whistles around his neck and something of the tired, impatient air of a boxing referee. The other was improbably tall, with a hatchet face crowned by a narrow-brimmed straw hat. He was as long-legged and deliberate as a praying mantis, and as brightly colored in his grass-green suit. His head rotated on an axis as he paused for a moment and inspected the *quadra*, chewing on a piece of gum with toothless jaws. Slowly his head returned to center and he resumed his crossing. As if the two men's presence were a command, several other men climbed onto a singers' tower placed at right angles to the drummers' platform, on which they were soon joined by Beto End-of-the-Night. Beto Fim da Noite, energetic, bald, and very black, announced the evening's events over a foggy microphone that stirred his words into the general soup of noise and confusion and only sporadically let some meaning through: "The harvest now commences . . . best team win . . . great Mangueira nation . . . this night memorable . . . end of the evening three finalists . . . competing for the glory of carrying our school to victory at carnival . . . now sing the Mangueira anthem . . ."

The drums slammed into action, there was a piercing short whistle, and as if released from coils the dancers bounced into the air. At the center of the dance space stood Alberto Pontes, the heavy-shouldered man with the whistles, looking now more like a gladiator ready to take on all the Colosseum's lions. He crouched menacingly and blew sharp commands on his whistle, and as a stream of hyperkinetic women charged onto the dance floor he growled, gestured, stamped his foot and pushed the herd away from the center of the floor and back toward the barriers. Unheeding, the women jumped and swayed and broke into frenzied little circles of movement, hips and jewelry flying in every direction; they surged forward and grabbed all the available space while Pontes cursed and ordered them back again with a righteous forefinger, Moses compelling the waters to retract, God expelling a thousand Eves. The samba pounded on and the women multiplied, but Pontes did not interrupt his labors.

"The shepherdesses," Marilia shouted over the commotion when I sought her out in the crowd. "They're called *pastôras*," she repeated. "By tradition, only women are allowed to dance in the central space during real rehearsals." But in fact it was Pontes who seemed more like their sheepdog, herding his flock away from their Dionysian instincts and back to a world of order and sobriety.

A skinny little man approached the central space, giddily drunk and full of gay mannerisms, dance bursting out of him. Swiftly he was scooped up by two youths in pink "Mangueira Security" T-shirts. It was not time for him to dance yet. It would not be time until the end of the harvest, when Mangueira began its more commercial round of "rehearsals" designed to fill the school's coffers. Then the dance floor would be open to all.

Meanwhile the men danced on the edges of the *quadra*, between the beer counter and the tables. The real bambas danced in all-male groups, whipping their legs in circular movements over the beer bottles set on the floor, knifing out with one leg to upset the balance of another male dancer, shifting from high to low movements and from sitting to standing to spinning positions like break-dancers.

Couples danced too, provocatively. A teenage girl sheathed in a tight white strapless dress circled her hips slowly to the floor in front of her enthusiastic middle-aged partner and then slid straight up again, her pubic bone pressed into the man's thigh. Eventually the man offered his place to a little boy who had been practicing samba off in a corner on his own. The boy kept his distance from the girl for a few seconds with elaborate dips and bops, a little out of breath with shyness. He stood still, hesitating, before diving into the space between her thighs. Chest level to her hips, he grinned awkwardly while she pulsated against him. Then he leapt away, laughing and proud and cheered on by a circle of observers.

A chunky gray-haired woman in a plain cotton shift and slippers stood at the center of a group of teenagers. Too old to jump or spin, she faced her adolescent partner and wiggled as hard as she could, bursting into great roars of laughter every time she managed to set her entire body shaking. "Vovó," the kids called her, "Granny." But she explained that she had no children of her own, and that the teenagers who had brought her here were children she had helped raise in her suburban favela.

Through the mad crowd that had formed at the center of the rehearsal space a serene dancer emerged. The flag-bearer and the major-domo, a royal pair, head the dancing section of every parade, and a candidate to the flag-bearing position was now just beginning her practice. She was very young, shy and hesitant. For a second she seemed to be floating alone, but out of the crowd her partner appeared, scything the air with his long bones, folding his limbs at the joints and then stretching them out again to full, preposterous length: Delegado, the green-and-brown praying mantis. Together they dipped and spun and circled for a few seconds, and then Delegado turned the flag-bearer over to her teenage coapprentice. The women marched behind, tirelessly, over and over, while the sound wave broke and shattered against the wall.

By now it was almost one in the morning. The song we had been listening to, someone said, was the samba from the previous carnival parade, in which Mangueira had won first prize. The contest for this season's samba had in fact not yet begun, but now that the song had come to its abrupt end the composers and singers on the tower shifted and cleared their throats and consulted. There was a great flurry of activity down in the table area, where Marilia and Guezinha and several other members of the directorate were sitting. A hopped-up, nervous young man named Rody came up and with a superb smile handed me a slip of pink paper with the mimeographed lyrics of his samba, a heavy crowd favorite. He had written it together with Verinha—a woman composer—and Bus-Stop Bira; the three made up a team that had written the previous year's winning samba. He shook hands earnestly with everyone in sight. "Give me a little strength," he asked Marilia, but I knew his fate was sealed. "We in the directorate are rooting for Helinho's samba," the women had said on the night I met them.

This is what Rody's song said:

> The black race came to this country,
> Bringing their strong arms and their roots.
> They planted their culture here,
> Yoruba, Gêgê and Nagô.
> In the refineries, mines and fields,
> Blacks were always oppressed,
> And in the rebel enclave of Palmares
> Zumbi our leader fought for freedom.

(Chorus)
Finally light dawned,
Reason prevailed,
And Princess Isabel
Abolished slavery.
Or did she?
Is it true, is it a lie?
Because to be born with a black skin
Has not given us the right to freedom.
One hundred years of liberty:
Is this reality or illusion?
Let's all wave our white handkerchiefs
And with Mangueira ask
For an end to discrimination.

(Chorus)
Throw off the ties that bind!
Please give people their freedom!

Rody's song ended, another samba began. A messenger broke through the dancing crowd, breathless and tragic. The music stopped, there was a moment of silence, and the singer at the microphone announced that Carlos Dória had just been murdered.

The news sent people whirling centrifugally toward the exit doors, concentrically into each other's arms. Mangueira emptied out. I stood on the stairs leading to the mezzanine and the directorate offices and watched Dona Zica being carried out in a half-faint. Marilia gathered her ten-year-old daughter and her friends off the dance floor and headed down the road for Dona Neuma's house. The school's vice-president staggered by, clutching at his chest with one hand. A large, fortyish woman, considerably drunk, screamed *"Meu presidente! Meu presidente!"* and flung herself repeatedly against a standing column at the foot of the stairs. A man climbed up to the directorate offices—slender as a knife, of indeterminate age, wearing a bright pink leather jacket and pitch-dark glasses at four in the morning, surrounded by bodyguards. He emerged again, sliced his way through the clots of hysterical bystanders on the stairway, paused at the landing to announce, "A lot of blood will run for this," and was gone. The last stragglers left. The *quadra* shut down.

Dória had been sitting in his car a short drive north from the *quadra*, waiting for the garage door in his apartment building to open, when someone came up and shot him four times through the head and chest. His murder was never solved. The few Mangueirenses I had met were not forthcoming on the possible causes or culprits, and I had to rely on the Rio papers, where the murder made the front page and then filled the crime section for almost a week with the latest speculations on the assassins' motives: that Dória had been involved with a drug group and was killed by a rival gang; that he had participated in one of the Rio police corps' notorious death squads and had been singled out for revenge by a victim's friends; that the entrenched leadership of Rio's League of Samba Schools had had him murdered after he threatened to set up an independent association. This last became the official Mangueira version, volunteered to all and just as vigorously denied by League leaders. In any event, Mangueira never resigned from the League, nor did the school or Dória's relatives ever press charges. Over the months, as carnival activity spread beyond the favelas and took hold of the entire city, the case faded from public attention.

In the wake of the murder Mangueira's carnival prospects were assumed to be nil. The samba harvest was suspended for two weeks. There was a funeral and then, eight days after the murder, a mass for the resurrection of the soul of Carlinhos Dória.

* * *

There were few tears during the resurrection mass for Dória. The young foreign priest from the church down the road set up an improvised altar in a corner of the nearly empty *quadra*, led his uncertain parishioners through the church rituals, and spoke about crime and the difference between forgiveness and justice, hinting broadly that those who knew who had killed Dória might absolve the culprits in their hearts but let the criminal justice system know exactly who it was they had forgiven all the same. The priest seemed realistic about the limits of his moral influence and kept the sermon brief. Shortly after he finished folding the altar cloth he was out the door.

The sambistas lingered in the drafty *quadra* until well after nightfall. There were people here who did not meet in the course of daily life except at rehearsal time, when the din of the *bateria* made real conversation impossible; but on this chilly evening, made nostalgic and vulnerable by the presence of death, they clustered together for comfort and in the congenial silence soon found themselves laughing at old stories, singing forgotten samba verses quietly to each other as they remembered this or that carnival or party. They talked about Dória and his brief tenure as Mangueira president, about his violent temper and his devotion to the school, and because the future was looming in the shape of an upcoming carnival with no president to lead it, they talked about the past, with special emphasis on the moments of glory.

"Mangueira was, after all, the first of all the schools to come out with a story samba," a trim old man said, to murmurs of agreement. "Other schools keep claiming that honor, but they know the truth." The speaker, Carlos Cachaça, was the last surviving founder of the Mangueira school, having outlived almost every other bamba of the period when samba first became popular and led indirectly to the invention of the samba schools. "Story samba" is the proper name for the song that sets forth the theme of a school parade, easily distinguishable through its speed and emphatic marching beat from song samba, counterpoint samba (known outside Brazil as "bossa nova") and the earliest form of the genre, call-and-response samba. Cachaça liked to remind people of Mangueira's historical if much-disputed claim to leadership in the field of story sambas because, as it happened, he had invented the subcategory himself back in 1933, when samba—the whole broad genre of highly ornamented two-by-four rhythms—was just establishing itself as Brazil's national music. Cachaça was in his early thirties then, Mangueira was a miserable stop on the suburban rail line, and Brazilian carnival was about to witness its great flowering, brought about by the fusion of black and white carnival cultures in the crucible of the newly created samba schools.

Brazilian whites today readily admit that carnival would not have amounted to much had it remained in their hands. The Portuguese colonizers' idea of enjoyment during the week before Lent was to spray each other with syringes filled with water, foul-smelling liquids, or worse. In the mid–nineteenth century someone came up with the only slightly better idea of beating a very large drum while a crowd followed him around the neighborhood. Carnival life began to improve only toward the end of Emperor Pedro II's progressive regime, when a restless new urban elite championed the abolition of slavery, which the emperor also favored; republicanism, which the emperor, understandably, was against; and a more sophisticated, "European" form of carnival to which Dom Pedro, as far as the evidence shows, did not object. Patterned on the elegant celebrations of Paris and Venice, elaborate costume balls quickly became the rage. "Carnival societies" were formed to parade through the main streets of the city dressed in complicated allegorical costumes, often designed to satirize the old regime and promote the liberal agenda. This was the carnival that blacks would imitate and preserve long after the tradition had died out among whites: a daydream vision of European elegance, of white aristocrats at their dazzling play.

* * *

It was getting late. The mass had ended hours before, and someone in the control room flashed the *quadra*'s lights off and on impatiently. A voluble conversationalist with an Assyrian profile and a sculpted beard to match was still eagerly talking to his friend Marilia, the Mangueira sociologist, about the political aspects of samba. Djalma belonged to the much younger samba school of Vila Isabel, and had come to Doria's mass to pay the respects due a school considered by many the last holdout against encroaching commercialization. "Because look here, the schools are dying: Do you know what some big companies are trying to do? They want the float-pushers—the only school members who are not in costume—to wear T-shirts with the company logo on their backs. The day is coming, I want you to know, when one school will belong to Coca-Cola and another to a supermarket chain. It's the same thing that happened to the soccer clubs, and I want no part of it. I live and die for my school, but for me the schools are the people on the hills, and watch out; the day the companies take over, I'm out of here." He had much more to say about the current state of samba, and the other groups of stragglers were also in no mood to end the evening. Someone suggested the party move down the road to Dona Neuma's house, whose doors remained open at all hours of the day and night. She had not attended the mass, and Djalma thought it would be a good idea to stop and pay his respects to her as well.

Dona Neuma was the daughter of a school founder who had died of tuberculosis and poverty many years before. Her husband had worked as a carpenter until his death, and for most of their lives Dona Neuma and her family had lived in a brick-and-wood shack on the same spot where their house now stood. One of the daughters, Chininha, had married well, to an airline attendant. Another, Ceci, had a government job with which to support herself, her daughter, and granddaughter, while Guezinha, married to a car salesman, also worked off and on at a store or at other clerical jobs. The family's combined incomes and a little money from carnival-related activities had built the house, which was magnificent by hill standards. Half a dozen people sprawled on a frayed living room set, watching television. New family members constantly emerged from a set of back bedrooms and joined the others on the couch. Someone made coffee. Beers were poured. Guezinha stored the week's shopping—beans, rice, macaroni, detergent, toilet paper, and gallons of cooking oil—in a carved wood highboy that formed part of a fancy and uncomfortable dining room set. I fidgeted, feeling both out of place and eager to linger in the household's chaotic warmth. Guezinha gave me an amused look. "You're here to learn, aren't you? Come here, I'll show you something." She led me to the huge kitchen, where an excited group of women was studying a sketch of a svelte creature in a feather-topped turban, sequined bra, and ankle-length, below-the-navel skirt, seductively draped and slit thigh-high up the front. The outfit looked like something the chorus girls at the Crazy Horse in Paris might wear for their presentation walk-on, but Guezinha said it was supposed to be a parade costume representing an *orixá*, or African goddess. Looking at the sketch I understood why the Portuguese word for costume is *fantasia*—"fantasy": all my life, I had wanted to look like that, if only for a few minutes, a few seconds.

"It's for my wing," Guezinha explained. "I have an all-woman wing, fifty of us, and this is the costume we'll wear. Do you like it?" I said I did. She gave me a sidelong glance, then looked around at the other women. "Well, how would you like to join my wing and parade with us at carnival time?" I said I would like that very much indeed. "But first," Guezinha said, with hardly the shadow of a smile, "you have to learn to samba."

One of the subtler forms of amusement for blacks at carnival time is watching whites try to samba. White people have had nearly the whole century to work it out, and most of them still can't quite get it right. It's not that blacks mind; that whites look clumsy while they're trying to have fun is a misfortune too great to be compounded by mockery, but it's also a fact that can't be denied. Whites are certainly given points for trying, though, and in the Samba Palace the ones who got up to dance seemed to be much more warmly regarded than those who tried to maintain their dignity. But I was terrified of what I might look like, and in the weeks before carnival, after lurking in the corners of the *quadra* at almost every rehearsal, I went home and practiced samba grimly and in secret.

HOW TO SAMBA (WOMEN'S VERSION)

1. Start before a mirror, with no music. You may prefer to practice with a pair of very high heels. Though samba is a dance that started out barefoot, and can still be danced that way, high heels will throw your spinal column out of whack and give your pelvis the appearance of greater flexibility. Platform shoes with relatively wide heels provide the best combination of stability and shock absorption.

2. Stand with feet parallel, close together. Step and hop in place on your right foot as you brush your left foot quickly across. Step in quick succession onto your left, then your right foot. Although your hips will swivel to the right as far as possible for this sequence, your head and shoulders should remain strictly forward. Otherwise you'll start looking like you're doing the *hora*. Practice this sequence right and left until you can do it without counting.

3. Test yourself: Are your lips moving? Are your shoulders scrunched? No? Are you able to manage one complete left-right sequence per second? Good! Now that you've mastered the basic samba step, you're ready to add music. Choose Zeca Pagodinho, Jovelina the Black Pearl, Neguinho of the Hummingbird or any other sambista you like and start practicing. The key thing at this stage is speed: When you are up to two complete sequences per second you are well on your way to samba. Aim for four.

4. A samba secret: Add hips. They're probably moving already, but if you are trying to hit required minimum speed they may be a little out of control. You want to move them, but purposefully. When you step on your right foot your hips switch left-right. When you step on your left they switch again, right-left. Two hip beats per foot beat, or about twelve beats per second, if you can manage.

5. Stop hopping! Keep your shoulders down! Face front! The magic of samba lies in the illusion that somebody is going like crazy from the waist down while an entirely different person is observing the proceedings from the waist up. Keep your torso detached from your hips and facing where you're looking, and practice with a book on your head until you can stay level at full speed.

You've mastered the mechanics of samba. Now you're ready to start dancing. If the following essentials seem a little daunting, don't be discouraged. Remember, you've come a long way from your beginning days. Dress appropriately for this next stage. Preferably something that emphasizes the waist, so that hip movement is maximized. Go for shine. Twelve hip beats per second will look like a hundred if you're wearing sequins.

Arms: If you are up to two to four sequences per second with a book on your head and your hips swiveling at least forty-five degrees in each direction away from the wall you're facing, you're ready to ornament your dance by holding your arms out and ruffling your shoulders as you move. Think of a fine-plumed bird rearranging its wings. Keep the movement flexible and easy. Reach out with your fingertips. If you can't shimmy without looking scrunched or panicky, drop it.

Smile: The key rule is, don't make it sexy. You will look arch, coy or, if you are working really hard, terribly American. Your smile should be the full-tilt cheer of someone watching her favorite team hit a home run. Or it should imitate the serene curve of a Hindu deity's. The other key rule: There is no point to samba if it doesn't make you smile.

Sweat: Obviously, you will produce lots of it. You will soon discover that it looks wrong when it is dripping off the tip of your nose. Don't let this upset you. Perseverance and practice have got you this far; keep at it. Practice. When you find that your body is moving below you in a whirlpool frenzy and your mind is floating above it all in benign accompaniment; when your torso grows curiously light and your legs feel like carving little arabesques in the air on their own for the sheer fun of it; when everything around you seems too slow for the rush that's carrying you through the music, you'll probably discover that sweat is clothing your body in one glorious, uniform, scintillating sheet, flying around you in a magic halo of drops, and you'll know that you have arrived at samba.

Two weeks after Dória's death, on a wet, cold Friday evening, the Mangueira samba harvest resumed with the selection of the story-samba semifinalists. Dória's murder had had a number of devastating consequences, not the least of which was a nearly empty *quadra* that mid-October night. Bereft of crowds, the Samba Palace looked garish and lonely in the late-winter drizzle. Garbage overflowed a dumpster between the *quadra* and Dona Neuma's house, and pigs and dogs rooted about in the soggy mess. The few hundred people from the hill who did show up looked chilled and uncomfortable among the puddles in the dance space. The sound system ground the music into mush, the singers repeatedly wavered off key and the *bateria* did the worst thing possible: It lost contact with the singers and went off the beat. When this happens during a parade the result is unsalvageable ruin; caught between the competing rhythms of the marching drummers and the singers, who travel separately on a sound truck, school members wander off on their own, and the parade's tight ranks soon dissolve into chaos. When this "crossing up" occurs in the course of a rehearsal, the result is simply to make the music unbearable.

Sometime around two in the morning I stopped by the table where Guezinha was sitting with a few of her sisters and friends, looking close to tears and very slightly drunk. We stared for a while at the dance space, where the shepherdess-herder Alberto Pontes was halfheartedly chivying a handful of women. "The samba is really hot tonight, isn't it?" Guezinha said, smiling at me like a television announcer. I said that it certainly was, and we sat together wordlessly for a while, listening to the *bateria*'s excruciating hammer. Guezinha pushed back her chair. "I'm going to bed," she announced, and went home.

The school's situation was no better in the daytime. When Mangueira was mentioned in the press, it was in the context of police interrogations and speculations on Dória's off-duty life: Had he participated in a death squad? Was he involved in the drug trade? Dona Neuma and Dona Zica, the two "First Ladies" of Mangueira, were interviewed by the press not on the usual colorful subject of carnival's early days but on the question of who had murdered their president. "If I knew, I would have chased the culprit all the way to Japan," Dona Neuma avowed, and tried unsuccessfully to get her questioners interested in the wonderful theme for the coming carnival.

Comment on the misfortune was generally avoided around the samba school, as if reference to it might attract additional bad luck. "Dória is dead but the school lives on," was one standard answer to questions about the current adversity. And it was a sign of how bad things were that the most devastating consequence of Dória's murder was the one that was never mentioned. Mangueira had won first place in the carnival parade for the previous two years running. With a striking theme and a first-rate story samba this year, there had been little doubt in the community's mind that the school could win a third time in the upcoming carnival, an achievement only two other schools could boast of and that was permanently associated with their names. That Mangueira, bereft of leadership, was no longer in the running for a triple championship was the great unstated fact casting its miserable spell on the harvest evening that followed Dória's murder. "Mangueira is going to have to parade any old way," Vila Isabel's Djalma had commented sorrowfully on the night of the resurrection mass. "And I, for one, am not looking forward to watching what will happen. It's going to be a very sad thing." The disastrous semifinal rehearsal was evidence of the school's depression and disarray. Now, less than twelve hours later, the *finalissima*, or final contest night, loomed ahead.

When I walked in at midnight, the Samba Palace was unrecognizable. The walls looked scrubbed and the floor was dry and spotless. Every table in the house had been set out and all were full. A huge crowd threaded its way among them, dodging radio reporters and school members busing trays of fancy appetizers to a section of tables that had been cordoned off for VIPs. The master sambista Delegado had clothed his long body in a hot-pink suit. Pontes the shepherdess-herder had an extraordinary array of whistles bouncing off his chest. There was a phalanx of standard-bearers: old ones, new ones, apprenticing adolescents. Guezinha, a woman I associated with hard work and practical clothes, stood smiling at the center of the dance area, enclosed in the halo of her own sexuality, dressed in a strapless sheath someone must have stitched directly onto her body, exhaling perfume with every movement, unapproachable as a shrine. "What happened?" I asked, bewildered. The goddess, remote and knowing, only smiled.

"What happened?" I asked another member of the directorate. He smiled too. That morning, he said, people had recognized that things looked bad and that a final harvest session like the previous night's would be fatal. A cleanup brigade was organized. Emissaries were sent to the radio stations with pleas for a little promotional help to get Mangueira back on its feet. The hill membership was asked to turn out in force. Dona Neuma and her family brigade worked overtime cooking up platters of special tidbits for the press and the VIPs. In short, Mangueira drew on the habits, discipline, infrastructure, and reflexes that wealthier and younger schools covet and cannot reproduce. After all, what sambistas call tradition is often simply the training provided by years of endurance.

The walls were aglow with paper banners in magenta and green for Helinho Turco's team—the school directorate's favorite—and green and yellow, the Brazilian national colors, for the other finalists. This was the team made up of the composers Ivo, Otacilio, and Sinval, and their song was a favorite with the *bateria*, especially because it included a catchy little drum riff in the middle. A huge white banner hanging from the metal rafters depicted this team's logo; a bare-chested black man with arms open in a victory sign. The directorate had in fact settled on the samba they preferred practically at the beginning of the harvest, but the teams whose songs were popular with the audience had continued lobbying among school members, hoping to overturn the decision with a display of enthusiasm on the dance floor. They had a lot at stake. The display of flags, the photocopied handouts of each samba's lyrics, the singers hired for the night to present the song, all cost money—perhaps as much as two or three thousand dollars in the course of the season. The school contributed some of the funds, but a composer who believed his samba was likely to win would invest as much as he could rummage, because the royalties for a winning samba would solve his financial worries for a healthy period of time. Now, caught up in the excitement, the claques for the two finalist teams shuttled between tables, egging their supporters on, flashing victory signs at each other, handing out bags of confetti to be thrown into the air at the appropriate moment. Even the sound was clean, and as the loudspeakers broadcast recorded sambas from the current hit parade the crowd was on its feet and dancing, wired so tightly to the music they seemed to anticipate and create every riff and flourish. Friends called greetings to each other across tables. The slouching young men in Bermudas looked alert and bright-eyed. On the mezzanine, the VIP balconies filled with men in white linen suits and women in skintight halter tops and miniskirts. Through the gap between the *quadra* walls and the corrugated metal roof suspended high overhead, the favela was visible, and in the houses that bordered directly on the Samba Palace spectators hung out of windows for the best view of the action below.

At a table near the VIP section an old woman who had been sitting with a group of young white men got up and began to dance. She was tall and ruined by age. Her hair was pulled back in a scrawny ponytail, and her generous grin showed few teeth. She wore thick glasses and a faded T-shirt over a pair of patched, much-washed blue jeans, but when she rose from her chair, the groups at the surrounding tables turned to her expectantly. Leisurely, she began her dance: shuffle to the left, shuffle to the right, circle all around and wiggle on down. Shuffle again, do it one more time, put your hands on your hips and shake them down the line. . . . The men at her table were grinning with her, waiting, clapping in time, egging her on as she smiled down on them. Standing in place, immobile, she began a shiver that climbed slowly from her heels to her calves, crawled up her thighs and settled in her haunches, dividing the samba rhythm into a hundred faster particles without ever losing a beat. Then, with her hips trembling in isolation from the rest of her body, she produced her pièce de résistance: bunching up her fingers, she blew a bouquet of kisses on each one and bestowed them on her admirable behind, first on her tremulous left buttock and then, with a second appreciative smile, on her right. Her audience went wild, and the woman, delighted, doubled over with laughter. When she saw me staring in captivated amazement, she performed the routine all over again and raised her bottle of beer at the end in a mischievous toast.

"That," said Marilia, "was Dona Nininha Xoxoba, one of the great Mangueira flag-bearers."

A burst of rockets interrupted her explanation. In the great open space between the *quadra* walls and the roof, the view of the favela was momentarily erased by a curtain of fireworks, exploding in constellations of silver, green, and gold. The *bateria* rammed its sound wave into the night, a huge cheer went up, and on the singers' tower Ivo, Otacilio, and Sinval's team raced into its samba, pursued by the drums. "Black men are outcasts,–But they're the kings of the parade!" they sang, and later, Helinho Turco's team answered, "They are the kings, pink and green, of all Mangueira!" And, "Has freedom really dawned / Or was it all an illusion?" To which Ivo's team answered, "It's going to change, or isn't it? / It's going to change, or isn't it? Who knows. . . ." The dance space filled to overflowing for both teams, the women sweating and pushing the samba on. Nininha stood up once again to dance. Guezinha made her way onto the dance floor, and Dona Zica, in her granny glasses and white hair, led the river of women, escorted by the preening Delegado. Both sambas were hot, the drums were brilliant, confetti filled the air, there was no stopping the dancers.

Beto End-of-the-Night announced the winner at dawn, and as light filled the *quadra*, a hoarse white man, Percy Pires, acting as rehearsal coordinator, evoked Dória's name and Mangueira's past and assured the happy, sweaty crowd that another school victory was on its way. His speech did not sound hollow. As the Mangueirenses streamed out through the turnstiles into a hazy, unclouded day, someone ventured a timid cheer: "Mangueira Triple Crown!"

CLAUDIO MAGRIS

TRANSLATED FROM THE ITALIAN BY

PATRICK CREAGH

Castles and Huts

I. At the Red Prawn

Bratislava. On the ceiling of the entrance hall of the old pharmacy called *The Red Prawn*, in Michalská Street, there is a fresco which portrays the god of time. The potions and mixtures surrounding him in that atrium like a confident challenge, and the learned tome lying open in front of him, threaten to exorcize his power and hold up his advance. That eighteenth-century shop—now transformed into a Pharmaceutical Museum—gives the impression of a military parade in its rigid symmetry, of an unassuming yet determined art of war displayed against Chronos. The pots on the shelves, in cobalt, emerald green, and sky blue, embellished with floral designs and biblical quotations, are like the ranks of tin soldiers in museum reliefs of famous battles; the tinctures, balsams, balms, allopathics, purgatives, and emetics are there at their battle stations, ready to intervene according to the requirements of strategy. Even the labels, with their abbreviations, are reminiscent of military contractions: Syr., Tinct., Extra., Bals., Fol., Pulv., Rad.

The art of the herbalist seeks to defeat the wastage of the years, to restore the body and the face as one restores the façade of a Renaissance palace. But it is nice in the little museum; it is quiet and cool in the midst of this torrid summer, as it would be in a church or under the pergola of a country inn. As one stares at the alembics in an alchemy laboratory, or the bust of Paracelsus erected to commemorate the period when he worked in Bratislava, the jars of aconite and Cinnamomum, the papers on pharmaceutics in the fourteenth to eighteenth centuries, and the wooden statue of St. Elizabeth, patron saint of herbalists in the baroque era, one is infused with a neat, modest middle-class sense of intimacy.

This museum of palliatives against the outrages of time is a museum of history, which is the mundane branch of time—the agent of its inception and of its ravages—but also the remedy, the memory and the salvage of what has been. On the shelves the Austrian magazine of the Pharmacists' Union is flanked by *Pharmaceutica Hungariae*, a very hefty volume, *Taxa Pharmaceutica Posoniensis* by Ján Justus Torkos, published in 1745 in four languages: Latin, Slovak, Hungarian, and German. Bratislava, capital of Slovakia, is one of the "hearts" of Mitteleuropa, with layer upon layer of centuries forever present, unresolved conflicts and lacerations, unhealed wounds, and unreconciled contradictions. The memory, which is in its way a branch of medicine, preserves all this under glass, both the lips of the wounds and the passions which inflicted them.

The Central Europeans are ignorant of the science of forgetting, of filing away events. That manual of pharmacy in four languages, and that adjective "Posoniensis," remind me of how at school, my friends and I used to discuss the city's name, which ones we liked best: Bratislava, the Slovak name, Pressberg, the German one, or Poszony, the Hungarian name derived from Posonium, the ancient Roman outpost on the Danube. The fascination of those three names bestowed a special glamour on a composite, multinational history, and someone's preference for one or the other was in a childish way, a basic stance taken towards the *Weltgeist*. That is to say, we had to choose between the instinctive celebration of great, powerful cultures such as the German, the ones that make history, or our romantic admiration for the exploits of rebellious, chivalrous, and adventurous peoples such as the Magyars, or else our fellow-feeling for what is more subdued and hidden, for the small peoples such as the Slovaks, who remain for a long time a patient, unregarded substratum, a humble, fertile soil waiting centuries for the moment of its flowering.

In Bratislava, a town famous in the past for its excellent watchmakers and collectors of these artefacts, now on show in the museum in Zidovská (Hebrew) Street, one is aware of the imperious presence of ages woven through and through with conflict. The capital of one of the most ancient of Slav peoples was, for two centuries, the capital of the Kingdom of Hungary when practically all the latter, following the Battle of Mohács in 1526, was occupied by the Turks. It was to Bratislava that the Hapsburgs came to don the crown of St. Stephen, and that as a young woman, after the death of her father, the Emperor Charles VI, Maria Theresa came to enlist the aid of the Hungarian nobility, bearing her newborn son Joseph in her arms. All that mattered in Bratislava at that time was the dominant Hungarian element, or perhaps to some extent the Austro-German one; the substratum of the Slovak peasantry had no standing or relevance whatsoever.

Until 1918 the Viennese thought of Bratislava as a sort of pleasant suburb, which they could get to in less than an hour and enjoy its white wines, a traditional product already flourishing at the time of the Slav kingdom of Great Moravia, in the ninth century, and watched over by St. Urban, the patron saint of vintners. As we wander round the city, through charming baroque squares and small, abandoned byways, we get the impression that history, in passing by, has left many things here and there, things still full of life, that flourish again for us. Ladislav Novomeský, the greatest nineteenth-century Slovak poet, has a poem about a year he lost in a café, just like leaving behind an old umbrella. But things turn up again, and the old umbrellas of our lives, left here and there over the years, one time or another end up in our hands again.

2. Where Are Our Castles?

This is the title of an essay written in 1968 by Vladimír Mináč. The *Hrad*, the Castle, soars above Bratislava with its mighty towers and robust symmetry, a massive fortress which combines the rough, indestructible loyalty of a sentinel with a fairy-tale remoteness. Slovakia is strewn with castles, fortresses, and lordly dwellings; here, we have impregnable castles on peaks and hilltops, with their turreted Disneyland fantasies (but genuine), and there, manor houses and low-lying outbuildings, usually of an ochre color, which dwindle little by little into the more familiar dimensions of large farm houses.

But what Mináč seems to say is that these castles are somewhere else, in another history that was not created by the Slovaks. Most of the gentlemen who resided in these mansions were Hungarian. The dwellings of the Slovak peasants were the *drevenice*, wooden huts held together with straw and dried dung. In the castle of Oravský Podzámok, in the Otava valley, there is a picture revealing the white complexion and plump hands of the Celsissimus Princeps Nicolaus Esztherházy, while the hands of the peasants in the village beneath the castle even today are the color of earth, wrinkled and knotty as the roots of trees writhing among the stones. The difference between those hands is a symbol of the history of these peoples. The Slovaks have for centuries been a downtrodden people, the obscure substratum of their country, not unlike the straw and dried dung which holds their huts together. We have no history, writes Mináč, if this is made up solely of kings, emperors, dukes, princes, victories, conquests, violence, and pillage. In a poem by Petöfi, the national poet of Hungary, the Slovak is depicted, though in a good-natured way, as a red-nosed tinker in a washed-out smock.

But what the nineteenth-century notion labeled "nations without a history," as if they were mythical communities destined by nature to a perennially land-bound, subordinate position, were nations which some political or military defeat had deprived of their ruling classes. Mináč argues furiously for the role of the Slovaks in this obscure but patient work of construction, in which destructive violence was never committed against others, but which has long been a losing game. In 1848, when revolutionary hopes set Europe ablaze, the Slovaks turned to their Hungarian masters (themselves at that time in revolt against the Hapsburgs) with the so-called "claims of Liptovský Mikuláš," a demand for the most basic rights for their people. It was answered by the Hungarian authorities with arrests and tough repressive measures. The Austrians, for their part, once they had quelled the 1848 uprisings, tried to make friends with the Hungarians and abandoned the Slovaks to their tender mercies. After 1867, with the Double Monarchy, the fate of the Slovaks was crushing oppression. Particularly on the grounds of the Hungarian law of 1868, they were considered nothing more than a sort of folk survival within the Magyar nation, denied their identity and their language, and impeded in the running of their schools, while their demands were quashed if need be with bloodshed, their social aspirations smothered, their delegates to parliament obstructed in every way. The figures given in a monograph by L'udovít Holotík clearly show an overwhelming Hungarian social and economic predominance, which confined the Slovaks to a rural way of life, putting them quite out of reach of cultural development or capitalistic enterprise, which is as much as to say the formation of a middle-class. This was the cause of widespread emigration, largely to America. More than any other element it was the Church—Catholic and Evangelical alike—which safeguarded the nation, set up schools, and defended the obscure, despised Slovak language.

The question of the language created difficulties even within the Slav brotherhood and its emancipation movement. A number of Czechs, who were the leaders of the Austro-Slav movement, called for the use of Czech as a written language even in Slovakia, with a view to giving unity and efficiency to the movement; but at the same time this relegated

Slovak to the status of a dialect spoken in the home, clearly a subordinate tongue. Even Ján Kollár, the great Slovak intellectual assimilated by the Czechs, upheld these positions; but they were contested by his fellow countrymen, who saw them as meaning the end of their identity, and demanded the independence of their language.

These tensions, still alive today in the rivalries between Czechs and Slovaks, undermined the unity of the Slav renaissance, and Austro-Slavism in particular. On one hand, in fact, in so far as they were a nation thrust into the sidelines and retaining their primitive character uncontaminated, the Slovaks considered themselves to be one of the original, genuine cradles of Slavia, of its ancient, unitary civilization, and for this reason felt particularly akin to the other peasant Slav nations, such as the Ruthenians and the Slovenians. As early as the eighteenth century Jan Baltazár Magin had words of praise for this flawless, pristine purity in the *Apologia* he wrote—in Latin—to rebut the denigrations of Michal Bencsik, a professor at the university of Trnava. Ján Kollár, who turned to the Czech language and wrote in Czech, but was a Slovak, expressed this exalted Slavophilism in his long poem *The Daughter of Sláva*, which dates from 1824. It was in Slovakia that messianic Slavophilism found its first expression, and not only earlier but more vigorously than among the Czechs.

These ferments were susceptible to different and even conflicting developments. One possible outlet was filo-Russian Panslavism, another was Austro-Slavism, as championed by such a pugnacious leader as Milan Hodža, who was close to the three-pronged ideas and projects of Francis Ferdinand. But if the Austro-Slavism professed by the Czechs could hold out some hopes of securing a position of consequence in the desired structure of the Empire, the Slovaks were in a different situation: Under pressure to become Hungarianized and at the same time rather firmly divided from the Czechs, it was hard for them to see any way of escaping their minority situation. Towards the end of his life the revolutionary poet and patriot of 1848, L'dovit Štur, wrote a book called *Slavia and the World of the Future*, in which he prophesied the dissolution of the Hapsburg Empire.

Štanislav Smatlák, an essayist and member of the Academy of Sciences, tells me that Slovak literature has been the plaintiff in the lawcourt of world history, bearing witness to its "tremendous power of annihilation," as Nietzsche put it. In one of his pieces, written for the conference on peace, which took place in Prague, Šmatlák commemorated these painful yet pacific traditions as the thread which runs through the entire literature of his country, from the *Gentis Slavonicae lacrimae, suspiria et vota* (1645) by Jakub Jacobeus, or the *Desiderium aureae pacis* (1633) by Michal Institoris—two Latin compositions which lament and indict the tragedies of war—down to the *Bloody Sonnets* published in the fateful year of 1914 by Hviezdoslav, one of the fathers of the nation's poetry, and whose statue may be seen in the main square of practically every town, large or small.

These themes emerge in recent literature as well. Mihálik writes a poem about the dreams of serving-maids, while Válek's lines speak of the life of an old grandmother whose days were marked as if by whiplashes or the plain grooved by the carriage wheels of the gentry—grooves imbued with sweat and blood. In a wonderful story called *The Priest*, that vigorous, fertile storyteller František Švantner describes the humble, uncertain awakening of an ethical-political consciousness during the nationwide uprising against Fascism in 1944, a thing that emerges gradually from centuries of the repetitive life of the peasantry, a life completely ruled by the seasons, the soil, the cycle of agricultural production. In a trilogy of novels Vincent Šikula brings the historical events of the nation back to life, but as seen from below, from the point of view of the obscure, oppressed classes. Even *L'Abeille millénaire*, the novel by Peter Jaroš which became famous thanks to the film version of it shown at the Venice Festival in 1983, is the sage of a family of bricklayers in the Liptov region.

The history of these peoples has not been an easy one. On a coat of arms in the City Museum of Bratislava the Hapsburg two-headed eagle is glossed by the words "sub umbra alarum tuarum," but the Slovaks did not rest under the shadow of any wings, they were not subject to the tolerant, fair-dealing Austrian administration, often raised by the Slav peoples to the level of myth, but to the markedly nationalistic dominance of the Hungarians. The Pan-Slavic ideology, or the claim to an ancient national identity, is explained by the need of the Slav peoples to defend themselves, by exalting the myth of their own indestructible essence, against power and against culture fascinated by power, which denies dignity and a future to those who have until that time remained in shadow.

The nineteenth-century philosophers who traced out the necessary laws of historical "becoming" were often neither tender nor optimistic with regard to the minor nations, as many of the Slav nations were minor. Those fascinated by the "great world" of politics often forget that even the great powers were once small, that the time of ascending and of decline comes for all, and that even for the smallest comes the time to raise their heads.

But a small people which has to shake off the disdain or indifference of the great—of those whose greatness may perhaps have only a little while to run—must also shake off its complex about being small, the feeling of having constantly to rectify or cancel this impression, or else totally reverse it, glorying in it as a sign of election. Those who have long been forced to put all their efforts into the determination and defense of their own identity, tend to prolong this attitude even when it is no longer necessary. Turned inward on themselves, absorbed in the assertion of their own identity and intent on making sure that others give it due recognition, they run the risk of devoting all their energies to this defense, thereby shrinking the horizons of their experience, of lacking magnanimity in their dealings with the world.

Kafka, in spite of being so fascinated by the life of the Jewish ghetto and its literature, sadly but sternly proclaimed that a poet must remain detached from the literature of any small people, which does not tolerate a great writer because it is forced to defend itself from outside influences, and is wholly taken up with this struggle for survival. Giuliano Baioni has written that Kafka consciously became that great writer rejected by a minor, oppressed literature, intent on defending its own national identity and culture and eager for positive and consoling voices; rejected because such a writer creates a void around himself, provokes schisms and imperils the compactness of the little community.

A writer is not the father of a family but a son, and he must leave home and find his own way. He is faithful to his harassed little country if he bears witness to the truth of it, or if he suffers its oppression unstintingly and takes it upon himself, and if at the same time he transcends it, with that stern distancing needed by every kind of art and every liberating experience. Even today the relation between Czechs and Slovaks has to free itself of a reciprocal spiral of suspicion and distrust, the shadows of old prejudices on the one side, but also persistent retaliations on the other.

The most lively trends in Slovak culture display this freedom, and simply because it is enamored of its own green and pleasant land it is able also to reveal its failures and shortcomings. In 1924 Štefan Krěméry complained about how difficult it was to write a Slovak social novel: Political conditions were too restricting and views and experience too limited. Today, in spite of the heavy hand of a police state, one gets the impression of a country in which people have retaken possession of their own history, or are in the process of doing so. It is as if the styles of the public buildings and the houses of the lords and gentry, the Austrian and Hungarian styles which tower above the Slav flatlands with their one-storey peasant houses, were gradually merging with the latter, and no longer crushing them with their loftiness and grandeur.

The castle of Pezinok, an ancient royal free town surrounded by vineyards, merges imperceptibly with the ramparts, where there is a local *vinarna*, which offers fairly rudimentary accommodation but good fish and good white wine. It may be that Justice—which is represented on the roof of a public building in Oravský Podzámok by a statue with the scales and, rather than a sword, a far more frightening scimitar—has cleanly cut a number of iniquitous Gordian knots, and has brought that fish and that wine, at one time the privilege of the overlords, to more accessible tables.

Slovakia, though it made some considerable contributions to the spring of 1968, was paradoxically spared and even benefited by the brutal Soviet and pro-Soviet reaction of that August, which suffocated and extinguished Czech culture. While Prague was, as it were, decapitated, the totalitarian restoration of 1968, while it was certainly savage in repressing civil liberties and the rights of the individual, nevertheless increased the political weight of the local population, either as a result of political calculation or out of faith in the Pan-Slavic (and therefore pro-Russian) tradition of the country. Slovakia today is therefore at one and the same time beneath an iron heel and in a phase of historical regeneration, with an expanding role in affairs. Ever since the events of 1968 the splendid city of Prague has given an impression of being under the spell of neglect and death, while Bratislava, in spite of everything, is sanguine and cheerful, a vital world in an expansive phase, looking not to the melancholy of the past, but to growth and the future.

3. That Obscure Object of Desire

Even though we are in Slovakia, which is proud of its wines, it seems perfectly legitimate to want a glass of beer, since Czechoslovakia produces some of the finest beers in the world. But this wish is almost impossible to fulfill, like attempts to make love or to eat in a famous film by Buñuel. Amedeo, though thirsty, is accommodating, but Gigi, whose brow is quick to darken, begins to live up to his fearful reputation. Whether in the most famous places, such as the *Vel'ki Františkani*, or in ordinary bars, the request for a beer seems to the waiter quite bizarre. In one bar we asked in vain for *pivo*, and were told elsewhere that perhaps we should have asked straight out for Pilsen or Budweis, two particularly well-known brands.

The *Kyjev* Hotel is one of those big hotels typical of the eastern European countries, luxurious and yet dreary and a bit disreputable; here foreigners can find anything at all, from the most expensive liqueurs to available female company—certain Arabs from Kuwait spend nights with them which are embarrassingly noisy for their more temperate neighbors. But even at the *Kyjev* beer is a chimera; one evening, from under the counter, the porter furtively produces a lukewarm bottle for us.

The length and breadth of valleys and rivers, through towns over hills, from the lowlands to the high Tatras, our search becomes nervous and disordered, while the guidebooks we consult go on for page after page, lauding the various beers of each single place, telling us about their degree of alcohol, the differing pressures in the barrels, the nuances of color and the subtly different ways in which the froth froths. Some of us attribute our failure to a sudden seizing up of the mechanisms of distribution, and begin to reflect upon our Socialist convictions, while others see it as a national Slovak Fronde in opposition to the Czech national beverage. When we enter an inn at Podbiel, a small town in the Tatras, there are foaming tankards on the tables, but when it comes to our turn the barrel has run out. At Trenčin, beneath the vast castle, a waiter finally approaches us with a few beers, but a few steps from our table he trips up, the glasses shatter on the ground, and long, methodical labors of gathering up the fragments, sweeping and washing the floor, drying it and putting the rags away, once more postpone the fulfillment of our desire until some other stop in the unknown future.

4. To Each His Hour

Gondola Ilica is the seat of the Philosophy Faculty of Bratislava University, which is named after Comenius, the philosopher and teacher whose *Orbis Pictus* is to be found, in old editions in four languages, in the library of the old Slovak towns. The dignity of these buildings reminds me of a singular figure to whom I owe my interest in German culture ever since I was a schoolboy, and my discovery of the world of the Danube. He taught in a secondary school, though in his young days had been reader in Italian at these universities in Mitteleuropa, whose atmosphere he conveyed with effective and intense ham acting. I will call him Trani. He was a little like Napoleon when already fat and a little like Shylock. His marked features, never well shaven or rinsed, formed the impenetrable mask of a great actor, a personage ostensibly destined to play a leading role in the great theater of the world, to be a great man, but whom fate had consigned to teaching German to schoolboys.

Pupils and teachers had many and justified reasons for complaining about him, for his eager, theatrical, reticent personality was not without shadows, and his open-mindedness could be very far from praiseworthy, but it is to his genius that we are indebted for a number of basic intuitions. He did not consider us an audience unworthy of his gifts, which could and should have given proof of themselves in far loftier places, but he studied the *coups de scène* of his actions for us as if we had been the audience at the *Comédie Française* or the Swedish Royal Academy, which confers imperishable glory.

With us he only spoke in German or Triestino dialect. To make us understand what poetry was, he read us those lines of Dante's about the siren in mid-sea who misleads sailors, and when he wanted to make us understand what poetry, in his opinion, was not, he read those lines of Carducci's about Tittì, who is not clad simply in feathers and has more than just cypress berries to eat. Only the bad taste of an Italian professor, he said, could grudge his daughter the few pennies that he had to fork out for her maintenance. There are certain conventions, he added, that must be respected: If someone should ring the doorbell at Professor Carducci's, the door cannot possibly be opened by the professor's daughter in the nude. You ought to have thought first, he said in dialect, because you don't have to have children, but now that you have a daughter, love her, enjoy her, maintain her. But he became most furious when he read the poet's nostalgic invocation immediately corrected for reasons of prudence and opportunism: "Ah with what warm heart would I stay with you . . . with what warm heart! But, little cypress trees, ah let me go . . ." Really and truly scandalous, was his comment. "It's as if I were to say, 'Magris, I'm going to Paris; shall I call in on your grandmother?'—'Oh, that would be splendid. Poor old dear, she'll be so pleased.'—'But, you know, I'm only there for two days, and I've a lot to do, and she's out in the suburbs, I'd have to change trains three times and then take a bus . . .'—'Oh go to hell then, who asked you for anything!' "

He wanted to teach us to despise the soppy mush of feeling, the false generosity that for an instant, and in all good faith, promises the sun, moon, and stars, convinced of its own generous impulse, but that for all sorts of sound, valid reasons draws back when it comes to the point. In his way he was really fond of us, and wished to prepare us for the pitilessness of life. "For tomorrow I want 300 lines by heart," he would say. "Anyone who doesn't know them gets a Fail. I know this is unfair, because it's impossible to learn 300 lines in a day, but life's unfair and demands impossible things, and I'm training you to put up with it and not to let it suddenly overwhelm you. So tomorrow it's sink or swim."

To that man, the butt of so many criticisms at the Parents' Meetings, I owe not only my discovery of Central European culture, but also of one of the most important and unusual lessons in morality. If it is true that he trafficked in private lessons, then he was unable to practice strict justice himself, but to us he taught the sense of what is right and contempt for what is wrong. Like so many classes, our class had its victim, a fat, very timorous lad who blushed and sweated at the drop of a hat, who was unable to trade insults and was the object of that unwitting but no less blameworthy cruelty that we all have in us; cruelty which, if not kept at bay by some precise law imposed from within or without, will flare up in spite of ourselves to the detriment of whoever is weak at that moment.

Not one of us was innocent in his regard, and none of us was aware of being guilty. One day, while with theatrical gestures Trani was teaching us the conjugation of the German strong verbs, this boy's next-door neighbor, by the name of Sandrin, suddenly seized his fountain pen and snapped it in half. I can still see the victim's face as it grew red and sweaty, and his eyes filling with tears at the injustice of it, and his awareness that he was incapable of putting up a fight. When the teacher asked him why he had done that, Sandrin answered, "I felt nervous . . . and when I'm nervous I can't control myself . . . I'm just made like this, it's my nature." To our astonishment—and to the delight of the aggressor and greater humiliation of the offended party—Trani replied: "I understand. You couldn't do anything else, you're just made that way, it's your nature. We can't blame you, it's just life, that's all . . ." And he went on with the lesson.

A quarter of an hour later he began to complain about the fug, to loosen his tie and unbutton his waistcoat, to open the window and slam it shut again, to tell us that his nerves were on edge until, feigning a sudden fit of rage, he seized hold of Sandrin's pens, pencils, and notebooks, snapped them and ripped them and threw them all over the place. Then, affecting to grow calm, he said to Sandrin: "I'm so sorry, dear boy, I had a fit of nerves. I'm made like that, it's my nature. There's nothing I can do about it, it's just life . . ." And he returned to the German strong verbs.

Ever since then I have understood that strength, intelligence, stupidity, beauty, cowardice, and weakness are situations and roles which sooner or later happen to everyone. Anyone who dishonestly appeals to the mischance of life or of his own nature will, whether it be an hour later or a year, be repaid in the name of those same ineffable reasons. The same thing happens with peoples, with their virtues, their periods of decline and of prosperity. It is unlikely that an official of the Third Reich concerned with the "final solution" could have imagined that only a few years later the Jews would create a state with enormous military capacity and efficiency. Bratislava, the bustling capital of a small people long trodden underfoot, brings to mind memories and thoughts such as this, including that lesson in justice from the distant past.

5. A Working Class Danubian Sunday

Nedel'a (Sunday) is the title of one of the most famous books by Ladislav Novomeský, published in 1927. From the very start of his career Novomeský posed himself the question of his nation's identity—ever since, as a young man, he had heard its very existence denied. And avant-garde poet and a militant Communist, in both his work and his political activity, he has fought parallel battles for the national culture and for the internationalist viewpoint, for the "melancholy of the East" which, as he says in one of his poems, runs in his veins, and also the Marxist revolution. In the struggle for this latter he saw the deliverance of all the oppressed, and therefore of his own people—an almost completely proletarian nation. The precarious frontiers of Slovakia, which have often left the country open to foreign domination, become in his lyric poetry the symbol of a world without frontiers.

But the "melancholy Danubian procession" which the critic Stefan Kreméry sees in *Sunday*, is not just a procession of the humble, sorrowful destinies celebrated by Novomeský; it is also the melancholy of a contradiction which pervades all his poetry, constituting its greatness and making it one of the nerve centers of Slovak culture and politics. In the beginning Novomeský's art is rebel art, *poésie maudite*, a symbiosis of the poetry of revolution and the revolution of poetry. It is that negation of what is, which pervades the avant-garde throughout Europe and which, in socially committed poetry, aims to overturn reality and create a new reality and a new mankind, free from the chains of alienation.

But if at the beginning the melancholy of poetry is its futility in an alienated world, later on—with the advent of real Socialism—it is the feeling of being futile in a world which needs the prose of labor and not the poetry of revolutionary expectancy, which the new system, according to how one looks at it, has either achieved or belied. And it would be sadder still, with the revolution as an accomplished fact, to have to repeat a phrase written years earlier, in a moment of depression while awaiting the revolution:

> "This childlike poetry
> Did not change the face of the world."

Novomeský has never been prone to this disillusionment, even when he was arrested in 1951 and condemned as a "bourgeois nationalist," remaining in prison until 1956. Seated at the pleasant table in the *Klastorna* cellars, among barrels from which they draw smooth, fragrant wines, Šmatlák talks to me at length about Novomeský, who represents not merely the poetry he has written but also an exemplar for the whole of recent Slovak history. Here the memory that still smarts is not that of 1968, of events in Prague in the spring of that year, but that of 1951, of the Stalinist trials of the 1950s which mowed down the flower of Communism. In the West, Communists only began in 1956 to become aware of Soviet totalitarianism. The trials and executions which took place in the early 1950s, all the more serious because they were perverse and unmotivated, at that time only shook a handful of militants.

Rehabilitated with full honors in 1963, Novomeský, who died in 1976, did not side with the spring uprising in Prague. To praise him today is, in part, to praise a figure who stands for what is claimed to be the continuity of Communism, a continuity violated by what are officially considered to be the bloody distortions of Stalinism, but not violated, nay restored, by the Soviet intervention of 1968—so preaches the rigid official ideology. Novomeský is thus the symbol of a poetry rooted in the Slovak, internationalist, anti-Stalinist humus, but foreign to the tumults of 1968. Paradoxically, his dramatic destiny supplies an alibi for the conservatism and authoritarianism of the regime.

One gets the impression—no more than an impression, in view of the reticence which is *de rigueur* on this subject—that people in Bratislava were more easily reconciled to the restoration carried out by the Soviets in 1968. As Enzo Bettiza wrote at the time, until the eve of that spring Bratislava had played the role of an effective opposition, combining a strong thrust towards internal democratization with an emotional and spiritual closeness to Russia. The changes, both real and purely formal, introduced since 1968, have increased the importance of Slovakia within the state and have given the Slovaks some measure of satisfaction and compensation, in comparison with the desert created among the Czechs and in Czech literature.

If Czech literature has been thrown out of office, and now survives only amongst exiles, while those writers who have remained in the country have to choose between being ghosts, parasites, or Kafka's animal which digs itself underground tunnels, Slovak literature today has its own effective organic unity, even when it clamors for a new "epic" and a new positivity, a political and social function of collaboration rather than of opposition. There is certainly a measure of opportunism in the criticisms leveled at Mňačko, the writer who emigrated to Israel, and whose *Belated Reportages* were in the 1960s a highly popular indictment of the Stalinist terror; but the story called *Fever*, in which Jozef Kot shows the uprising of 1968 in a critical light, cannot be compared at all with the servile encomiums with which, in the 1950s, certain intellectuals in Czechoslovakia gave their assent to the elimination of friends or Party colleagues.

The assertive epic quality now frequently to be found in Slovak literature is not acceptable to the poetic taste of Western countries, but perhaps it is appropriate to a nation under the weight of an oppressive bureaucratic elite, which nonetheless feels itself to be the subject of its own history to a greater extent than in the past, and is therefore in a phase of initiation, not of imitation. The world has been changed, even though in all probability not by the poetry of Novomeský.

6. Roadside Cemeteries

One of Novomeský's poems is about a Slovak cemetery. In many mountain villages the cemetery has no wall, or one that you would barely notice. These places are unconfined and spread into the filed, or border the roadside as at Matiašovce near the Polish frontier; or else they are simply there at the edge of the village, like a garden in front of a house. This epic familiarity with death, found again, for example, in the Muslim tombs in Bosnia, quietly set in the orchard of the dwelling—things which our own world neurotically tends more and more to set apart—has the measure of how things ought to be, a feeling of the relationships between the individual and the generations, the earth, nature, the elements which compose it and the law which presides over their combination and dispersal.

In the windows of the shacks beside these cemeteries appear broad, good-humored faces, resembling the good, sound wood of which the houses are made. Those cemeteries which know nothing of sadness tell us how deceitful and superficial is the fear of death. As these cemeteries are located side by side with everyday life, rather than in a place remote from it, maybe we ought to learn to look at death from the other side of it. A poem by Milan Rúfus contains the lines:

> Only before us does death strike fear.
> Behind us
> it is suddenly all beautiful and innocent.
> A carnival mask in which,
> after midnight, you collect water
> to drink or, if you are sweaty, to wash.

7. On the Tatras

In the violet of an inexpressible sunset the high Tatras are already black outlines, sharing the profound mystery of all great mountains. Amedeo and Gigi are commenting on the play of light, the effects of refraction, the relation between those distant things and the perception which we have of them. At this moment we are all convinced that this blue and violet evening must exist somewhere, and in some way, forever, in the hyper-uranian world or the mind of God, as the incorruptible and everlasting Platonic Idea of Evening. It seems to us that those outlines, that light, that splendor materially contain in themselves these days through which we are passing, and their secret, like a fairy-tale lamp or ring that one only has to rub for a Genie to appear.

As we drive through the dark wood the headlights suddenly flash onto a signpost marked "Matliary, 2 km." In the sanatorium at Matliary Kafka spent the months December 1920 to August 1921. The moment the lights unexpectedly pick this sign out of the darkness I remember a photograph showing Kafka in a group, with a timid, almost happy smile; and in the background are these trees of Matliary. That photograph, with that dark and utterly mysterious foliage, and this same wood which we are passing through this moment, are like walls of infinite thinness that have been blown away. That life which the photograph fixed in one of its instants has vanished forever. Not even Kafka's work renders up its secret entirely, because it too is paper, though far more real and substantial; but it is still unequal to the vanishing of existence, as even to the shadows of the wood we are passing through.

The holiday resorts in the Tatra Mountains, such as Tatranska Lomnica, sport a *belle époque* luxury tourist décor. Apart from Czechoslovaks, most of the present clientele comes from East Germany. The elegance of these resorts is not without some of the ostentatious unreality of places which only exist in the holiday season, or where the latter has overwhelmed or completely erased the original existence and life of the community. Vulgarity triumphs, showy and sophisticated, when people go to a town not simply to enjoy tranquil or prohibited pleasures, but rather to celebrate a rite which they consider necessary to their own rank and style. A libertine who indulges his own inclinations is not vulgar; but he becomes vulgar if as he does so he is concerned not only with enjoying his pleasures, but also with making a meaningful gesture which raises him a cut above other people.

A specific elite which carries out its historical and political function—an aristocracy still in command or a military caste in power—can even be odious and criminal, but it is neither gross nor snobbish, because it is doing a real, impersonal job which transcends each individual member. The visiting celebrities who created the myth of Capri have very often been stigmatized as vulgar, in so far as they constitute a dreary crowd of eccentrics, not representative of anything at all, but convinced of representing something thanks to their predictable capriciousness and ostentation of elegance. We are therefore not too unwilling to leave the restaurant of a big hotel in the Tatras, even if the meal was decent and at last—thanks to the international atmosphere—we have been able to drink a decent glass of beer.

8. Old Books, Life and Law

In the post-war years the second-hand bookshops in Czechoslovakia were a gold-mine for people interested in German studies. Families of German origin, but resident here for centuries, were expelled: a stupid act of injustice which, aimed at avenging the infamy of Nazism, simply deprived the country of one of its essential components. These families left the country, and they sold their books. In the second-hand book-shops one could reach out and touch the liquidation of German culture in Czechoslovakia. Now many years have passed, the traces of that tragic exodus have been all but erased, and few of those books are to be found. On the other hand we come across bound volumes of *Lecture illustrée*, a delightful French magazine published at the end of the last century, and two Latin tomes of *Ethica catholica (Generalis* and *Specialis)* by Dr. Josepho Kachník, professor in the theological faculty at Olmütz in Moravia, issued at Olomucii (Olmütz) in 1910.

Dr. Kachník's work is a treatise without any claim to originality, but presumes only to expound the doctrine of the Church. He embraces the whole range of human actions, the alternatives they offer and the rules to be followed; he studies and classifies the freedom and the necessity to act, the order and nature of human and religious laws, obligations and exceptions, customs and departures, circumstances and passions, distinctions between the various sins and the various virtues. He gives a survey of adultery and of the phenomenology of drunkenness, he deals with moral and social values, with all the impediments, the attenuating and aggravating circumstances, the phantoms which cause bewilderment in the conscience and the insidious self-deceits with which the conscience tries to bamboozle itself.

One chapter, of extraordinary psychological insight and rhetorical expertise, is devoted to the over-scrupulous conscience, to the neurotic disability of those who are obsessed by sin and see it everywhere, who confess themselves with maniacal insistence to one confessor after another without allowing themselves to be convinced by any of them, or cured of their groundless fears; and who lose themselves and wander off into the desert of their own anguish and pride, into moralistic quibbles about what is fair and what not, their opinions vacillating from one moment to the next.

The logical Doctor, who is not without his comic pedantries and naively clerical conclusions, sees acutely that these obsessions of the overly rigorous conscience, which the Church considers an evil and a sin, are in fact a disease, a mental disposition which comes "e corporis constitutione," from a melancholic temperament and organic malfunctions. Depression tending towards feelings of remorse is the result of some evil affection of the nerves and brain, "nervorum atque cerebri mala affectio" which corrodes the psychophysical integrity of the individual.

The over-rigorous conscience has nothing to do with morality, but with a mixture of stubborn pride, unwilling to allow itself to be persuaded that it has not sinned, and neurotic *Angst*. A person with such a conscience "without any reason fears that he is sinning, both before and after acting, discovers sin in places where it in no way is, tortures himself uselessly over the most insignificant causes and, even when he is assured that a thing is licit, persists in believing that it might be wrong."

Timorous boys and girls, observes the Doctor, might out of ignorance be disturbed by scruples relating to the matter of the Sixth Commandment, but proper instruction can easily free them from this. He urges confessors to be patient with the over-scrupulous, though not to ponder to their phobias, but rather to give them the firmness they require, preventing them from indulging in their obsessive, self-satisfied guilt complexes, and during confession going at length into all their fancies, manias, and supposed sins, especially "si de turpibus agitur." To the over-scrupulous themselves, among various remedies he exorts them not to keep company with other neurotics, but above all to overcome that horror of society and love of solitude which are false signs of profundity and spiritual election. He urges them to accept human intercourse and sociability which, as even Goethe's Mephistopheles knew, are the conditions in which each one of us truly finds himself.

In one volume of *Lecture illustrée* a French physiognomist describes the mouth of Cléo de Mérode, the voluptuous actress—"broad, avid, curious" at fifteen, but latterly "shut tight . . . as befits a self-satisfied person with nothing to learn . . ." The French physiognomist and the theologian's high-flown Latin seem to be set in contrast—both full of charm and wisdom—as two days of understanding and living life. The story which the physiognomist reads from the mouth of the lovely actress is a story which one can sense but not explain, a life which without wishing it or knowing it has tended towards melancholy. It is a life of the dark depth and the fleeting surface, which comes and gives the impression of not being able either to choose or to explain. The moral theologian, on the other hand, does not allow himself to be drawn or dismayed by the indistinct flowing of existence, by the vague shadow or contradictory murmuring of a state of mind. He wants to make things clear, to establish laws, to fix the universal nature of the concept.

It is more fun to side with life than with law, with mobile, spontaneous creativity than with the symmetry of a code of regulations. But poetry dwells more in Dante's triplets than in any vague formlessness. Moral creativity is the ability to find a law and establish it freely. Only the power to put order into the fluctuating contradictions of life can do justice to those contradictions; they are rhetorically falsified when we see in them and their ill-defined vacillations, the supreme truths of existence and mistake them for mental activity. Marcus Aurelius warned otherwise.

When we confuse all gestures and actions, putting them all on the same plane in the name of the philosophy of "that's just life" which Professor Trani refused to let my schoolfellow Sandrin get away with, then the face of justice is darkened and vitality itself grows sad, shackled with falsehood. The sense and rigor of law do not suffocate passion, but endow it with strength and reality. If Cléo de Mérode had studied Latin, and Dr. Kachník's treatise, maybe the shadow of sadness might not have fallen across her lovely mouth, because the Doctor of Olmütz taught above all that we must not allow ourselves to be overcome by sophisms and the weaknesses of "indoles melancholica . . ."

PETER MATTHIESSEN

Congo Basin: The Search for the Forest Elephant

[Part I]

January 1, 1986

On the last evening of the year, the all-but-empty flight from Dakar-Monrovia-Lagos to Nairobi is crossing the lightless forests of the Congo Basin, passing at midnight over the Central African Highlands of the Zaire-Ruanda border, where the earth's last bands of mountain gorillas sleep in their nests. Down there in the dark, the enraged Africans who murdered the gorilla researcher Dian Fossey just a few days ago are still in hiding; Fossey is being buried there this very evening. On the screen is a South African movie, *The Gods Must Be Crazy*, a simple-hearted tale (though politically disingenuous, with its slapstick guerrilla squad of foolish blacks led by a caricatured Cuban).

At 2 A.M. in the new year, I am met in Nairobi by the savanna ecologist David Western, a husky, trim, and well-kept Kenyan citizen of forty-two. Dr. Western is the resource ecologist for the New York Zoological Society, best known for its Bronx Zoo and New York Aquarium; he is also pilot of the N.Y.Z.S. aircraft in which we shall embark the day after tomorrow on a survey of the rain forests of central Africa, paying special attention to the numbers and distribution of the small forest elephant, which may be seriously threatened by the ivory trade. As Dr. Western—known since a small boy as Jonah—wrote me in a letter last September, "We still know remarkably little about either the forest elephant, which now accounts for 60 percent of the ivory leaving Africa, or the Congo Basin, an area including about 20 percent of the world's tropical equatorial forests. The forest elephant is something of an enigma, and reason enough for the entire trip."

The African elephant, *Loxodonia africana*, has been seriously imperiled by ivory hunters; recent analyses of market tusks show that the poaching gangs, having reduced the savanna or bush elephant, *Lox-*

odonta africana africana, to less than a half-million animals, are increasingly concentrating on the much smaller forest race, *L.a. cyclotis*. Unlike *L.a. africana*, which is easy to census by light plane, *cyclotis* spends most of the daylight hours hidden in the forest, and estimates of its numbers have been mainly speculative. Proponents of the ivory trade maintain that the forest canopy hides very large numbers of small elephants, while ecologists fear that in this inhospitable habitat the numbers have always been low. It is generally agreed that an African elephant population of two million or more animals could probably sustain the present slaughter for the ivory trade, which until very recently, at least, has produced about 750 tons each year. However, computer analyses indicate that if fewer than a million elephants are left, as many authorities believe, then the species is already in a precipitous decline in which half the remaining animals will be lost in the next decade. The future of *Loxodonta* may depend, in short, on an accurate estimate of the numbers of the forest race, which would lay the foundation for a strong international conservation effort on behalf of the species as a whole.

"There will be a large gap in our understanding of the forest elephant until we understand the forest better," Jonah Western wrote. "That is one of the purposes of this survey. The truth is, we know very little about forest ecology. Only in recent years, with the realization of how rapidly the rain forests, with their great abundance and variety of life, are disappearing, especially in South America and southeast Asia, have we come to realize that the forest is a very important biome that cannot be ignored by anyone committed to conservation and the future of the earth. Because of its inaccessibility and low human population, the Congo Basin is still largely intact, but there is no reason for confidence that it will stay that way."

As for me, I am interested in both the forest and the forest elephant, and I enjoy the company of ecologists, who teach me a great deal that I wish to know about the origins and structure and relationships of the natural world, which have filled me with awe and fascination all my life. Throughout our journey we shall be working with ecologists already in the field, and an elephant biologist will meet us in central Africa and accompany us throughout the first part of the journey. Later we shall accompany okapi biologists and Mbuti Pygmy hunters into the Ituri Forest of Zaire.

Since our main destinations will be wilderness regions of the Central African Republic, Gabon, and Zaire, we will travel nearly 7,000 miles, from Nairobi, in Kenya, to Libreville, on Gabon's Atlantic coast, and back again. So far as Dr. Western knows, this transcontinental forest journey has never before been made in a light plane, but this feat interests us much less than the discoveries we might make along the way. With luck, for example, we shall learn more about the mysterious "pygmy elephant" in C.A.R. and Gabon, widely reported for almost a hundred years. With the problematical exception of the mokele mbembe, an elusive dinosaur-like denizen of the vast swamps of the Congo Basin, the pygmy elephant, *Loxodonta pumilio*, is regarded as the last large "unknown" animal in Africa. In a forest of such size and inaccessibility, it would be unwise to dismiss the pygmy elephant out of hand; the gorilla was reported for nearly a century before its existence was scientifically accepted, and the okapi, a large forest relative of the giraffe, eluded detection entirely until 1908.

January 3
Dr. Western and his wife, Dr. Shirley Strum, the distinguished social anthropologist and student of the baboon, have a new baby and a new house that faces across the Mbagathi River, which forms the boundary

between the Nairobi National Park and the Kapiti Plain, in Maasai Land. Driving out the Langata Road, passing the demolished car of a New Year's celebrant, Jonah assured me that early in the morning I might see black rhino from his guest room window.

Calls of the ring-neck and red-eyed doves reminded me as I awoke that I was once again in Africa. Now it is sunrise, and I see no rhino, but there are eland, impala, and giraffe, and a small herd of buffalo on the thorn landscape, still green and fresh after last month's short rains.

The bureaucracy in the new Kenya, which by comparison to a few years ago is stable and quite prosperous, is under stern instructions from President Daniel Arap Moi to serve the people rather than abuse them, as has been the popular custom on this continent, and preparations for our air safari go quite smoothly. But this morning the Directorate of Civil Aviation was down to a single airport clearance form, though six were needed, and all the copiers in the Ministry were out of service, and by the time we filled out the lone form and took it downtown to be copied, and completed the strict airport preparations and procedures, and passed through customs, it was already two in the afternoon, with a long flight across Kenya and Uganda into northern Zaire to be made before nightfall. "You're leaving too late," Shirley remarked when she came to see us off, and we both knew this, but by now we were frustrated, anxious to get going.

The New York Zoological Society's aircraft is a single-engine Cessna 206, which normally can go six hours without refueling. It is specially fitted with a cargo pod and extra gas drums to give us a range of fourteen hours, very critical in the vast reaches of central Africa where sources of fuel are problematical.

Jonah, an experienced bush pilot of thirteen years' experience, reckoned that we would still reach the airstrip in Zaire's Garamba Park before dark. There we will refuel the aircraft from our spare fuel drums and spend a day with Kes and Fraser Smith, who are studying the last northern white rhinos. The following day we will head west to our first destination in the Central African Republic.

Leaving Nairobi, the plane turned northwest across Kikuyu Land and the Rift escarpment, heading up the great Rift Valley between the Mau Range and the Aberdares. As it crosses Lake Naivasha, I peer down upon the bright white heads of fish eagles and a shimmering white string of pelicans; off the white soda shores of Lake Nakuru is a large pink crescent made by thousands upon thousands of flamingos. Then we are crossing the equator, droning northwestward over the Kakamega Forest, the easternmost outpost of the equatorial rain forests that extend all the way into West Africa. Off to the north rises Mt. Elgon, on the Uganda border, as a great migratory flight of European storks passes south beneath the plane, on their way, perhaps, to winter range in the Serengeti.

The high winds of the new monsoon, blowing out of Chad and the Sudan, have shrouded the rich farmlands of Uganda in a haze of dust. The sun looms, disappears again, behind bruised clouds that are thickened by the smoke of fires in this burning land. Whether or not the rebel forces of Yoweri Museveni bring peace and stability to this bloodied country, the countryside below is still under the control of the violent soldiery of the beleaguered Milton Obote, who is now known to have presided over the tribal slaughter of many more thousands of his countrymen than had his predecessor, Idi Amin. (Even among African countries, Uganda seems especially beset by bloody-minded tyrants, who were already ruling when the first explorers came up the Nile; in the days of Henry Morton Stanley, the despotic ruler was a man named Mwanga, for whom Idi Amin named his son.) The long red roads are strangely empty of all vehicles, for the countryside below, so green and peaceful in appearance, is in a state of utter anarchy and fear, with all communications broken down and the hated, vengeful army of the latest tyrant in retreat across the land, looting and killing.

From Murchison Falls, we take our last bearing for Garamba. Twenty-five years ago, when I passed through here, hitchhiking south from the Sudan, this park (later named Kabalega but now Murchison again) was famous all over the world for its legions of great-tusked elephants and other animals. Most of the animals are gone, cut down by the automatic guns of marauding armies, including the Tanzanian Army that helped to depose Idi Amin, but the booming white falls of the Victoria Nile, which descends from the broad morass of lakes and swamps called Lake Kyoga, thunder undiminished in an empty and silent land.

The day is late, the skies in all directions dark with haze and smoke, as we set out across northeastern Zaire. Air charts of Zaire are out of date, and therefore misleading, and Jonah, frustrated, must resort to my small relief map for his navigation. On this large-scale map, in the poor light, he confuses the town of Arua, on the Uganda side, with Aru in Zaire, so that none of the scarce roads and landmarks seems to fit, and the light fails nearly an hour earlier than we had expected as the sun sinks behind a dark shroud of smoke and desert haze off to the west. We are now disoriented, with only a very rough idea of our location. Small clusters of huts below, in the old fields and broken forest of rough hill country, are already dimming in the shadow of the night, and suddenly we know without discussion that we will not arrive this evening at Garamba, that even a forced landing in rough country is much better than finding ourselves with no place to come down, in the pitch dark. (Not all pilots, as he told me later, feel confident about landing in the bush, and tend to hesitate until the light fails entirely and *any* landing becomes very dangerous.)

The dirt roads are narrow and deeply rutted, and we must choose quickly among inhospitable rough fields. Jonah banks for a quick approach, slowing the plane right down to stalling speed, nose high, as we settle into the stiff grass. Because the high grass hides the ground, and the field is small, he is forced to touch down quickly. The plane strikes the bricklike laterite with a hard bounce and hurtles through bushes with a fearful whacking of stiff branches against metal. Missing the hidden termite hills and ditches, it suffers no worse than a few dents in the tail planes.

To make such a wild landing without mishap is exhilarating, and I congratulate Jonah on his skill, grateful to be wherever the hell we are still in one piece. All we have to do, I say to cheer him, is refuel the wing tanks, lay out our bedrolls, and be off again at dawn. But this is the first time in thirteen years as a bush pilot that Jonah has been lost at nightfall and forced down, and though he is calm, with scarcely a blond hair out of place, he is not happy. As a man who neither drinks nor smokes and is before all orderly and neat, he takes pride in his preparations and efficiency, and he has not yet figured out where things went wrong. "Getting off again, Peter, may be quite another matter," he says stiffly, descending from the plane and standing, hands on hips, staring about him.

From every direction, Africans come streaming across the country. We had seen some running toward the scene even before the airplane touched down. Within minutes, they surround the plane in a wide circle, and a few come forward, offering long, limp, cool, callused hands. They touch the wings, then turn to look at us again, eyes shining. Everyone is scared and friendly—the children run away each time we move, women smile and curtsey. "It is like an apparition to them," says one young man gently, separating himself discreetly from these hill peasants who have never seen an airplane before.

Many of these Bantu folk of the northeastern region known as

Haut-Zaire (Upper Zaire) have some French or Swahili, and so we are able to converse freely, and a good thing, too, because otherwise we might have found ourselves in trouble. The first group of several dozen shy onlookers has swelled quickly to a noisy crowd of hundreds—at least seven or eight hundred, by the end—all of them growing more and more excited in that volatile African way that can lead very quickly to irredeemable gestures, and sometimes violence. Politely but firmly, our well-wishers warn us to move away into the dark, to let the people calm themselves a little. We are told that we have landed near the village of Dibwa, and soon the village headman, who is drunk, asserts his authority by demanding to see identification. An ad-hoc committee draws our passport numbers on a scrap of paper amidst random officious shouts and cries of bewilderment and suspicion.

In 1903, when the first Baptist missionaries penetrated this huge region west of the Nile—said to have been the last region without whites in the whole dark continent—it was known to other Africans as "the Land of the Flesh-Eaters," due to the rampant cannibalism of its inhabitants, and the reputation of these local Azande people (of northeast Zaire, southwest Sudan, and southeast Chad) has not improved much since that time. After the Belgian Congo achieved independence (and became Zaire), in 1960, there began a six-year struggle for power, and Haut-Zaire was pillaged by waves of undisciplined soldiery, guerrilla bands—the Simba rebels—and South African and Rhodesian mercenaries. Because of this recent memory of bloodshed and famine, and because Zaire is surrounded by unstable, often hostile African states, the Zairois are highly suspicious of unidentified white foreigners. But as in most Africans, their excitability is offset by a great courtesy and gentleness, and throughout this experience we were treated well by almost everyone in this remote community.

Now it is dark, but the people do not disperse. Increasingly it becomes clear that we will not be permitted to sleep here at the plane, that we are, in fact, to be taken into custody. "After all," my confidant explains, when I protest, "our people are very simple, they do not know why you have come here suddenly like this, or what you will do during the night." I look over at Jonah, who is getting the same message in Swahili. Having no choice, we agree to be escorted to the nearest hut, a quarter mile away, where in a yard swept bare as a defense against night snakes, granary rodents, and mosquitoes, a fire is built and well-made chairs of wood and hide provided.

"We *have* to keep you here, we *have* to report you!" the headman explains, somewhat mollified now that we have decided to come peaceably. We sit surrounded by admirers, who wish to hear our story over and over. Soon we are shown inside the hut, where cane mats have been spread for us on the earth floor. "This is not what you are used to," one man suggests shyly, not quite sure of this, and anxious to inquire about our customs. Two men ask to borrow my flashlight and have not yet brought it back when, still in good spirits, I doze off.

Toward midnight we were woken up and led outside. Someone had run across the country to fetch some sort of district secretary, and we gathered once more at the fire. Once again we produced our passports and told our story, which was duly recorded. The secretary had made a long night walk to gather this information. "I have done it for the security and welfare of my people," he informed us.

Another messenger had been sent by bicycle to the town of Aru, thirty kilometers away, to notify the district commissioner, who arrived in a van with his aides and soldiery about one-thirty in the morning. This time a gendarme in green uniform banged into the hut, shouting abusively, shoving Jonah, and loosening his belt, to demonstrate his eagerness to move us faster. Outside, the calm, cold-faced commissioner had already been seated in a chair, and the foreigners were led to two chairs placed directly in front of him. Once again we showed our passports and accounted for ourselves, but this time the passports were not returned. Though we said we wished to stay nearby, to watch the plane, the commissioner informed us that a soldier would be assigned to guard it, and that we were to be taken back to Aru.

Under armed escort, we were marched across the fields toward the road. Without my flashlight, which had never been returned, I could not see the hard-baked ground, and I made a fatal misstep at a ditch edge, with a searing pain as ligaments tore from my ankle. I fell to the hard earth with a mighty curse, aware that at the very outset of this trip, which would involve a lot of forest walking, I had resprained an ankle already injured in cross-country skiing. The pain was so violent that I did not notice the safari ants that everyone else was slapping: I simply hobbled ahead while I still could, gasping in anger and shock. Not until I was inside the van, seated opposite a sullen African with a machine pistol and another with two carbines, did I feel the *siafu* attacking me under my pants. I dealt with them all the way down the rough road to Aru.

Beside me, Jonah seemed as stunned as I, and we did not speak.

Jolting along in the dead of night, with no idea what was coming next, there was little to say. With each new development, our predicament seemed to be worsening. We had no clearance for landing in this region, only at Kinshasa, where we were scheduled to arrive a few weeks later, and Zaire, with its reputation for violence and corruption (it is sometimes referred to as a "kleptocracy"), was no place to have one's papers not in order. Also, an investigation might identify me as the author of an article about a previous visit, a few years before, in which I was sharply critical of Zaire's puppet dictator—reason enough in this feverish climate to be arrested as an enemy of the state, if not a suspected mercenary or spy. Twenty-five years ago to the very month, scarcely a hundred miles east of this place, on the Sudan border, I had also been in custody, under much worse circumstances (the murder of Zaire's Prime Minister, Patrice Lumumba, in January of 1961, had rightly been blamed on American and European influence, and had inflamed Africa, turning the friendly Sudanese into fierce enemies), and I had no wish to repeat any such experience.

In Aru, to our great astonishment, we were not locked up—we could not go far, after all, without passports or airplane—but were dropped off almost casually at the quarters of a British pilot for the United Nations' High Commission for Refugees, which is kept very busy in this part of the world. Our host, routed out at 3 A.M., kindly showed us where we might lie down, observing in passing that Zaire was paranoid these days about "mercenaries," which has been a dread word in this country since the anarchy and massacres of the 1960s. Rumors had implicated Zairois soldiers when seven French white-water boatmen who had entered the country without permission disappeared on the Zaire River a few months ago. Officially they perished in the rapids, though their boats were found intact and right side up, and the one body that turned up had been beheaded.

The pilot was flying to Nairobi at daylight, now two hours away, and Jonah, concerned that Kes Smith at Garamba might radio an alarm when we failed to appear, sent off a message to his neighbor Philip Leakey to notify his wife that we were just fine.

At 8 A.M., the pilot's Ugandan assistant drove us around to the District Commissioner's house to inquire about our passports. We were referred to the Chief of Immigration, who referred us to the Chief of the Police, who said he had reported our arrival to his superiors in the regional capital at Bunia and could not return our passports without their permission. Bunia would check our identities at Kinshasa, where we were expected two weeks hence by the Minister of National, Parks, but since it was Saturday, it now appeared that we might be detained throughout the weekend.

Meanwhile, the authorities had no objection if Dr. Western returned to his airplane and brought it here to Aru; they assumed that he would not vanish, leaving me and his passport behind. As Jonah wished to take off with an empty plane, the obliging police chief returned with him to Dibwa, where the people were ordered to chop brush, knock down termite hills, and fill up ditches while the plane's extra fuel and other cargo were unloaded for ground transport to the strip at Aru. As it turned out, the same pair that had absconded with my flashlight the night before had used the flashlight to off-load all they could find in the unlocked cargo pod under the fuselage, including three jerry-cans of fuel, a computer printer destined for Garamba, and a duffel containing all my clothes and personal belongings. The duffel, minus some of its original contents—toilet kit, malaria pills, spare flashlight and sneakers, sweater, hat, and every pair of socks and underwear—was retrieved eventually, but the fuel and the printer were gone for good.

Jonah made a skillful downhill takeoff and followed the road eastward to Aru, where word came at mid-day from Bunia to let us go. By early afternoon, we were in the air again, and headed north.

January 4

Nagero, on the Dungu River, forms the southern boundary of Garamba National Park. At its small airstrip, we were met by Alison (Kes) Smith, a pretty woman in her thirties with dark-red hair. Dr. Smith, born in England and now a Kenyan citizen, is the biologist on the Garamba Northern White Rhino Project, which is funded by various conservation groups and private donors, and has won at least vocal support from Zaire's president. Her husband, Fraser Smith, is in charge of restoring to good operating order the logistical system of Garamba, which was the first of Zaire's parks, established by the colonial authorities in 1938. Accompanied by Chyulu, their infant daughter (named for the Chyulu Hills in Kenya), the Smiths escorted us in the afternoon to the flat rocks by the hippo pool where they were married just a year ago, in a roaring and blaring serenade from these hundred hippos. Perhaps on that day as well as this one, the silver limbs of the dead tree across the Dungu were decked with a winged red influorescence made by companies of carmine bee-eaters, which, with their blue heads, cobalt rumps, and long stream-ing tails, are among the most splendid of all birds in Africa. Among them were smaller, only slightly less spectacular red-throated bee-eaters, and by its nest on a high tree sat a thickset white bird, the palm-nut vulture. Already we are far enough west so that endemic bird species of East and West Africa are overlapping; I last saw this aberrant bird in Senegal.

Fraser Smith has constructed a small house on the banks of the Dungu, and the household presently includes a large dog (a second dog was taken by a crocodile), two cats, and a banded mongoose, which formerly enjoyed the run of the camp but must now be caged to keep it from attacking people, including its mistress, who has been severely bitten by it twice. Since Dr. Smith had mentioned its bad character, I was unpleasantly surprised to see the snout and beady eyes of this large weasel relative appear beneath the wood stockade of the outdoor shower into which I had limped just before dusk to wash away the memory of the night before. There was no mistaking the intent of its opened mouth, which was to bite me as speedily as possible, and sure enough it whisked into the shower and nipped my heel before I could take defensive action.

As anyone knows who has read Kipling's *Just So Stories*, a mongoose is much too quick for any cobra, let alone a crippled man in a cramped space. With my inflamed and swollen ankle, I was already a bit rickety on the uneven wet bricks slippery with soap, and this evil-tempered viverrid, renewing its attack, had me at enormous disadvantage. Jonah and Fraser were away from camp, refueling the airplane, and I called to Dr. Smith, more or less calmly, that she could find her mongoose near the shower. She had meant to take "Goose" for a walk, she said, and now began to call it, but the mongoose ignored her, darting in and out of sight under the stockade. I flicked hot water at it and made frightful growling noises, all to no avail; it backed out of view, came in swiftly from another angle, and sank its teeth into my toe, eliciting a sharp cry of vexation. "Is Goose biting you?" his mistress called. "So sorry!" It seemed that she was nursing her baby, but would come and fetch the mongoose in a minute.

For the nonce, I seized up a steel bucket and banged it down in front of my tormentor. This drove him back a little but did not deter him. Hopping mad, he dug furiously at the sandy earth—what field biologists call displacement activity, in which strong emotions are vented inappro-priately. My toe was bleeding, my ankle hurt, and I, too, was full of strong emotion. Though loath to execute a household pet by bashing its brains out with my bucket, I was considering this last resort when it darted out of sight, made a flanking maneuver, and shot in again from yet another angle, affixing itself to the top of my left foot with a terrific bite. There it remained until I kicked it free, emitting a wild oath of rage and pain.

Fearful, no doubt for her pet's life, my hostess appeared at once, joining me in the shower without warning. On the soapy floor, her legs flew out from under her, and she landed on her bottom, careening into the stockade as the mongoose disappeared beneath. Looking up, soaked by the shower, she found herself confronted by the frontal nudity of her amazed guest, covered a bit late by the bucket. "Sorry," she said, starting to laugh, and I laughed, too. "I have no secrets," I said, groping for a towel. "Just remove that mongoose." I pointed sternly at my bloody foot. And with suspicious speed, or so it seemed to me—as if, in this camp, an emergency mongoose-bite repair kit was ever at the ready—Dr. Smith was back at the shower door with bandages and disinfectants. "Sorry," she said. "Better take care of that. Might turn septic quickly in this climate."

The mongoose episode occurred at exactly the same hour as the forced landing at Dibwa, and considering all that had taken place so early in our journey, I felt the need of a stiff whiskey, in which Kes joined me. I asked her first of all to explain her nickname (it's from "Kesenyonye," or "Live in Peace," a name given her by Maasai tribesmen when she and her first husband, Chris Hillman, who was working on an eland study, lived in Maasai Land south of the Ngong Hills) and, second, for details of the white rhino project—specifically, why she felt so strongly that such a large international effort should be expended in a probably doomed attempt to save the last seventeen animals of the northern race, when the very similar southern race is well protected, and the species as a whole not currently in danger.

Dr. Smith pointed out that the southern white rhino (the originally described race, *Cerathotherium simum simum*) was already endangered by the turn of the century and virtually exterminated in the 1920s by South African hunters; it was reduced to a remnant hundred animals before its protection was seriously begun. This number has now been increased to approximately 3,000, most of them in South Africa's national parks; white rhinos have also been reintroduced in Botswana, Zimbabwe, and Mozambique (though the Mozambique animals were probably massacred in that land's recent wars). This recovery lends at least faint hope for the recovery of the northern race, which is worth saving not only for itself but as a symbol of the conservation effort.

January 5

Kes, whose own plane is out of commission, was anxious to go on an air survey of Garamba, which she had been unable to make in several months. In the early morning, before breakfast, we flew north across a vast plain of savanna grassland, already browning in the dry season, interspersed with shining, languid rivers. In the grassland stand large isolated trees—mostly the sausage tree, *Kigelia*, and a *Vitex* of the verbena family. The more permanent water courses are enclosed by gallery forest—sometimes called "finger forest," because it penetrates deep into the savanna in long fingerlike extensions of the rain forest farther to the south. The rich green strands, which shelter many forest animals and birds, are set off by lovely lavender leaves of a combretum liana that here and there climbs to the canopy.

In comparison with the East African savanna, which has many medium-sized animals, including zebra and both large and small antelopes, this northern grassland has very few, a discrepancy mainly attributable to climate. Equatorial East Africa has two rainy seasons of about three months each, with corresponding dry seasons in which herbivores can crop back the new grasses, whereas in this northern savanna, with its mixed woodland, a single long rainy season produces and sustains a high, rank, thick-stemmed grass ten to fifteen feet tall. Such grass cannot support herds of small herbivores, being not only unpalatable but too coarse to be managed except by large browsers with big guts; there are no zebra, and the few antelope species resort to flood plain grasses and burned ground.

On the flood plain are fair numbers of antelope—tiang, kob, and waterbuck—together with buffalo and warthog and a few small herds of elephant. The Congo giraffe is also here though we do not see it. Kob and buffalo are by far the most common animals, and large flowing herds of big black buffalo may be seen along most of the many streams that flow south to the Garamba River.

The northern region of the park, which adjoins the Lantoto Park in the Sudan, is rocky and hilly country, with only a small animal population, vulnerable to poachers. Unlike elephants, which are wideranging, rhinos are sedentary and are very easily tracked and killed, and the horn can be bashed off with a stone in a few minutes by local amateurs. Ivory poaching, on the other hand, is always risky and a great deal more difficult (time is required to remove tusks from a fresh carcass, and tusks are heavy to transport through roadless country), and requires an efficient organization. But the park rangers have not been provided with the means to patrol this remote area, with its poor roads, rivers, and precarious log bridges, and such animal protection as exists is concentrated on a thirty-two-square-mile area in this south third of the park, entirely composed of savanna and slow water courses. This region contains almost all the remaining rhino, but even here they are threatened: A captured poacher recently admitted having killed two rhino in 1983 and another two in 1984, effectively eliminating, all by himself, any increase that the animals might have made.

In an hour's flying, we count ourselves lucky to spot three white rhino, a lone male and a cow with calf; seeing our plane, the calf moved closer to its mother, which raised her head toward the sky but did not run. Among all land mammals on earth, white (from the German *"weit,"* or wide-nosed) rhinos are second only to elephants in size. The huge, placid pale-gray creatures with their primordial horned heads might have been standing on the plains of the Oligocene, seventy million years ago, when they first evolved. Except for a lion rolling on its dusty mound, they were the only creatures at Garamba that did not flee at the airplane's approach. Kob scattered widely through the tall coarse grass, and the buffalo herds, panicking one another, rocked along aimlessly in all directions, and the big bush elephants of the savanna, wariest of all, hurried along through the high grass in their stiff-legged, ear-flapping run.

Toward mid-morning, Jonah and I head west across the Garamba River, on a 400-mile flight to Bangassou, in the Central African Republic. We have left the rivers that flow toward the Nile; the Garamba is one of the many headwaters of the Congo (now the Zaire River). In the nineteenth century, when the Zanzibar slaver Tippu Tib sent his expeditions up the tributaries of the Congo, and Arab slavers came westward from the Nile, this savanna belt at the north edge of the rain forest was a great slaving region, and captured tribesmen carried ivory tusks back to the coast. Stanley's journals from his 1887 expedition—part of which was spent traveling with Tippu Tib—draw early attention to the devastating cost of the ivory trade:

> There is only one remedy for these wholesale devastations of African aborigines, and that is the solemn combination of England, Germany, France, Portugal, South and East Africa, and Congo [Free] State against the introduction of gunpowder into any part of the

Continent . . . or seizing upon every tusk of ivory brought out, as there is not a single piece nowadays which has been gained lawfully. Every tusk, piece, and scrap in the possession of an Arab trader has been steeped and dyed in blood. Every pound weight has cost the life of a man, woman, or child, for every five pounds a hut has been burned, for every two tusks a whole village has been destroyed, every twenty tusks have been obtained at the price of a district with all its people, villages, and plantations. It is simply incredible that, because ivory is required for ornaments or billiard games, the rich heart of Africa should be laid waste at this late year of the nineteenth century, signalized as it has been by so much advance, that populations, tribes, and nations should be utterly destroyed.

The region was all but emptied of human beings, and the few that were left, infected with syphilis by the slavers, were beset by an infertility that has kept the population low to the present day. More recently, the withdrawal of the colonial administrations and their clinics has brought a resurgence of sleeping sickness to both Sudan and C.A.R. For these reasons and others not well understood—superstitious memories of the dark era, and fear of Azande witchcraft and cannibalism, may have kept other groups from moving in—most of this vast region of Haut-Zaire and eastern C.A.R., with its immense woodlands and savannas, swamps, and rivers, shows no sign that man has ever been there.

In the great silence that settled on the land, the elephants prospered, and long after King Leopold II's Congo Free State was taken over by the Belgian government, this region remained the greatest ivory-hunting region in all Africa. Because it is remote, without roads or towns, its elephants were relatively untroubled even when, in the late 1960s, the price of ivory escalated, and a wholesale slaughter of elephants throughout East Africa began. The amount of ivory exported from Kenya rose 86 percent in a single year between 1970 and 1971, 81 percent more the following year; within five years, Kenya had lost half of its elephants, or about sixty thousand animals, and by 1980 Uganda's elephants were all but gone. In Somalia, northern Tanzania, Zambia, Mozambique, Angola, and throughout West Africa, the populations were reduced by 50 to 90 percent. (Zimbabwe, Botswana, and South Africa, which were farthest from organized poaching gangs and ivory depots, were much less affected.) Inevitably the poachers turned to the Sudan, in which the herds were reduced from 135,000 animals in 1976 to less than 30,000 in 1983. In recent years, the pressure has intensified in Chad, Zaire, and

C.A.R., from which the bush elephant is rapidly disappearing. Here as elsewhere, corrupt regimes have encouraged and controlled the trade in ivory.

The eastern two-thirds of the Central African Republic, like northern Haut-Zaire, is classified by ecologists as "guinea savanna," after the broad belt of grass and woodland extending eastward from northern Guinea, in West Africa, all the way across the continent into south Sudan and Ethiopia. North of the guinea savanna lies the Sahel, a dry grassland which, in the great drought that began about 1970, has been steadily invaded by the Sahara Desert. To the south lies the tropical rain forest, which extends from southern Guinea along the West African coast to Cameroon, widening out in the great Congo Basin and spreading eastward to the highlands of central Africa.

This broad savanna with its sinuous reaches of riverain forest, stretching away northward toward the Sahel, is entirely beautiful and awesome, and yet the great silence that resounds from a wild land without sign of human life, from which all of the great animals are gone, is something ominous. Mile after mile, we stared down in disbelief; we had not been prepared for so much emptiness, for such pristine and undamaged desolation. Beyond Garamba, we had encountered a few elephants, but these must have strayed out of the park, to judge from their great scarcity farther west. In hundreds of miles of unbroken wilderness, without so much as a distant smoke in sign of man, we saw no elephant whatsoever, nor any sign of the elephant trails that give away the presence of these animals even from high in the air.

With its notably sparse population of human beings (the whole country has less than three million people, and a third of these, by present estimate, have crowded into the few cities and towns), C.A.R. would seem an ideal environment for elephants. Before 1970, there were thought to be well over a hundred thousand in this country, and as late as the mid-seventies, when elephants were disappearing almost everywhere else, it was hoped that this region in the heart of the African continent would survive as a last stronghold of the species. Instead, the animals were exposed to unrestricted slaughter, and official exports of ivory jumped from four tons to a hundred and sixty-five tons in a single year. In just five years, here in the east part of the country, it is thought that four-fifths of the elephants were killed.

Jean Bedel-Bokassa, the "Emperor" of what he called the "Central African Empire" until he was deposed in 1979, is said to have ordered the slaughter of thirty thousand elephants by helicopter gunships and other means. He wished to support his family enterprise, La Couronne (The Crown), in its near-monopoly on ivory exports, which, according to the elephant biologist Dr. Iain Douglas-Hamilton, who made a continental survey of African elephants in 1979, were largely based on ivory illegally imported from Zaire and the Sudan. (Zairean elephants, he discovered, were also being massacred by government troops.) In 1980, after Bokassa was deposed, bans on ivory exports were announced in both C.A.R. and Zaire, but neither was meant to be enforced, and the slaughter continued unofficially and unabated. With official reopening of the ivory trade in 1981, as Douglas-Hamilton pointed out in a paper presented at a wildlife conference at Bangui in late 1985, C.A.R. was the only country left in Africa in which ivory hunting was "entirely legal, authorized, and operational."

In addition to the local people, the massacre attracted tough poaching gangs from Sudan and Chad that had run out of elephants in their own countries. The Sudanese favored camel transport and automatic weapons scavenged from the wars all around the region, while wild desert horsemen from Chad stuck to traditional methods, riding up on the great beasts from behind and ramming their sides or crippling their legs with long sharp spears. (Out of thirty-two animals examined by a Peace Corps group in 1983, twenty-five had been cut down by spears.) Already "big ivory" was hard to find, and between 1982 and 1984, exports declined from two hundred tons to forty. In 1984, an air survey of C.A.R.'s northern parks sponsored by several international conservation organizations could locate no more than forty-three hundred elephants, indicating a decline of nearly 90 percent in just four years. As Douglas-Hamilton observed at Bangui, "What happened in northern C.A.R. was caused by a regional crisis involving not only C.A.R. but Chad, Sudan, and Haut-Zaire. Ten years ago, this regional resource was beyond compare, five years ago it was in serious danger, today it is largely destroyed." In recent years, Sudan, Gabon, and C.A.R., responding to international pressure, have ordered an official ban on ivory export, but nobody thinks that this has slowed the killing.

What was rapidly becoming clear was that much of the recent ivory was coming from the smaller forest elephant, whose straight tusks are composed of a harder, whiter ivory that is easily detected in the shipments. Ian Parker, a wildlife entrepreneur based in Nairobi and a student of the world ivory trade, maintains that about 60 percent of the ivory turning up in Hong Kong and Japan (which together represent roughly four-fifths of the world market), much of it illegal ivory being exported through Burundi, comes from the forest elephant. Yet Parker, a longtime promoter of and participant in the trade, claims that elephants are still so numerous that tusks harvested from natural mortality alone would adequately support this commerce, which handled an annual average of seven hundred and fifty tons in the ten years between 1975 and 1985; except locally, he says, there is no such thing as an elephant crisis, since at least three million elephants are still at large in Africa. Douglas-Hamilton, on the other hand, has estimated a population of 1.3 million, and is convinced that *Loxodonta africana* is endangered as a species, despite this seemingly large number.

Dr. Western believes that even the smaller figure may be too high; the most recent analyses of ivory-trade records indicate that elephant numbers can no longer exceed one million, far less three. Between 1979 and the present, he says, the average weight of marketed tusks declined by one half, which meant that roughly twice the number of animals had to be killed to maintain that seven-hundred-and-fifty-ton harvest. It also meant that more than half the slaughtered animals were females, which in the old days were rarely shot at all. Analysis of ivory exports shows that the average tusk weight is about three kilos, in an animal that formerly produced tusks of a hundred kilos each; computer analysis has shown, he says, that once average tusk weight falls below five kilos a collapse of the entire population is at hand. The main source of these little tusks are juvenile males between five and ten years old—well below the age of reproduction—and mature females, twenty to twenty-five years old. Not a single tusk came from an animal over thirty-five years old, in a species which may attain four times that age. If there are really three million elephants, as Parker claims, why is no one shooting mature males? And why did the tonnage drop off drastically in 1985 to four hundred and eighty tons, despite dedicated killing by ivory hunters all across Africa?

By using an arbitrary equation that correlates elephant density with average rainfall, Ian Parker concludes that very large numbers of forest elephants—about two per square kilometer—are hidden by the forest canopy, a figure higher than the highest density found anywhere in the savanna. Dr. Western, whose own data Parker borrowed to construct his estimates, reminds me that elephants may eat three hundred pounds of fodder in a day, and defecate fifteen to eighteen times in the same period. "If you think of Parker's density figures in terms of a dung fight," he says wryly, "I can only say that you would never be out of reach of ammunition."

We put down quickly and refueled our tanks at the Bangassou airstrip—we had no clearance—then take off again and continue west across savanna and forest to our next landmark, the Oubangi River. Below the Kouimba Rapids, the Oubangi makes a great loop north. We do not follow it but maintain our course, crossing the river and flying 300 miles over the jungles of northern Zaire in order to meet the Oubangi once again where it sweeps south on its last descent to the Zaire River. On this leg of the journey, like the one before it, there is scarcely a sign of human presence—no tracks, no huts, no smoke, near or far—though an artificial city is being built for Zaire's billionaire president somewhere off there to the north, at Gbadolite. Nor are there tracks of animals, nor visible life of any kind except huge black hornbills with broad white on their wings, flapping and sailing over the forest canopy and slow green rivers. Then the forest opens out on the great Oubangi, where the few pirogues hold more human beings than we have seen in the 800 miles since we left Garamba. The river slides south to a great bend, and here rocks part it into rapids presided over by Bangui (the Rapids), the small capital of the erstwhile Empire of Central Africa. According to my trusty map, Bangui, a pretty town inset in small steep hills, lies just upriver from two villages, Bimbo and Zongo.

January 6–7

Bangui, with its fine river prospect, is a typical colonial town turned capital city in the new Africa. Its decrepit villas, European cars, and modern-type commercial buildings housing the remnants of colonial enterprises are set off by potholed red earth streets, traditional peasant dress and colors, radio music and impromptu dancing, flavorsome markets, head cargos, and flowers, and, everywhere, a restless proud humanity in bright clean clothes, streaming along under the trees to quarters that, for more people than not, will be tin-roofed shacks without electricity or plumbing.

The capital is set about with triumphal arches, erected in his own honor some years ago by the Emperor Bokassa, for whom the imperial boulevard into the city from the grandiose and empty airport was also named. It is now called the Avenue des Martyres, after the 200 schoolchildren who were slaughtered on imperial whim, with the Emperor's own wholehearted participation. Because Bokassa was a "charismatic" Francophile (he onced presented a gift of diamonds to French Premier

Valérie Giscard d'Estaing), this by no means isolated episode disappointed his many French admirers, who for investment reasons had supported him long after his bloodthirsty predilections became known. When the schoolroom adventure drew international attention, the Emperor and most of his country's money were hurried off to La Belle France, where he lives today in the greatest comfort and "is very popular," or so we were told by his bewildered countrymen.

Our main business in Bangui is to urge the creation of the country's first forest park and promise coöperation from the New York Zoological Society to Raymond Mbitikon, Minister of Waters and Forests, Fishing and Hunting, who asks us to prepare a survey and recommendation while we are down in the Bayanga region. The park was originally proposed last year by Richard Carroll, a former Peace Corps volunteer in C.A.R., now a doctoral student doing his thesis on lowland gorillas. M. Mbitikon dispatches a Ministry vehicle for Bayanga with a week's provisions and drums of aviation fuel. The journey is about 500 miles and fourteen hours over a rough road, and the truck will meet us there tomorrow.

To venture very far outside Bangui, according to a brochure of travel in these parts prepared some years ago by Air Afrique, "it is necessary to equip oneself seriously and be prepared for rather long delays." Since we are flying out tomorrow to Bayanga, in the far southern corner of C.A.R., we have seriously equipped ourselves with traveler's checks, to pay not only for provisions but for aviation fuel, for fuel comes very high indeed in what people living here believe to be the most expensive city in the world. We have lunch on the Oubangi River with the kind and helpful Ambassador and officers of the American Embassy, and the Ambassador's wife, Katia de Jarnette, escorts me to a Peace Corps clinic, where my mongoose bites are thoroughly cleansed and a tetanus shot administered by a cheerful nurse appropriately named Kandi Christian.

We are also "prepared for rather long delays," and a good thing, too, for at the airport next morning we find that the compressor on the gas pump has broken down. Gasoline in drums that cost three dollars a gallon yesterday will, for not entirely mysterious reasons, cost us five dollars per gallon today. We protest this piracy, and wait, and eventually the compressor is resuscitated. Before the plane can be refueled, however, a general failure of airport electricity knocks out the gas pump for a few more hours, and not until three-thirty in the afternoon, after flight clearance from the airport tower, customs, and immigration, do we clear the ground. We are accompanied on this flight by the British elephant biologist Richard Barnes, who made all the arrangements for us here in Bangui, and also by Gustave Doungoubey, Director of Management of Wildlife, who is kindly escorting us to Bayanga.

Immediately southwest of Bangui, the plane crosses a huge palm-oil plantation and heads out across the rain forests of the Congo Basin. There is no savanna anymore, the rare patches of swamp are small, the rare red tracks are narrow, shrouded by trees. Except for the rivers, which are not always in view, there is no place to come down in one piece. Years ago in eastern Zaire I flew over this Congo Basin forest in a light plane, from Bukavu to Obaye and then to Goma, and the sight of its monotone expanse of green, undulating in all directions to the green horizon, is as disturbing now as it was then.

Even so, the rolling foliage is magnificent. Forest green and gray-green, jade, emerald, and turquoise, pond-green, pea-green—all the greens of the world unroll below our wings, set off by bright fire-red leaves of the *azobe* (or *bois de fer* or "ironwood"). Here and there in the wet sloughs is a strand of raffia palms, said to be a favored haunt of pygmy elephants. Just once in the whole flight between the Oubangi and the Sangha did I see a sign of human habitation, two poor huts in a clearing near a forest stream.

The first glimpse of the Sangha River is a silver sliver among darkening hills in the late afternoon light. The plane swings south over slow rapids, the trees of the river islands mirrored in the silted water, and then the river opens out onto broad sandbars that in the dry season appear in front of the Bantu village called Bayanga.

Bayanga lies in the Lobaye Forest, in the furthest southern territory of C.A.R., surrounded by forests of the Congo Republic and Cameroon. Originally our plan had been to swing well east over the Congo Republic and count the elephants along the swamps and rivers, but M. Doungoubey received word this morning that Congo soldiers were crossing into C.A.R. in a border dispute, and might shoot at a small circling airplane, not realizing that elephants and not themselves were being studied. (Later we learned that the Congolese soldiers had withdrawn to their own border post, down the Sangha River, which flows due southward through that country to its confluence with the Zaire. "They put up their flag in our territory and we take it down again," I was told by a C.A.R. soldier.)

Bayanga is named for the Yanga fishing people ("Ba"—"Wa" in East Africa—is a Bantu prefix signifying plural man or "people") attracted here by Slovenia Bois, a Yugoslav lumber concession whose mill lies at the south end of the settlement, and whose acting manager, Janez Mikuz, was kind enough to meet us at the airstrip and refresh us with cold beer at the company mess overlooking the river before installing us at a comfortable guest house in the compound. But to our embarrassment our friend Gustave Doungoubey and his cousin, M. Babisse, who had now arrived with a soldier-driver in the truck, were installed separately in lesser quarters. Gustave, a bright, equable fellow who permits nothing so small as this to trouble him, seemed not to mind; he had many friends here, all of whom came to embrace him. Next morning at breakfast, there was more discomfort when M. Babisse and the local forestry official polished off a half bottle each of Slovenia Bois's good Côte du Rhone white wine, pouring it into man-sized tumblers and drinking it straight off like mountain spring water. Our friends showed no effects of their glad refreshment, then or later, but the Yugoslavs, who do not seem fond of Africans (Jonah remarks that this tends to be true of most Eastern Europeans), were clearly irritated, plainly regretting that the natives of this country were now permitted at their European mess. However, they were polite to the Africans, and kind and hospitable to the whites throughout our stay.

January 8–12

From the settlement a bright red road runs southwest through the forest, crossing a bridge in a big thicket of bamboo and climbing a steep hill to a forest ridge. Manioc and lone papaya fend for themselves in the thick weeds grown up around the unbranched columns of black skeletal trees 150 feet in height. Like all forest Bantu, the Yanga practice the primitive slash-and-burn agriculture that has already destroyed most of the rain forest of West Africa. Often a forest garden is abandoned and a new one started even before the poor soil is depleted, since slashing and burning is easier than keeping up with the fierce weeds. In regions of dense population, such as West Africa, primitive agriculture leads inevitably to total degradation of the forest together with the disappearance of the animals, but in Central Africa, where the human population is so low, the random agriculture, by encouraging second growth, makes forage more accessible, and, where not intense, may actually increase wildlife populations.

The dust of the road is patterned by the shifting coil patterns of thick vipers, and the snake patterns are interspersed with tiny human prints of Babinga Pygmies. Lost in the woods between road and field are the Pygmies' low leaf-thatched huts, which are woven of a strong latticework of saplings stuck into the earth to form the walls, then bent over and lashed together as the roof, giving great tensile strength to a light structure while obtaining the maximum space of a rounded dwelling. (Huts constructed on this principle are also made by the Turkana and Maasai and are in fact found all over the earth. Even the Inuit igloo is quite similar, including the long tubular entrance on one side, and so are the modern tents we carry with us.) Though the huts are scarcely four feet high, the tiny sleeping platforms of bamboo are often set one above another, in order to keep more people clear of the earth floor.

The middle-sized descendants of those Babinga who have interbred with their Bantu neighbors have inherited few of the fine points of either race, seeming neither as handsome and husky as the Bantu nor as alert and merry as the forest people. By our rather narrow Western standards, most Babinga are unprepossessing, seeming stunted and bent rather than small, with scared, uncomprehending faces and the slightly averted gaze of uneasy animals. At a roadside camp, three naked little boys, feeling behind them with their hands, withdraw into the foliage in the slow way of wild things not wishing to be seen, and one drops to all fours before disappearing into the leaves, peering back at the huge white men over his shoulder.

Last night after dark we listened to Babinga drums, and this morning near the airstrip we hear raised voices, a simple wistful three-note descending chorus, *Dee-do-do*, like a human echo of the sad sweet song of an emerald-green bird, Klaas's cuckoo, which I watched this morning at the forest edge. According to the Bayanga people, the Babinga come here only in the dry season, to take advantage of old manioc plantations, and perhaps work in the lumber mill, erecting their leaf huts outside the mill and the Yanga village. Like most Pygmy groups, they have a certain interdependence with their Bantu neighbors, who live mostly in rectangular wattle-and-daub huts, with tin roofs brought in by the lumber company, and are served by makeshift shops and a small bar. (Outside the "Bar Patience" is a decrepit jitney bus on which is painted "Sangha Eagle." As a parting shot to those left in its dust, a message painted on the rear reads "Good Will Never!" It has been quite a while since the Sangha Eagle traveled anywhere. How it got here or where it used to go is quite unknown.)

Early in our visit to Bayanga, I accompanied Drs. Barnes and Western on a reconnaissance flight across the "Dzanga-Sangha Reserve" proposed by Richard Carroll, which would include an area of 2,700 square kilometers. We hope to persuade M. Mbitikon to enlarge Carroll's proposed reserve with the idea that in the future, when the timber leases have run out, it might be given the fully protected status of a national park.

After a few preliminary circles at high altitude, we descended again to a few hundred feet above the forest canopies; the trees flow down to the gallery forests along the Sangha River, bursting and shimmering with morning light. The ironwoods were burning bright in the sea of greens, and the strange semaphore of white-winged birds turned out to be groups of the huge brown-cheeked hornbills, crossing the cool glades of the forest.

Our first forest elephant, a bull seen in a slough near the Dzanga Pan, shook its head at the banking airplane in disapproval, but it did not run—a sign that ivory poachers must be rare here. Another good sign was the almost total absence of forestry scars other than narrow logging roads already overgrown, and later we learned from Slovenia employees that this advanced lumber operation, which exploits only four of the myriad tree species (three red hardwoods are cut for export, and a white wood is used in local construction), rarely removes more than one tree every few acres.

Selective logging, excellent in principle, often does great damage to the forest because of the network of forestry tracks and roads required to remove the trees, but to judge from the minimal effects observable from the air, Slovenia Bois was taking unusual pains. By opening many small new clearings, this selective operation may have the same beneficial effect as the fall of ancient trees, which from the air look like giant skeletons on the forest floor. The sunlight streaming down through the tear in the forest permits a burst of second growth, providing accessible browse for many animals that cannot reach the nutrients high in the canopy.

Richard Barnes, who did his master's thesis on the bush elephant in Tanzania's Ruaha Park, is being sponsored by the N.Y.Z.S. in a study of techniques for censusing the forest race, which is far more difficult to observe. Until now, the vague estimates of its numbers have been influenced by the bias of the guessers, and a much more accurate census will be needed before international conservation efforts can be mustered on its behalf. Dr. Barnes's study area, which we shall visit, is in the Ivindo River region of northern Gabon, perhaps 300 miles southwest of Bayanga, and before he is finished he will have made the first comprehensive census of forest elephants in Gabon, the methods of which can then be applied to the African rain forests as a whole. "We haven't worked out precise figures as yet," Barnes informed me in his usual precise tones. "There are certain anomalies in our dung-density data having to do with dung decomposition rates." Here at Bayanga, Dr. Barnes will use his techniques to arrive at some estimate of elephant densities in both primary and secondary forest, and on our first day he and Dr. Western, with M. Doungoubey and Babisse and three Babinga trackers, set off on the first of his foot transects, in which elephant droppings over a predetermined distance provide the main basis of the count.

At Bangui the nurse had warned me that I must not walk more than absolutely necessary until my spectacular ankle swelling had gone down, and since I wished to be more or less fit by the time we arrived in the Ituri Forest, I decided to limit my forest walking to the afternoon. Slaus Sterculec, the man in charge of Slovenia's local construction, had kindly offered to accompany me to the Dzanga salt pan, a haunt of elephants perhaps two miles by forest path off an old logging track. Mr. Sterculec, a lifelong bachelor and wiry jungle veteran of a breed less often seen these days in Africa, has been out here since the founding of Bayanga thirteen years ago, and he has not left the forest in the last five years. He turned up to fetch me with two Babinga hunters, Bisambe and Lalieh, who were markedly smaller than the three who had gone off with the other party. Bisambe, the elder of the two, is yellowish and hunched, with a big head, and both have incisors filed down to sharp points. I was not displeased that Mr. Sterculec had brought along his rifle. "It is not for hunting," he explained disarmingly. "It is for my fear."

At supper the night before we had discussed the pygmy elephant *(Loxodonta pumilio)*, which is known to the native peoples throughout the tropical forest as a creature even smaller than the small forest race of the African elephant that we are here to study. Richard Barnes tells us that in Gabon nobody doubts the existence of this reputedly pugnacious little elephant, which is called *assala. A Field Guide to the Mammals of Africa,* published in 1977 by two German authorities, provides a detailed description of this creature and cites its widespread reputation for aggressiveness.

The first description of a "pygmy elephant" appeared in 1906, based on a small animal (1.2 meters at the shoulder) taken in Gabon the previous year and shipped to the New York Zoological Society's Bronx Zoo. The would-be discoverer, Theodore Noack, a German professor, claimed it as a new subspecies of the African elephant, *Elephas* [*Loxodonta*] *africanus pumilio*. Unfortunately, it had doubled in size and was a normal forest elephant when it died nine years later—still an adolescent—but by that time it had been forgotten, its place in the scientific limelight having been usurped by a second "pygmy" of an allegedly separate subspecies, *E.a. fransseni*, collected in 1911, and also a well-received report of a herd of five miniature elephants. All six of these were from the north bank of Lake Leopold II, in the Congo, where the exciting new animal was known as the "water elephant," and was alleged to have amphibious habits, like the hippopotamus. Two more small elephants killed in the same locality in 1923 were identified as pygmies by no less an authority than the New York Zoological Society's celebrated director, Dr. William Hornaday, and in 1936 another two "midget pachyderms," arriving alive in New York City, caused a great stir in the press and among the populace. One of these was still alive in 1947, by which time, like Dr. Noack's specimen, it had grown remorselessly to full forest-elephant dimensions.

Nevertheless, reports by reputable observers continued, and, as for the African population, the local people in all equatorial rain-forest countries without exception had two different names for two distinct elephants, the smaller of which was notoriously less wary and more aggressive than the larger. Furthermore, they said, it made a different sound, had more sedentary habits, and generally preferred swampy terrain, often in association with raffia palms, leading some authorities to speculate that even if it was not a separate geographic race—it appeared to share almost the entire known range of the forest elephant, and did not seem to occur where the latter was absent—it was separate ecologically, and therefore entitled to subspecific status.

Those who doubted the existence of a separate race of "pygmy elephant" pointed not only to the tendency of captive specimens to grow up in captivity but to the absence of dependable sightings of juvenile animals in reports of pygmy herds.

But if the existence of such a creature was unproved, so was the statement that it did not occur where the forest elephant was absent. Or so claimed its partisans, including a controversial Belgian zoologist, Dr. Bernard Heuvelmans, author of *On the Trail of Unknown Animals*, in which he states that "to deny that the pygmy elephant exists, even as a subspecies of *Loxodonta cyclotis* [sic] is absurd." Also, the late W. D. (Karamoja) Bell, among the most celebrated of all African elephant hunters, described a herd of pygmies from Liberia. Bell made a drawing of these animals from memory, and the drawing revealed a female pygmy with a baby alongside. Others had also reported evidence of baby pygmies—the afterbirth of a killed female, a female in lactation—to which the naysayers retorted that evidence of sexual reproduction was no evidence of maturity, and that these reproducing females would continue growing and exceed the six-foot limit usually applied to the hypothetical adult *pumilio*.

In the course of our trek into the forest, I asked Bisambe if he knew about the pygmy elephant, and he said he did. Asked if it was "plus méchant"—nastier, more aggressive—than the others, he murmured, "Ils sont *tous* méchants!" at which both he and Lalieh burst out laughing.

The trackers were wearing ancient shorts and child-sized and decrepit red plastic sandals, but entering the forest both went barefoot, carrying their sandals with great delicacy between their fingertips. Bisambe, who took the lead, stopped frequently to listen, poising right in the middle of a step, foot off the ground, turning his head to pick up some fleeting sound or smell amidst the raucous squawk and hooting of turacos and hornbills, the pungent dung and foliage aromas of the forest. "Moku," he would whisper with a slow mysterious smile, or "gandi," eyes dancing with delight. Moku is monkey and gandi—to judge from his deft mime—a species of duiker, a small forest antelope. Like many traditional hunters, the Babinga communicate in the bush with what seems to be a kind of soft ventriloquy; sometimes Bisambe, twenty yards ahead of me on the leafy path, would murmur something in his deep soft voice without bothering to turn his head, and there would come an answering soft sound from Lalieh, twenty yards behind.

Dancing ahead of us along the narrow path were male diadem butterflies with big white dots on black wings (the female, very different, has her own name: yellow pansy) and big cobalt-and-black striped daneids. Smaller forms have cobalt spots or are entirely cobalt, and the same brilliant color—perhaps the one that shows up best in the forest darkness—flares again in the rump and tail of a green-breasted pitta, a secretive bird of the forest floor which I felt very fortunate to see.

Nearing the Dzanga Pan, Bisambe stopped short again, and a moment later the snap of a heavy branch, like a pistol report, resounded in the silence, signaling the presence of a browsing elephant or a gorilla. Bisambe remained motionless for a little while, long fingers pointed like antennae. Then he moved on in dead quiet to a place where the thick canopy opened out, and afternoon sunlight poured into an open pan, perhaps 400 yards in length and a hundred across. There he turned his big head with a smile to end all smiles, his hand pointing straight ahead between the trees.

From the west end came a family group of elephants, a cow and three juveniles, and to the east a female with small calf and a large bull skirted each other. To my astonishment, the large bull had the high shoulders, huge ragged triangular ears, and heavy forward-curving tusks of the bush elephant. Another gathering of perhaps ten animals was far down at the west end of the pan. Directly in front of us, two very small male elephants with disproportionately big tusks were snuffling deep in a mudhole in the pan, which was broken by shallow pools of stagnant water.

I had scarcely focused on this odd pair with my binoculars when I saw the faces of two Africans in the trees behind them. *Poachers!* I thought, but a moment later I picked up a white face behind binoculars, observing the same two little elephants, and I soon found another doing the same thing. Richard and Jonah, completing their transects through the forest, had been led into the Dzanga Pan from the far side. Just prior to my arrival, they said later, one of these feisty little tuskers had actually skirmished with the large savanna bull. Though there were other elephants in the pan, these small males with outsized tusks turned out to be the most intriguing of all the elephants we were to see throughout our journey.

In the near-windlessness, the female with three young had caught our scent and led her small group without hurrying into the forest, as Gustave Doungoubey and his armed men, spotting our Pygmies for the first time, came hurrying across the pan, suspecting poachers. Slaus and I stepped out into the open, eliciting sheepish grins from our African friends, and soon Jonah and Richard came across the pan and compared impressions of our first forest elephants, in particular the big "bush elephant" and the two small males.

Just as the forest elephant may follow the river trees into the savanna, and sometimes is observed in open country, the bush elephant penetrates deep into the forest. Richard Carroll had also seen "bush elephants," assuming that they were fugitives from the ivory trade slaughters to the north, but Jonah thinks it is the savanna genes that have penetrated so far south; this particular animal, in all likelihood, had never seen the open grasslands.

The other elephants, in varying degrees, displayed the characters of the forest race, *L.a. cyclotis*, in which the highest point of the body is behind the middle of the back, and the head tends to be held lower, so that the small rounded ears on the small head (which make them look like very young bush elephants) do not reach higher than the neck. In *cyclotis*, the tusks tend to be narrow, straight, and vertically inclined, that is, pointed straight downward. Presumably the low head and small ears are adaptations for forest travel, but the function of the vertical tusks, like so much else about *cyclotis*, is not yet known. (I speculate that straight tusks might be used for digging tubers, in the way that the walrus uses its straight tusks for digging clams, but Jonah appears unimpressed by this brilliant theory.) Nor is it known why the forest race lacks pronounced sexual dimorphism; in the bush elephant, a big male may be twice the size of an average female.

"I suspect," Jonah says, "that dimorphism in elephants, as in other polygamous species, is related to male competition for females, and that in the savannas, which are strongly seasonal, herds aggregate during the rains, females come into estrus fairly synchronously, and bigger males will of course win out. Here in the equatorial forest, the seasons are much less pronounced, and food and water are more evenly spread. Under these conditions, we suspect, female elephant herds are tiny and more evenly distributed, and probably breed all year round. If this is true, males would also be widely spread, and would not compete so strongly in one place and at one time, so that the advantage of size is less."

Richard, in his careful, reserved, and taciturn way, is discernibly elated by these interesting elephants, seen in the open, at close range. Never before has he had such a look at forest elephants, and today was only the second time he had ever been able to get photographs. "In Gabon," he had told me over breakfast, "they are always hidden, sometimes only a few yards away. We can be right on top of one and not know he's there. And even when we *are* aware of them we make noise to drive them off, because"—and here he had shrugged, as the relentless candor which is one of his likable qualities overtook him—"because, well, I'm *afraid* of them. I'm not prepared to take the risk of approaching strange elephants in the forest, and my fiancée has extracted a promise from me that I will not do so."

If Drs. Barnes and Western were surprised to see a "pure" bush elephant so deep in the forest, they were positively astonished by the tusk size of the two young males just in front of us, which, to judge from their height—no more than five feet at the shoulder—were probably about five years old. These creatures answered perfectly the description of the "pygmy elephant," even to an aggressive nature, displayed when the larger of the two had instigated that brief skirmish with the savanna bull, which was several times its size. But a few minutes later, the same little male had approached a female in the large group at the west end and engaged in unmistakable filial behavior. Thus in an instant he had demonstrated that he was not a mature elephant of pygmy size and outsized tusks but an extraordinarily independent young forest elephant. The reason for that independence may well lie in the complete absence of lion, hyena, and wild dog, the only predators that might attack young elephants of this size in the savanna (the leopard is simply not large enough to bring one down). Freedom from predators permits a very early independence from the mother, and might account for obstreperous groups of juvenile *cyclotis* that are reported as "pygmy elephants."

It is encouraging that these elephants are comparatively tame, a sign that they are harassed little if at all, and a point to be made in our recommendation of this place as a national reserve. The foresters say that elephants are more numerous farther south, and that gorilla and bongo are common in the region, though usually difficult to see. What Dr. Western will probably recommend is a park far larger than the proposed reserve, occupying the whole triangle of C.A.R. that lies between Congo and Cameroon, with contiguous reserves or parks in those two countries—the first international forest park, preserving hundreds of square miles of undamaged habitat.

Since we had flashlights, Slaus and I, with Lalieh and Bisambe, decided to remain here until dusk. Our friends had scarcely disappeared when four more elephants, golden-yellow with caked clay from another bathing place, walked out of the deepening evening greens onto the east end of the pan. Soon they were joined by the big gray savanna bull, whose size, color, and configuration made him look like a different species altogether. All five crossed over to our side and re-entered the forest, and we wondered if we would encounter them on the way back. Another elephant came and went. Then, quite suddenly, the Babinga were gesturing.

The vanished five had reappeared at the edge of a grassy swale just to our right. Not catching our scent, they kept on coming, passing too close as they headed toward the center of the pan, where they bathed and drank for a little while before the female caught our scent in a subtle shift of wind. She lifted her trunk high, then directed it straight at us like a blunderbuss. Silently, in unhurried hurry, the elephants moved out of the pan, and the sand plovers, the green sandpipers from Europe, and some blue-winged, chestnut-colored ducks shifted just enough in the wash of mud and water to escape being flattened by the great round feet. I had never before seen this beautiful forest duck (labeled Hartlaub's duck through no fault of its own), the nest of which has never been located. "Faunistically," as Jonah says, in uncharacteristic resort to eco-jargon, "the rain forest of the Congo Basin is very little known."

Two days later, while Richard continued with his transects, Jonah and I returned to Dzanga Pan, arriving at two in the afternoon so as to be ready when the elephants came in; we were interested especially in large-tusked "pygmies." The day was hot, the pan dead still: I watched a sun bird, a green shiny lizard, and a pair of chortling gray parrots catching the sun in their red tails. (This species is the loquacious favorite of the parrot fancier.) Not until midafternoon did the first group of elephants appear, looming suddenly out of deep green shadows in the forest wall across the pan, lifting their trunks to sniff the air, swinging a forefoot several inches above the ground, ears uncoiling, thin tails switching, in the constant flowing motion of the elephant, even a calm one. "The first ones in are always suspicious," Jonah whispers.

This first group, which appeared to be almost "pure" *cyclotis*, was scared off by two Babinga hunters who emerged from the forest to the southwest with big leaf-wrapped packets of fresh meat and whacked a tree hard with a panga to scare the elephants away before crossing the pan. Twenty-two elephants came in once they were gone—mostly hybrids, with pronounced bush characters such as bulging brow, long back, and sharp-cornered ears. The sole young male was even smaller than our "pygmy elephants" and lacked their heavy tusk development, yet he was even more independent in behavior, coming into the pan early, all by himself, traveling the length of it past other groups, and departing the pan, still entirely on his own, in another direction. "On the savanna," Jonah said, astounded, "elephants are eight years old before they leave their mothers. That one can't be more than three! In the savanna he wouldn't last one day!"

The forest west of the Sangha River is entirely roadless, stretching away across an unmarked boundary into Cameroon. Perhaps for want of first-hand knowledge, blacks and whites agree that the gorilla is most plentiful in that region, which is dense and treacherous, so Gustave says, and ridden with swamps aswarm with crocodiles. Its only inhabitants are Pygmies, and our own Babinga won't accompany us, since they say that these Pygmies, who come in from Cameroon, are "très méchant." (Cameroon is the westernmost territory of the Pygmies, who are thought to number about 200,000. The largest group—about 25,000—and the one most culturally intact is the Mbuti, which we shall meet in the Ituri Forest of Zaire.) International boundaries are of no concern to Pygmies anywhere, but possibly the Sangha River is a natural barrier separating Pygmy bands. Or perhaps, being people of the forest, they are afraid to cross such a broad water at the mercy of the Yanga fishermen, who stand in the stern of their pirogues to paddle their narrow leaf-like craft up and down the currents in the shadow of the gallery trees.

Under the circumstances, Jonah and I decide to go on a gorilla hunt alone. Since the pirogues are too delicate and leaky to carry two big passengers, Slaus Sterculec offers to take us across the Sangha in his river boat, a decommissioned metal landing craft from the Second World War. Soon we are rounding the broad sandbars that appear in mid-river in the rainy season and crossing the heavy current to a break in the forest wall where elephants come occasionally to water.

Slaus is concerned that without a tracker we may lose ourselves in the dense forest, and on the far side he conscripts a young Yanga fisherman, Aliende, who agrees to guide us. Heading inland, Aliende skirts a broad and grassy marsh, perhaps an ancient oxbow of the river, and arrives at an overgrown, treacherous swamp perhaps a hundred yards across, all tussocks and tangled undergrowth, rotten footing and hidden holes, into which we sink well above the knee. On the far side, the rain forest has been much modified to their own advantage by the elephants, to judge not only from plentiful droppings but the numerous small clearings with abundant second growth that provides them fodder. This browse is also very useful to gorilla and the big forest antelope called the bongo, and before long we come upon gorilla signs—beds, feeding areas, old droppings. Continuing westward perhaps two miles more, we find fresh green droppings and a sweet whiff in the air left behind from the night before. But the gorilla, who rarely shows himself until he wishes to have a look at his observers, remains hidden in the rank and heavy cover.

From the north, across the river, comes a shot; three or four more ring out in the next half hour. Aliende stops and shakes his head; any animals nearby are sure to flee. He is not a Pygmy, and he grows unsure as he goes farther from the river, for there are no paths. He has marked our course rather too casually with flicks of his panga, and two or three times on the way back, we realize he has misread his own signs even before he backtracks to pick up the trail. Near the river, there is a sudden burst of rufous animals out of a thicket in the grassy swale—Bohor reedbuck, an antelope we know well from East Africa.

At the river, Aliende slips away in his pirogue, and, waiting for Slaus, Jonah and I sit on the bank gazing out over the water. So far we have gotten on extremely well, perhaps a bit better than I had expected, though we have been friendly for fourteen years. Increasingly, we can laugh at each other and have fun, and since, on this journey, we share many interests and concerns, we are rarely short of conversation. There by the river, sharing an orange, we are full of well-being and contentment, and in the same way that I now feel free to make inquiries, Jonah feels free to answer. He tells me about his father, a British building surveyor and city planner thirty years ago for the colonial administration in Dar-es-Salaam. In his spare time, Arthur Western was a hunter, but, like many hunters in East Africa, he was also a conservationist, and he was instrumental in the establishment of Mikumi National Park in what in those days was still Tanganyika. He was also an "honorary ranger" who was sometimes called upon to dispatch dangerous rogue elephants, and he was killed by such an animal in the Kilombero Valley, north of the Selous, in 1958, when Jonah was fourteen.

Jonah, who was born in England, returned there in 1961 to find work and complete his studies. "I was only anxious to get back to Africa," he says. In 1967, he took up residence in Amboseli Park, in Kenya, to complete his thesis ("The Structure, Dynamics, and Changes of the Amboseli Ecosystem"), and for the next ten years he lived mostly at Amboseli, under Mt. Kilimanjaro, which he still considers home.

On a reconnaissance flight on our last afternoon, we are sorry to see no elephants whatever in the pans to the south near the Congo frontier, and only a single herd of forest buffalo. But once again there are elephants at Dzanga, which seems to attract most if not all of the local population.

During the flight over the forest, the plane develops a mysterious whine, and there is also some sort of minor oil leak from the propeller filming the windshield. I notice that on the return flight Jonah crosses over to the Sangha River and follows it back upriver to Bayanga. On the ground, as we refuel and prepare the plane for tomorrow's four-hour flight, I ask if coming back along the river had been a precaution, and he said it was. He tells me that that whine is nothing serious, the motor was overhauled completely before we started on this voyage, perhaps we will have it checked in Libreville.

Jonah seems preoccupied and even downcast, he says he is fighting off an achy flu. Walking down the twilight road toward the village, we discuss for the first time the fine points of a forced landing in these jungle rivers. "No margin for error out there, is there?" Jonah murmurs, managing a grin, and I nod, relieved that he realizes this, too, and feels relaxed enough to say so. He describes how Douglas-Hamilton once conked out over the forest, and, with the usual amazing luck that has rescued our friend from one scrape after another, peered down to see the only village clearing in the region, which he glided into.

Since Jonah is nothing if not stiff-upper-lipped, he rarely mentions the awesome inhospitality of the equatorial forest from the perspective of a single-engine plane, perhaps because there is nothing to discuss: In the event of engine failure or forced landing, unless a swamp or river is within gliding range, a light plane would disappear into this greenness like a stone dropped from the air into the sea. (Even if by miracle the plane managed a pancake landing on the canopy without disintegrating or exploding, there are no low limbs on the forest trees, and the injured passengers might find themselves confronted with a jump of at least a hundred feet into the gloom below.) It would do no good to worry people by telling them our course, and we are usually remote from radio contact, even if radio contact would be useful, and one's best hope, all things considered, would be death on impact, since survivors could never be found, far less assisted. In short, why talk about it—the less said, the better.

January 13–18

The morning is hazy, and we do not take off until 9:30 A.M., after bidding adieu to our cheerful C.A.R. associates and kind Slavic hosts. Climbing above a lens of cloud, the plane heads southwest, crossing the invisible frontier and drifting out over Cameroon. An hour later, by rough estimate, Cameroon's border with northwestern Congo falls behind. Occasionally we glimpse the green snake of a slough or a dark gray-brown jungle river, the scar of a burned clearing, or even an overgrown red road with the glint of a tin roof at the end. (Later Jonah estimates that we were in sight of a swamp or river or some other such place to attempt a landing about a third of the time—optimistic in Richard Barnes's opinion and my own, and not heartwarming odds in any case, quite apart from one's prospects during and after any such unwelcome ending to our journey.)

In Congo, we peer down at Souanke, a small village at the bitter end of the most remote road in all the world, perhaps an hour from the Karangoua River and the Gabon border. We cross the northernmost province of Gabon, then the southeast corner of the erstwhile Equatorial Guinea, a Portuguese colony currently known as Rio Muni, then back again over Gabon, crossing the steep green Monts de Cristal, from which fierce white-water streams course down to the Atlantic. The Gulf of Benin comes in sight within the hour, a dull streak on the gray tropical horizon. A rough crust on the sea edge is Libreville, the capital of Gabon, where we will seek permission to visit the forests we have just flown over.

Makoku, on the Ivindo River of northeast Gabon, lies in full tropical forest, less than fifty miles north of the equator. The Institut de Recherche en Ecologie Tropicale station at Makoku, founded originally by the French, seems just the place for Richard Barnes to perfect techniques for censusing the forest elephant, a task in which he is cheerfully assisted by his fiancée, Karen Jensen; Ms. Jensen has trained herself carefully in analysis of dung, which provides forthright and honest evidence of elephant numbers. An easygoing and informal young American from Long Beach, California, she appreciates Richard's rather formal personality (and vice versa) and suits herself up in full jungle regalia for their expeditions, just as he does.

Richard and Karen met a few years ago at Dian Fossey's gorilla camp at Karisoke, in Rwanda, where Richard was director of research and Karen was a research assistant. Both were impressed by Miss Fossey's fierce commitment to and thorough knowledge of gorillas, and both were alarmed by her misanthropic personality, which expressed itself most disagreeably in her violent prejudice against Africans, including her own cowed and frightened staff. "They lived in dread of her return," says Richard, "and when she arrived, the morale went all to pieces. She liked to abuse and humiliate African men, and because they had families and jobs were scarce they had to take it. We were told she would have poachers stripped, then thrash them head to toe with nettles; when she was drunk, she fired her pistol over people's heads."

One cannot question the veracity of Dr. Barnes, who goes out of his way to be conservative in his opinions, and Miss Jensen supported him in all he said. "At the end," he told us, "she rarely went out into the field unless cameramen or reporters were in camp. She loved gorillas, perhaps, but she had no love for human beings. We were certain there was going to be violence, with which, on moral grounds, we didn't wish to be associated. It never occurred to us that she might be the victim until we spoke with the American ambassador, whose comment was, 'One of these days, they're going to come after her with pangas, as they did Joy Adamson.' Finally I went to the authorities and advised them strongly not to renew her visa. They had already heard how serious things were, but they said she attracted interest and tourist income to Rwanda, which were badly needed, and they couldn't refuse her. Under the circumstances, we resigned; we felt we could not work there any longer."

Karen Jensen nodded her agreement; she has unpleasant memories of her own. That a colleague who started out so well (and won the admiration of such peers as George Schaller and Jane Goodall) should have come to such an ugly end was very upsetting, but their impressions of the last years of Dian Fossey are widely shared by others who had dealings with her. At a primate conference in San Diego last year, Miss Fossey informed Dr. Western that the only meaningful approach to conservation in Africa was to hand out condoms. "I thought I was talking to a crazy person," Jonah says. "I told her I didn't think we had much to talk about, and walked away. She was spitting mad."

In his years at Amboseli, Jonah worked continually with Africans, in particular the Maasai, whose cattle competed with the wild animals for the scarce grass, and he is convinced that conservation that does not coöperate with the local people is of limited value, confining the preservation of animals to the artificial limits imposed by the boundaries of a national park. "Putting a boundary around Amboseli did not protect it. If you work with the people, show them the benefits that may come to them, show them the compatibility of human use and conservation, they will support what you are doing, even help with anti-poaching. This way, wildlife conservation can extend beyond park boundaries." Jonah shrugged. "Things still go wrong, of course. The Maasai *morani* are forbidden to kill lions these days, and so last year, to prove themselves, they killed forty elephants instead. Nevertheless, coöperation with the other interests, with the farmers or pastoralists, or with the foresters, is far more effective in the long run than fighting everyone, as Dian Fossey did. For one thing, the governments can support both interests, instead of always having to choose."

One day we joined Richard and Karen in a walk of ten kilometers through the forest, led by an old Bakota hunter named Bilombi. Though supposedly not a Pygmy, Bilombi is so small that much of the day was spent ducking under vines that the old tracker had not slashed aside because he himself passed easily beneath them. This was not a failure of courtesy but of spatial apprehension, for he is an amiable old man. For a Bantu, he seems very easy in the forest, and familiar with all the nuts and fruits consumed by forest inhabitants, including man. One fruit the size and color of an orange comes from a liana called *mbolo*, which also produces a white sticky resin sometimes used in rubber manufacture. The *mbolo* climbs hundreds of feet to the top of some great tree in the canopy, where its bright fruits are consumed by monkeys. "Monkey candy," Bilombi says. Another small fruit, the *atanga*, is shiny purple-blue, and Bilombi stopped to gather up a pocketful, which he wrapped carefully for his family in the wide thin leaves that characterize the light-starved plants of the forest floor. "Everybody eats it!" Bilombi exclaimed, with an utterly open smile of delight, as if in approval of all life. Then he said, "If you wait here, all the antelope will come!"

Bilombi referred to the small forest duikers, but the sitatunga is also here, deep in the marshes, and so is the bongo of the elegant lyrate horn. Crossing a marshy stream, Bilombi pointed out the print of a larger antelope, which he said had been made by a sitatunga. Jonah shook his head: "Not long enough." And a swift green snake with a red belly which shoots from the leaf litter into a log Bilombi calls a mamba, though it is not. Probably Bilombi is mistaken in much of the information that he offers us, and tends to err on the side of what his white companions wish to see, but all the same his eye is sharp and his bushcraft expert. And so we learn about native medicines such as this tree sap which, when boiled, will deal with urinary mischief in all women, and this peculiar paste with thin white fibers, created somehow by a tortoise eating mushrooms; he draws our attention to a strangely swaying bush where a departing mandrill had not eluded his keen eye. At one place he whacks free a three-foot section of rattan that he calls "water liana," from one end of which, miraculously, a small but steady stream of pure good water flows into one's mouth. At another, the old man stops short and commences a weird nasal honking, used by the forest hunters to call duiker, and, sure enough, a small blue duiker, large-eyed and delicate-limbed, hurries in across the narrow shafts of sun before whirling to flee with a great thump and scatter.

Today we record all signs of elephant seen in each kilometer of our walk, footprints and scrape marks on trees as well as droppings, which Karen, compiling her "dung-density data," has got good at assessing as to age. Most of the droppings found today are old ones and well scattered, scarcely more than a round dark shadow of soft soil. "There are a lot of bush pig here," says Richard, "and they do a hell of a lot of rooting in this tembo dung. For that reason, our dung-density data"— and here he gives Karen an affectionate, sardonic glance—"may depend more on the density of bush pig than it does on the density of tembo." (Richard's use of the Swahili word for elephant, an echo of his days in Ruaha Park, is affectionate and not an affectation; a man with fewer affectations would be hard to find.)

That elephants were here last month is borne out by the droppings, but there is no question that they are scarce here. "Soils and plants determine where an elephant *can* live," Richard said, as we paused to inspect the remains of a cooking fire near a stream, where people had been fishing, "and man determines where an elephant *does* live." Elephant scarcity at Makoku is attributable to scarce fodder as well as to the occasional hunters from the Makoku settlement who make camp in these glades. (The men go hunting while the women fish the slow, dark forest brooks by constructing rough mud-and-log dams, braced with upright sticks, braced in their turn by lone Y-sticks planted at an angle.)

Of all countries in the Congo Basin, Gabon is thought to be the most intact, with the highest percentage of undisturbed forest and the least disrupted wildlife populations. Even so, wildlife seems scarce compared to the plentiful life in the savanna. "I'm not a forest man," Jonah said later, "but it seems to me that the available food produced here is much less than the food produced in the savanna, even if the mass is counted that is far out of reach of the elephants, up in the canopy. And much of the food that *is* within their reach is unpalatable, having developed secondary compounds—(cf. bad-tasting chemicals not related to the plant's growth)—to keep elephants and other creatures from eating it. Richard is unwilling to give out premature figures, but from what I've seen, both here and in C.A.R., he's getting about one point five droppings per kilometer of walking, which—allowing time for decomposition—works out to a rough count of one elephant going by each month.

"I doubt if this will improve very much anywhere in the equatorial forest, whether the region is occupied by man or not. According to Ian Parker's figure of five elephants per square kilometer, there should have been 2,000 animals in that area we investigated at Bayanga, which includes the high-density concentration around Dzanga Pan as well as a number of smaller pans and water courses. I very much doubt if there were two hundred altogether, and the average across the Congo Basin must be far less than that. Perhaps there were more originally, but I don't think forest elephant numbers were ever as high as people wished to think.''

It is here near the equator that we thought a pure population of *cyclotis* would be found. We were mistaken. A young male shot yesterday by local authorities as an alleged crop raider was immediately butchered and eaten by the people, but enough was left to determine that it was a hybrid, with bush tusks extending well forward, and round, small cyclotiform ears.

The rain forest communities are the oldest on earth, with hundreds of insect species specific to each of the many species of its trees, and almost half of the earth's living things, many as yet undiscovered, are confined to this green world that is shrinking fast to a small patch on the earth's surface. Man has already destroyed half of the rain forests, which disappear at an ever-increasing speed, and a mostly unknown flora and fauna disappear with them.

Therefore, at every opportunity, we explore the forest, and often I go out alone, for walking in solitude through the dim glades, immersed in silence, one learns a lot that cannot be taught in any other way. The canopy of huge trees is closed, so that even at midday its atmosphere is cool and dark, too dark—too *mysterious*, it almost seems—for photographs. The forest silence is impermeable, entirely undisturbed by the soft bell notes of hidden birds, the tick of descending leaves and twigs or soft thump of falling fruit, or even the far caterwaul of monkeys, or the unearthly squawks of great blue turacos, hopping and clambering along the highest limbs like *Archaeopteryx*.

Increasingly uneasy in one's own intrusion, moving ever more quietly so as not to wake things, one grows aware of an immense beauty. The dust of the world spins in cathedral light in the long sun shafts falling from on high. The light touches a brilliant bird feather, an armored beetle, a mighty bean pod husk, silky and red, or hard and shiny as carved wood. The silent processions of the army ants, in their myriad species and deadly strength, glisten in dark ribbons on the forest floor; the taut webs of jungle spiders shine and vanish. High overhead, a bright orange *mbolo* fruit swells with sun in a chink of blue sky like a clerestory. But this underworld is brown and green, and green is the color of the stifled air.

Man hunts in this forest, but a few creatures are still left—monkeys, mandrills, squirrels, duikers, tree hyrax, several pangolins—more than enough to sustain the leopard whose scats I found yesterday near a forest pool. The scat was too old to attract butterflies, which lose all caution and are easily caught when feeding on the protein in carnivore dung. Like a beautiful lotus growing out of mud is this strange blossom of cobalt, red and black and forest green; it closes and opens as the butterflies palpitate, drawing their life, their very color from their reeking feast. And they are hurrying, for in a climate that permits ceaseless reproduction, certain butterflies may begin and end their days in a single month.

The enormous sound that has resounded through the silence all along suddenly fixes upon one's awareness. It is the fierce wing shriek of cicadas, thick-bodied and green, each shriek as painful to the ear as a blade sharpened on stone, yet joining together in electric harmony and smoothing out in a wild ringing from the canopy high overhead. The cicadas are ventriloquial, Jonah says, and I wonder if this is not also true of those hidden forest birds whose beautiful voices seem impossible to trace. Most of the birds remain high in the canopy, but bird armies, or "ejaks," of mixed species—leafloves, wattle-eyes, malimbes, greenbuls—come flitting through the understory, and if one stands still long enough one of the hidden singers will appear.

Late one afternoon the yellow-cheeked trogon, a shy uncommon forest dweller with emerald mantle and crimson breast and yellow spots behind the bill, flew from the shadows and perched dead still on a limb over the path. Like a spirit of the forest, it remained motionless even when we walked beneath it, and it did not turn its head to watch us go.

[*The concluding section,* "Part II," *will appear in* Antæus *64, to be published in Spring 1990.*]

HAROLD NORSE

A Tangier Episode

The Hotel Carlton in the Socco Chico was a dump, with carpetless, creaky wooden floors and dismal, drafty halls. It was so dark that you literally could see nothing when you entered. Your eyes had to grow accustomed to the dimness. Every morning I phoned Paul Bowles, but his wife Jane always answered. I thought it odd that each time she put me off in the same way, repeating the same questions. She did not remember that we had been through it all before.

"Hello. May I speak to Paul Bowles?"

"Who *are* you?"

"A friend."

"Yes, but *who?* Don't you have a name?" She always forgot it. I didn't want to mention my name again because I thought she was prejudiced against me, but she would insist.

"Harold Norse."

"Oh . . . the name is familiar . . ." The vague voice hesitated, sounded dubious; then, heavy with suspicion: "Do *I* know you?"

"I don't think so."

"Well, then, what do you *want?*"

"I want to speak to Paul."

"But we don't *know* you."

"Paul would know me, if I can just—"

"If *I* don't know you, I'm sure Paul doesn't either."

"Would you please tell me when I can reach him?"

"No-o, I couldn't do that. . . . If we spoke to *everybody* just off the boat. . . ."

"I'm not *everybody!* We have lots of mutual friends. I'm a writer—"

"Oh, everybody's a writer! Everybody has friends."

I ticked off some names: Burroughs, Corso, Ginsberg . . .

"*Friends!*" her voice dripped sarcasm. "They are not *my* friends!"

"Let Paul be the judge of that. They told me to look him up, if you don't mind!"

"But I *do* mind!"

At this point I'd swear, unable to control myself, and hang up.

Then, about a week later, when I had abandoned the prospect of ever softening Jane up, she suddenly relented.

Some twenty years after my visit to Tangier, and ten years after her death, Jane became posthumously famous. She is now compared with Colette, Doris Lessing, and Gertrude Stein, admired as an amalgam of Zelda Fitzgerald and Louise Bryant. New generations worship her for her flamboyant, witty, bohemian life-style, her uniquely original prose.

"The greatest writer of our century in the English language," rhapsodized Tennessee Williams in his memoirs.

"One of the really original pure stylists," said Truman Capote.

And, most recently, William Burroughs, writing of Denton Welch, said, "I think the writer to whom Denton is closest is Jane Bowles. Both . . . are masters of the unforgettable phrase that no one else could have written . . . each has a very special way of seeing things."

At Jane's death in 1973, she had an imposing list of establishment admirers, but not a wide reputation. Now she has both.

What was Jane like when I knew her? Certainly unlike anything this postmortem adulation would suggest. I saw not a glamorous legend but a disturbed, ailing woman, desperately unsure of herself. As for wit, there was little evidence of it. She was petulant, fussy, irritable. Bohemian? Suburban seemed a far more apt description. Her background was clearly one of ease and privilege. In fact, both Paul and Jane Bowles (by contrast with all the other writers, mainly Beat, whom I knew at the time) seemed conventional in their social life, dress, and behavior. Whatever their intellectual and artistic attainments or political philosophy, they exuded a distinctly cosmopolitan air of "café society" New Yorkers.

The Beat writers never referred to Jane's work. But what is even more curious, Paul never spoke of it either. I assumed it wasn't worth mentioning. Paul, on the other hand, was highly respected as a precursor of the Beats; his novels and stories dealt with altered states of consciousness through drugs and themes of incest, "under-age" homosexuality, and other taboos long before any mainstream American writer dared to touch them. I can understand in retrospect why Jane must have felt so completely obscured by Paul's fame and by his friends—although Paul surely could not be held responsible for such feelings. She did much to create her own isolation and neglect. In fact, without Paul's constant badgering and encouragement and, not least, his superb critical eye, there is evidence that she might have produced even less than she did.

Small, lame, morose, and anxious, Jane led a claustrophobic, hot-house existence, full of phobias. Whenever I saw her—and I never saw Jane without Paul—I was struck by the peevish tone with which they pursued, during an interminable colloquy, the subject that never changed: what they would have for dinner. This bizarre ritual, carried to the point of absurdity, was an obsession that they must have secretly enjoyed, although I can't imagine why.

Jane's apartment, situated on the floor above Paul's at the Inmueble Itesa, an apartment building in the Marshan (European quarter), was neat but featureless, lacking the taste and character, not to mention the fastidiousness, that marked Paul's existence. Like Jane herself, the place looked rather plain, with bare light bulbs and dowdy furnishings in the Moroccan manner. Each time, upon arriving, after I had steeled myself in advance against a comatose hour or so, sometimes even longer, my appearance was invariably greeted with the same complaint.

"You only come here with Paul. You *never* come to see me."

To this I had no answer; the accusation was just. But it was also unfair. It did not occur to her that when I arrived in Tangier she had discouraged me from doing this. Yet with a note of anguish in her voice, she would cry irritably, "*Nobody* ever comes to see *me!* You're Paul's friend, not mine! Everybody is Paul's friend! I have no friends! I used to have them, but nobody comes anymore."

Paul would respond to this tirade as he responded to everything: with irrefutable logic.

"Janie, you know that's not true! There's Sonya and Narayan and Ellen to start with. And there's David and Isabelle and Ira. There's Tennessee and Libby—"

"Paul, stop it!" she'd protest, looking more injured. "You know very well what I mean! All the literary people who come to Tangier look *you* up. They're not interested in me!"

"Some of them become your friends too, like Ira."

During such arguments she would cast baleful, accusing glances in my direction, which only succeeded in making me feel more uncomfortable. She would sulk awhile with a look of defiance, her crippled leg protruding straight out in front of her, as she'd slouch against the wall like a disgruntled waif, peering at a hostile world from behind horn-rimmed spectacles. Having vented her irritation on the subject of being abandoned by everyone, she'd watch Paul intensely, both of them puffing cigarettes, and then he would broach the subject for which he had come: what they would have for dinner. Almost immediately their faces would assume the rapt expression of players in a game of chess, while I nodded over a book or magazine.

Once I asked Paul whether she was mentally ill. He said she wasn't, but that she had never been the same since her stroke.

In the background hovered Cherifa, Jane's companion, tight-faced, hostile, chain-smoking, a silent spook in trousers, her thick black hair bound tightly at the nape. She was extremely withdrawn, hard-looking, and masculine. I can't recall that Cherifa ever greeted us or said one word, though Paul and I would stop in to see Jane quite often before we set out, with my friend Mohammed, on some trip or other in my Fiat 600, around the countryside or to small, sometimes distant, villages where we visited cafés and listened to white-turbaned musicians play and sing their native music, a custom that was rapidly dying out, said Paul, and would probably be extinct in Morocco in one more generation.

When I asked about Cherifa, Paul said she had poisoned Jane. Jane, on the other hand, would never give her up. She felt protective of Cherifa, believing that in spite of Cherifa's selfish character, she was like a child who loved and needed Jane. Paul loathed Cherifa and was convinced that she was waiting for an opportunity to poison him, too.

"She has actually threatened me," he said, "on many occasions. 'Paul, I'm going to kill you.' She would say it coldly, when Jane wasn't around."

It was a Charles Addams household, and these sophisticated Manhattanites lived in constant fear for their lives. Yet in some perverse fashion they seemed to be enjoying themselves immensely in this backwater North African port, at the mercy of superstitious illiterates who could not read a word they wrote. The Bowleses formed the closest bonds with them, making them part of their intimate personal life, and refused to give them up. Paul had done exactly the same with Ahmed Yacoubi, whom I got to know quite well. Yacoubi also feared and hated Cherifa.

As for Jane, she disliked (was jealous of) Paul's friends—especially Ginsberg, Kerouac, and Corso. They had preceded my visit to Tangier by a few months. It was very likely that when I announced over the telephone that they were my friends, she lumped me with them and set herself against me. She may have resented them because, as a writer, they ignored her. One thing is certain: She could not have disliked them for their behavior—she was notorious for creating public scenes herself. She had a knack, Paul said, for livening things up in restaurants and cafés.

In time Jane's attitude toward me softened. Paul put it this way:

"Well, you know Janie. She has pro-Norse days and anti-Norse days. Mostly, I guess, anti-Norse days."

At some point I lent or gave Paul a copy of my most recent book, *The Dancing Beasts*, published earlier that year by Macmillan. He made a complimentary remark and indicated that Jane also admired it. I think this established me in her mind as a poet she could take seriously. Shortly after she had seen my book Paul reported, "Janie says if she had to choose between you and Gregory as poets, she wouldn't be able to because you're both equally good. But if she had to choose between you as people, you'd win, *faute de mieux*."

"A Pyrrhic victory," I muttered.

Paul, who was usually cheerful and brisk, and whose resentments (not so near the surface as the vulnerable Jane's) were mitigated by his inexhaustible fund of humorous anecdotes and odd information, startled me once by grumbling quite sullenly when Tennessee Williams arrived, "Tennessee doesn't come here to see me! He's only interested in Janie. He wouldn't even bother to come to Tangier otherwise. They positively *adore* one another."

He commented peevishly that they had an almost mystical union, believing that they alone among American writers possessed a rare poetic sensibility.

"An alcoholic *participation mystique*," Paul observed drily.

That summer of 1962 Tennessee Williams arrived, moonfaced and florid, one arm hugging a bottle of whiskey, the other outstretched in greeting on the busy thoroughfare between the Socco Chico and the Café de Paris, where he was headed. As I descended the inclined street toward my hotel, we met head on. "Harold! *Harold!*" he shouted effusively. "Paul told me you were here! C'mon, baby, let's have a drink! Let's go to Jay Haselwood's!" Haselwood's bar was frequented by the Anglo-American colony.

Tennessee's large blue eyes, barely focusing despite several operations, still had a trace of strabismus and looked more watery and fishlike than ever. Also fishlike was the way he kept gasping for air as he talked, his speech thick with drunken exuberance. Now in his fiftieth year, he had aged considerably since I had last seen him, a few years earlier, at what he called his "naughty rumpus pad" in Rome, where, as I recall, the rooms were painted brothel scarlet.

Since I had a prior engagement I could not accompany Tennessee but said I'd be at the beach the following day with Gregory Corso.

"Oh, is Gregory here? Remarkable boy! I'm very fond of Gregory. Let's meet on the beach around noon!"

Before Gregory's arrival I had moved to the Hotel Villa Muniria, a run-down stucco building in the casbah. I had a dark gloomy room on the ground floor, entered from an unkempt garden by French doors. There was a narrow bed and nothing else. The walls were a murky repulsive green. I had one suitcase and a small spirit stove with camping equipment. The adjacent room was occupied by Corso. The proprietress, a fierce old Frenchwoman, had been a whorehouse madam in Hong Kong.

When Paul first came to see me there he exclaimed, "This is Bill's old room! When he occupied it empty Eukodol bottles, garbage, and manuscript pages littered the floor. The pages blew into the garden with every breeze. Madame swept them away with the trash. Hundreds of pages must have been lost."

When Paul inquired about the pages, Burroughs muttered laconically, "That's my work!" Tight-lipped and poker-faced, Paul mimicked him perfectly, burring the r. The "work" was *Naked Lunch*. "I never cleaned or dusted the room," said Burroughs much later. "Empty ampoules and garbage piled up to the ceiling."

I was forced to sell my burnoose to Paul for twenty dollars. It was a dove-gray princely garment that had belonged to a sheik, for which Ahmed Yacoubi had bargained on my behalf in the souk at Arcila. When Paul first saw the *silhem* he inquired, "Where did you get it? It's a very fine robe!" When I told him that Ahmed had bargained an hour in the hot sun and dust on a dirt road in Arcila, and got it for twenty dollars, Paul said, "That's a very good price. If you ever want to sell it I'd like to buy it. I'll certainly give you twenty dollars for it."

"It's a deal," I said, "but I don't think I'll ever sell it."

I now took him up on the offer.

"What do I need another djellabah for?" said Paul, looking noncommittal. He was seated on a hassock puffing his cigarette, dangling the holder at a rakish angle. "I've got twelve djellabahs."

"But you *said* you'd buy it if I ever wanted to sell." I was shocked that he had forgotten.

"Well, it *is* a beauty. How much are you asking?"

"Thirty dollars."

"I really don't need it," said Paul. "Besides, Janie wouldn't let me. She'd be furious. She says I've been spending too much recently."

He continued puffing his cigarette and blinking rapidly, his thin pale face slightly perplexed, as he often looked when disagreement arose. Of all the people I had known in Tangier, I had been closest to Paul, whom I liked and admired immensely, and knew to be completely trustworthy. I couldn't believe that he, too, would break a promise. I had reached the door when he called my name. I turned, startled to see him trembling all over. He had risen to his feet and his voice shook. He said he would honor his word and buy the burnoose. "But you're asking ten dollars *more* than you paid for it?" he said in an outraged tone. I sold it to him for twenty.

"I hope Janie doesn't find out," he said guiltily.

Sometimes I thought that living in the Arab world most of his life had sharpened the shrewd, relentless bargaining skill that lay just beneath his cool, composed, New England Yankee demeanor.

My entire stay in Tangier was made unforgettable by Paul. Though we did not reveal much about our inner lives, as I got to know him better I began to see him on a gossamer tightrope (stretched like a silken spider's thread over an abyss) poised in a precarious balance between desperate angst and sheer delight.

Once, when we went together with my friend Mohammed to a mountain village called Jajouka, where the ancient Greek Pan ceremony was still performed annually by the native priest-musicians, the music of which Paul recorded, we watched him prepare for sleep in the adjacent cot. He plugged both ears with stopples, placed a packaged blindfold over his eyes, and swallowed sleeping pills. I, who could not sleep without barbiturates and stopples myself, realized that Paul was even more troubled about losing consciousness. He may even have detested noise more, if that was conceivable. I recognized a fellow equilibrist on the tightrope between being and nothingness.

Better than anyone I knew, however, he filled the void with music and conversation, producing endless pleasure. Once he took me to a town called Chaouen where we sat in a ramshackle café made of weathered gray boards on an unpaved dirt road. We watched young dancing boys in shimmering female costumes, multicolored, while old men lounged on pasha pillows smoking kif and hashish with their long-stemmed, segmented *sebsis*. With sinuous erotic movements, their smooth arms braceleted with colored beads around white turbans, the boys danced and sang. Between nine and fourteen years old, their dark eyes heavily painted with kohl, their lips and cheeks rouged, they were incredibly beautiful. Everyone sat transported, relaxed and happy, smoking cannabis, while the musicians never let up their nasal wail and hypnotic sound of ouds and wooden flutes.

From time to time the boys sat on the laps of the white-bearded old men (like an old Persian print), who fondled them tenderly, feeding them sweets, kissing and caressing them, and giving them money. I had never seen such an affectionate interchange between generations—this was mammal nature herself, the unspoiled natural condition of the human primate, uninfluenced by false preachings. Here was a tiny remnant of a bygone era, stashed away in a remote corner of North Africa, off the beaten tourist track, keeping alive what once had been widely prevalent all over the eastern Mediterranean, from Turkey and Byzantium to Morocco, an irrepressible instinct allowed to express itself openly. For this sight alone I would have been eternally grateful to Paul Bowles.

"Dancing boys must behave like women in every way to arouse the man," Paul explained. "That is the point of the dance. This is how they earn more money—the goal of it all. Like other boys in Morocco they are not a bit effeminate. It is merely custom, a highly stylized ritual." I felt like Lawrence of Arabia, like an adventurer. "It won't be around much longer," said Paul, a trifle ruefully. "It will be gone by the end of the century."

With only twenty dollars to get me through Spain and back to Paris in my little Fiat 600, I made preparations to leave. It was nearly noon. Groggily, I prepared brunch with some Quaker Oats I'd found in an open box on the dusty floor. I had never covered it and had no pantry or refrigerator. I stirred some water into the oats and idly watched it puff for several minutes on the alcohol stove, then poured some milk into it and began to eat. Something crunchy and tasty was mixed with the oatmeal. Peering into the box I saw what I took to be tiny chocolate chips. Ah, Nesselrode, I thought vaguely. Then it dawned on me. The last time I had seen Nesselrode was in my boyhood in Brooklyn. I examined the package—not a word about Nesselrode. Puzzled, I closely scrutinized some dry oats in my palm; then suddenly knew. Mouse shit. Tiny black pellets of mouse shit.

I spat and gagged in horror.

I pulled on my pants, tore upstairs to the hotel telephone, and frantically dialed Paul. No answer. I dialed Jane. Thank God she was home. In great excitement I sputtered out what had happened.

"Jane, I need a doctor at once! I've swallowed mouse shit! Yes, I said *mouse* shit. Maybe rat shit! No, I didn't *know* what it was! I wasn't trying to commit suicide, Jane. I was just eating oatmeal for breakfast and tasted something that I thought was Nesselrode. My God, what if I get convulsions? Spasms? The bubonic plague? Yech!"

I choked, retching with disgust.

Jane made sympathetic noises, saying she knew all the European doctors in Tangier. She told me to drive over while she phoned them. I leapt into the Fiat, sped to the Inmueble Itesa. Jane greeted me with a shot of whiskey, which I gratefully gulped. She told me her Swiss physician, Dr. Roux, was out. In the sweltering heat we raced to another doctor—also out. We drove from doctor to doctor, but not one was available. It must have been around 120 degrees Fahrenheit. Sweat poured down my face, armpits, and crotch. Jane was a marvel of patience. I don't know what I'd have done without her. She suggested that we return to her place, noting that I hadn't exhibited any horrible symptoms so far.

"You probably sweated all the poisons out of your system," she said, handing me another shot glass at her apartment. "You must have avoided any dire effects by boiling the oats. You'll live, so relax."

I wasn't so sure. But by then the panic had begun to subside. It was more than an hour since we had set out on our quest, and a few more shot glasses brought on a rush of warmth for Jane. Her concern, her reassuring tone and manner, and above all, the feeling of *Gemütlichkeit*, a homey New York feeling that I liked so much in Paul, melted me with gratitude. Furthermore, she had behaved sensibly, something I had never expected of her.

"You don't know how grateful I am," I began. "If it hadn't been for you—"

"So stop kvetching," she interrupted with a wry but charming smile. Suddenly she became a real person. Until then I had seen her as only a neurotic, compulsive invalid. "If you still think you need a doctor this evening, we can probably get Dr. Roux—if she hasn't expired from heat prostration."

That evening in Paul's apartment he told me that Jane had been hysterical with laughter all day. "She phoned everyone she knew in Tangier, telling them how Harold Norse ate mouse shit for breakfast thinking it was Nesselrode. And how, on the hottest day in memory, you shlepped with her all over town for a doctor, finally getting drunk at her place. And how sentimental you got over Janie, probably because you never thought she had the sanity and presence of mind to be of assistance in a pinch."

I was flabbergasted. Was there one writer in the whole world that you could trust? While professing sympathy to my face, Jane couldn't wait to laugh behind my back.

In disbelief, I asked, "She said all that?" Paul nodded.

"But if I hadn't boiled those damn oats—"

"Oh, you'd still be around to tell it. Haven't you heard of people eating rats during wars and famines? They didn't always *boil* them." He passed the kif pipe imperturbably. "They ate 'em raw," he said, after coughing out the green smoke. "And they survived."

"Do you think Jane knew that?"

"Who knows what Janie knows or doesn't know?"

"Not even you?"

"Certainly not me."

"Well, it was mean of her to make fun of my predicament."

"Why? You were in no real danger. And there was no malice in it. She loves situations like that. Well, you know Janie, she—" He put down the kif pipe and slapped his forehead. "I'm forgetting what I wanted to *say!* Lost in the middle of—a sentence. I'm kiffed!"

He started laughing. Then I began to laugh. I laughed and laughed, at myself, at the whole nutty episode, at Jane and Paul. I couldn't stop. It was a splendidly relaxed feeling. I was stoned, glad to be alive, to be sitting with Paul again, perhaps for the last time. What a fascinating year it had been! But did I really know Jane Bowles? Or Paul for that matter? Did I know *myself?* Anyone? Everybody—friends and enemies—the world—weren't they, we, all of us, gaga? Absurd? Wasn't I weaving a rope of sand?

JOSIP NOVAKOVICH

Crossing the Border

On the train approaching the Swiss border my fellow passengers stare at the black forest where patches of deciduous trees are radiant with sunshine. I have a sensation of homecoming because I am about to visit one of my best friends, whom I have not seen as long as I have been away from our native country, Yugoslavia, more than five years. Yet, instead of being joyful, I am nervous. I always grow nervous when approaching a border. Sometimes I dream I am being taken off a train to a police station of a border town, to be tortured with burning cigarettes.

I think that many exiles dream similarly. The border crossing arouses a feeling of doing something illicit, of violating the mythic line between one land and another. In many countries the very possibility of such transgression has been turned into fantasy, a surreal possibility (which is to say impossibility): a form of transcendence into the beyond. The transgression of borders becomes an obsession with many Eastern Europeans, and it is this challenge rather than their dissatisfaction with the lack of potatoes and apples in stores that entices many of them to cross the borders. The border in their minds becomes a frontier between the real and the imagined, between a technological junk yard (East) and a computerized perfection (West), between the drab and the brilliant.

Leaving your motherland for the first time is a rite of passage, a sort of birth: You establish your being-on-your-own. Abroad you find a precise, concrete, artificial, alienated fantasy land in which the trains run punctually and without clanking, in which all the reality as you know it has been scrubbed away, the friction of matter is gone, and gloss shines and glares at you. You drift and slide like a child left in a hockey rink on skates for the first time. Now the reverse challenge occurs: to come back. Now you live the Odyssey, the ode of the essay of return, and to do it you must cross the borders from your surreal deodorized laundered permanent-press existence back into the old country, where you feel you sucked life directly out of the crumbling dirt of the soil. The borders are again obstacles, more mythic than real. Breaking through them back into Motherland, the sphere of your childhood, is incest. You shudder at the thought of that body that you somehow feel you must not penetrate.

Now the thought of the border arouses my body and mind. Images of exiles who must not cross borders come to my mind: a pale sleepless East German woman in West Berlin walking the streets and telling me how much she yearned to go back to East Germany, but her plea to return had just been rejected by the East German officials, and she was doomed to hang around the wall and to look over Alexander Platz, the ugly Muscovite space with high-rises, toward a green brass roof of a church next to her old home.

An Albanian who ran across the border to Yugoslavia in a suit he had made of rubber tires so the barbed wires would not electrocute him. In a storm, when police dogs could not smell him, he stumbled over stones, branches, holes. Now he works in a New York pizza parlor, pretending to be an Italian, because he thinks it's better for his business to be an Italian.

An East German mathematician I met in Budapest, where he hoped to sneak into a Greek truck and hide among hot green peppers and tires, to pass the Hungarian border into Yugoslavia, that exit land of Eastern Europe. He didn't have enough courage to follow through with his plan. Two years later by marrying a West German teacher he got his exit visa. I don't know what he does these days. He owes me 200 dollars, and I guess to him communicating with me isn't worth that much. At any rate, he cannot go back to East Germany.

A Rumanian who swam across the Danube to Yugoslavia, almost freezing to death and drowning in his spasms of shivering, but he made it, and went to New York. Though he was an architect in Rumania, because he has lacked the proper papers in the States, he is a construction worker. I bet he dreams of borders. He deserves to. He is a real exile, unlike me, who probably could not even attain the status of official exile, exiled from exile.

I could list many cases of people gazing across the Hungarian-Yugoslav border, into freedom, and I have done the same, except in my case, I was staring, or at least I thought I was, from freedom into the almost certain enforcement into the military service. I am there at the border near the bank of the river Drava, whose waters after many rains are light brown. No border patrol in sight. All I see on the other side is a muddy peasant riding a muddy bicycle unsteadily, and a muddy dog limping after him. I expect the slivovitz drunk, which I surmise him to be, will fall any moment, but he pedals on. Could you imagine? This is the celebrated Iron Curtain! It looks more like a mud curtain.

But no reason to think of the Iron Curtain now: I am approaching Switzerland, the land of absolute liberty. I reproach myself for the pounding of my heart. I expect dark blue police and laugh at myself. And lo and behold, a policeman comes straight toward me. "Passport please!" I show him my Yugoslav passport, he looks carefully through it, slaps it across his left palm (which I experience as if he were whipping me), and puts it into his pocket. "You get off at the border, Badischer Bahnhof, next stop, please!" I feel robbed without my passport. Something must be wrong with my appearance. Whenever I am tired—and after bumming through Europe for two months I certainly am—I think I look very much a Slav. These "free-world" policemen are like dogs trained to smell us out, which in many cases quite literally should prove possible! I am the only one dragged into the police station, while others admire what a free country Switzerland is, where nobody even bothers so much as to look at your passport.

The police ask me to empty my pockets. I turn them inside out and lay my miserabilia on the table. Two policemen quite unashamedly feel my thighs and ass, which tickles me. With clinical concentration they examine the stuff on the table. It is an obscene invasion of my privacy, more so than if they had turned my asshole inside out and inspected it under a microscope—any microbiologist could tell you that there we are remarkably similar. In pockets turned inside out you can see how we differ. They take my old student ID from which a sticker has fallen off, leaving an incriminating word: VOID. My picture plus my name equals void.

My ID dreams flash through my mind. Asked to show my identification papers, I hand over an empty white card. Not that, a real ID please! I give them another one, with my picture but no name. The officer is angry. I search my pockets and with a sense of salvation feel the plastic of a card. The officer examines it through a magnifying glass, and shows it to me in a rage: my name and above it a Chinese face. I snatch the ID and find another one. My face and Li Hao Chu below. Then my name and a picture of a chimpanzee. And so on until I wake up.

Recalling the melange of my ID dreams, I begin to chuckle. The policeman looks at me as if it were illegal to chuckle. "What for would you like to visit Switzerland?"—"To visit an old friend." "His name? Address?" I give the information. "His occupation?"—"An exile." "There is no such occupation," the cop hisses. "Yes, there is; it's a full-time occupation, day and night," I say. The cop goes to the computer, looks for my name, does not find it, and enters it; his two index fingers hit the keys like the beaks of two slow woodpeckers; his eyes stare at the keys with the same type of green light as on the computer screen. Now I am in their records. "What do you have in your bag?" I offer my bag for rape like Lot his daughters to the mob of Sodomah. There is plenty of linen there. I hope that pieces of my shit stick to the cotton and that the cop's fingers sink into them. But my linen looks spitefully clean; I had been scrupulous about my linen and washed it just before the trip through Germany.

They look at the contents of the bag with squeamish disgust thinning their lips; they look through the French and German bank notes of low value in the heap, at the addresses on torn pieces of paper, mostly people I've met on the trains, in the streets, pubs, at the Siberian conference in Paris, etc.; all the addresses that I would regret throwing away but do not have enough enthusiasm to enter into my address book. I would still like to write to these people one day; their traces accumulate in my pockets, warm them up, make me feel like I need not be alone, call me to write. All that is childishly innocuous, but now exposed on the table it looks immoral to me. It seems wrong, and if it is not wrong in my eyes, it seems to me it must be wrong in their disapproving eyes; everything about me one way or another must be wrong and illegal. I've had it. I'm angry.

"Your occupation?" the green-eyed policeman asks me. Though I often become witty when angry (perhaps the only times I do), his question leaves me with a speech impediment. I mumble and stumble over words. Ordinarily I would meet the question with cheerful insolence: "I am a bum," the effect of which would be that I would not be believed. Now I feel guilty I have no ostensible occupation. I feel as the unemployed must have felt under the Pharaohs of Egypt who, according to the liar Herodotus, asked that once a year each citizen of Egypt demonstrate to have made a living in an honest way during the year; whoever could not do so was to be executed. Though I'm on a writing fellowship from Vassar, I cannot say I am a writer since I haven't been published. I cannot say I am a minister, since despite taking a degree in divinity, I haven't been ordained. My life is being assessed, and reckoned worthless. My German fails me, English and Croatian spring up in my mind, and I break into eloquence in English explaining that I have just finished my religious studies in the States and am touring in Europe for personal edification. It sounds so simple and acceptable that

I immediately translate myself into an easy-going and thoroughly incorrect German, and the cops laugh and beg me to spare them.

They tell me I am free to go, and they show in a bearded relic from the sixties and order him to empty his pockets. They don't even look at me to see whether I am leaving, and though I could not say that I miss their attention, I feel curiously abandoned.

I am in the streets of Basel, quite free to go wherever I want in Switzerland, and I enjoy the privilege of treading the cobbles and of climbing into the tram, which takes me past gilded buildings on to a sooty stone bridge over the poisoned river Rhine. The dark old architecture surrounds me as historical ghosts.

The border crossing has shaken me up somehow. Without it the city would appear free and beautiful. But rather than to take the border harassment merely as a necessary evil that misportrays the free country, I suspect it to belie a police state.

That crossing into Switzerland took place in 1984. I've had many border crossings before and since, each one distinct in its own way. Crossing the German borders from Holland I was thoroughly searched for drugs; a bony cop squeezed out one third of my toothpaste before he began to believe it did not contain cocaine. Crossing from West Berlin to East Berlin, I was interrogated for a couple of hours, my address book was seized to be photocopied. I was asked about my whereabouts, whom I knew in East Germany, why I visited, would I like to visit again, what I thought of the country, etc. I was sent back from Dover to France because I did not have enough money to be allowed into England; thrown off a train in Denmark because I did not have a Swedish visa(!?). In my entry into Hungary a customs officer looked through my papers, mostly diaries and stories, sat down and read them for quarter of an hour, making cynical comments and laughing whenever the narrative struck him as stupid. My luggage was searched through in my crossing to Yugoslavia for smuggled coffee (!). A Soviet border policeman ate all my bananas.

Almost whichever border I cross, the police take out their books and search for my name among the names of terrorists, murderers, rapists; and not finding it, they look at me as if meaning, "All right, not yet, but we'll catch you some day!"

I wonder what the borders of the new EEC will be like in 1992; there won't be any within the Community. This summer it annoyed me that I needed a French visa on my U.S. passport, but a Frenchman said to me: "When a Frenchman wants to go to the States, he has to undergo the insulting process of obtaining a visa, so why shouldn't it work the other way round?''

It strikes me now in 1988 that I've taken my border crossings too seriously; after all, since I am past the drafting age and have a U.S. passport, I can go back to Yugoslavia. For many people border crossings have been more trouble than for me. For example, after World War II it was nearly impossible to leave Yugoslavia. A man from my town often attempted to leave Yugoslavia and was always caught. On one occasion he cut the ceiling of the train and hid in the narrow ''attic'' between the roof and the ceiling. In the darkness he couldn't read his watch. To make sure that he would get off the train abroad, he waited as long as he could and when he got off he was right back where he had started from: in Zagreb. The coach had been to Vienna and back. Getting out of the roof in Zagreb, he was caught and sentenced to several years of enforced labor; the fiasco killed his spirit. He was raving mad once he left the labor camp.

Before World War I my grandfather attempted to emigrate from Austria (the part that is now Yugoslavia) to the United States. He could not obtain a passport. He thought it was so absurd that his cow had a passport (for sale abroad) that he took a preposterous chance. On the passport of his cow he traveled to the United States and was admitted into the country! It was before photographs became essential for passports. I wonder what the U.S. immigration officials thought when they saw ''450 kg'' for my grandfather's weight.

Nowadays the U.S. consulates do their best to frustrate potential visitors: In India thousands of people wait for days in front of the U.S. consulates to petition for visas; if you are lucky you get an interview with a petty official, which turns out to be an interrogation. Many people enter illegally, through fraud—buying passports, green cards, copying visas, or plainly crossing the borders where they are least attended, risking a not-so-gentle treatment by the U.S. border patrol. People are driven by poverty, or by a desire for wealth, or by hardship of one sort or another, greed of one sort or another, to move to another country and seek a new life. Even where life is not hard materially, it may be hard spiritually. You can run into many Dutch, Swedish, German, Japanese, etc. immigrants in the States and other countries. It's not that materially they didn't have good chances at home, but they just needed a throwing away of their strict upbringing in a country where different customs rule—a breakthrough into a new life, through borders not as obstacles but as thresholds to freedom.

JEAN REDWOOD

Chekhov and Food

I have been asked, why Chekhov and not another? Why not Nikolai
Gogol, who so often wandered into people's kitchens, peering into sim-
mering saucepans, giving them a stir and tasting the contents, and who
took a great interest in preparing food for himself and his guests?

My answer is that Chekhov's interest was of a more general and
scientific turn. He went into many a humble kitchen in his capacity as
a doctor and in hundreds of peasant huts when he helped to conduct the
general census in 1897. He looked with a beady eye at all the cock-
roaches he saw there, the dirty dish cloths, the ill-managed stoves creating poisonous fumes, and pigs running in and out. "Man is the dirtiest
animal," the artist proclaims in one of the debates in his long story *The
House with the Mezzanine* (1895–96).

Chekhov was very conscious of what man lives by; and few of his
stories and plays are without some timely reminders, usually slipped in
by a seemingly chance and insignificant remark, of prevailing economic
factors, of the great "out-of-doors," of where food comes from, whether
it is from the fields or from the slaughterhouse.

The irony of "rational agronomy" in the dry south steppeland did
not escape him when he wrote his long story *Steppe*. "Here they kill
swallows, sparrows, bumblebees, ravens, and magpies, so that the fruit
blossoms should not be damaged; and they fell trees so that they should
not impoverish the soil." This has a familiar ring, as does the chopping
down of trees described by Dr. Astrov in *Uncle Vanya*, which leads to the
drying up of streams and upsets the balance of nature.

The lot of the peasants, who constituted three-quarters of the population in 1897 when Chekhov wrote his long story *Peasants*, was a sad
one. Their numbers were increasing at a time when grain was being
exported relentlessly, and when they themselves had not enough to eat.
By the time Lent came most families were out of flour. In short, the
peasant was being squeezed to pay for rapid industrialization.

Chekhov enlarges on the theme of "upset nature" when traditional
pasturage was being changed into wheatlands in his story *The Reed Piper*

in 1887. The irony that such changes often produced the opposite effect to that intended is brought out in the story. Here an old shepherd tells a passing bailiff of the gradual disappearance of wild duck and geese, of fish and bees and even birds of prey. The bailiff racks his brains to think of some reply, but can only say: "But man is getting cleverer and cleverer." To this the shepherd rightly responds with the question, what good is that, if man loses his strength through the impoverishment of the soil and the cutting down and burning of forests?

In *The Cherry Orchard* (1904) trees are also cut down but for different economic reasons. The owners have neglected it and frittered away time and money. The orchard was once renowned for its beauty and the quantity of cherries produced. But the trees no longer bear and the art of preserving the cherries has been lost.

At the end of the play the orchard is chopped down to make way for building summer datchas for the new commuters on the expanding railways. There is one illuminating remark made by the theorizing student Trofimov that all Russia will be their orchard, which makes one wonder about possible ensuing devastation and development.

Like many other writers Chekhov found that food and the daily gatherings round the Russian table served as an admirable literary device to bring about dramatic denouements, and he made use of it for creating atmosphere and for showing the social positions, divisions, and temperaments of his characters.

Bourgeois snobbery, for instance, is seen in a table scene from *A Boring Story* (1889). Here a professor is deprived of his usual simple Russian fare by his ambitious wife when he becomes dean of his faculty. His favorite cabbage soup and accompanying savory pies, goose with apples, bream with buckwheat, are replaced by refined puréed soups and kidneys in Madeira.

On a humbler level, the story *At Christmas-tide* (1900) is about an old couple who cannot read or write and who seek out a scribe in order to write to their daughter whom they haven't heard from for four years. The letter writing takes place in the kitchen of the local tavern where a pork casserole is spluttering on the stove. The atmosphere is stifling and the old woman is distracted by the strange hissing and "flu, flu" noises emanating from the casserole so that her thoughts are confused and she doesn't say anything of what has been in her heart—that they hadn't enough bread to eat for Christmas and that they had to sell the cow.

Pork was the most commonly eaten meat by the peasants at festival times. In his story *Pecheneg* (1897) a discussion takes place on the question of vegetarianism and Chekhov raises some interesting points. An old man, reputed to like philosophizing, gives a young man a lift from the station, where they had met by chance, and presses him to spend the night at his house. The "philosopher" is a terrible bore and keeps his guest from sleeping, and moreover treats his wife like a servant and neglects his children's education. He observes the healthy young man, who is a vegetarian, and thinks that maybe it would be a good thing for him too as he is in poor health. Then he wonders what would become of the domestic animals if everyone became a vegetarian, and the young man says they would go back to the woods and live in the wild. "But what about the pigs?" asks the old man, "they trample the fields and woods and orchard and uproot everything." At this insoluble problem they fall silent.

Comic relief is provided by Chekhov's description of many of the foods consumed by characters in his stories. He himself loved good food and was quite critical of what was offered to him on his travels. Overeating, to which Russians were prone, especially at festival time and on special occasions, forms the basis of a number of stories, notably *In the Ravine* (1900) where, in an obscure village, a Deacon had once consumed a whole four-pound jar of the best nonpressed caviar when attending the funeral of some rich merchant. The Deacon, we understand, subsequently died. In another story, *Victory Celebration* (1883), the *bliny* (pancakes) were so splendid that it was difficult for the narrator to describe their golden puffiness. They seem to leap into the mouth of their own accord, dripping with hot butter and accompanied by *smetana* (soured cream), caviar, and other fishy delights. This is all washed down by a sea of wine and vodka. After this comes fish soup *(ukha)* and partridges with a complicated sauce. But *bliny* are seen to be the "temptations" leading the eater down the slippery slope.

In contrast to such festivity, Natasha, the joy-stopping wife of Andrei in *The Three Sisters*, puts her husband on a diet of yogurt, ironically just at Maslenitsa, the week before Lent, when everyone else would normally consume *bliny* and a good deal more in preparation for the great fast that was strictly kept until Easter.

The Siren is perhaps Chekhov's best known food story and is a splendid account of a meal, summoned up in the imagination of a secretary of a local magistrate's court. Certainly the effect on the reader is a desire to bustle off to the kitchen and prepare something. It is a kind of culinary drama amusingly strewn with a few phrases of a legal turn.

In this story Chekhov's little legal clerk Zhilin lets his fancy roam on the consumption of a meal of almost banquet proportions and is so eloquent that he completely disrupts the thoughts of the Chairman of the Legal Committee, who is unable to finish making his assessment of the recent legal proceedings. The other committee members present are also distracted and eventually all disperse at great speed, presumably to their respective dinner tables. The story gradually reaches a culinary crescendo and along the way pies are discussed so caressingly, viewed as temptresses, shameless in their nakedness and so on, that one feels that the clerk is making a plea in court and that the criminals have been transposed into food. However, Chekhov describes all this so subtly that it is better to read the entire story yourself.

Chekhov's attitude to food is ambivalent. He relished good food but sees danger: Satiety can produce complacency; gluttony can lead to illness and decay. He shares our wistfulness when we think of what should be and what is. But, as in real life, so in his stories Chekhov rubs in his lessons with a light hand. His artistic vein leaves "Doctor Chekhov" far behind. "Look at yourselves," he says, and forces the reader to do just that in his skillful allusions to nature and man's place in it.

Before I join the ranks of hungry philosophers or stray into unknown paths, perhaps it might be well to finish this article with a glass of Russian tea (without the standard piece of sugar held between the teeth and of which our dentists would disapprove) and perhaps a spoonful or so of gooseberry jam and a delicious little pancake, not so slippery or buttery as the ones described above, but delicate lacy ones made with buckwheat flour. Lacy, like Chekhov's prose, as Tolstoy once described it.

The pancakes are made as follows, Armenian style, with more than a dash of brandy beaten into the yolks.

ARKANJ: BLINY, ARMENIAN STYLE

8 oz (225 g) each of plain flour and buckwheat flour	2 tbs castor sugar
	4 oz (100 g) butter
3 egg yolks	pinch of salt
4 tbs brandy	

Beat the brandy and egg yolks, gradually sift in the flours and salt and mix to a soft dough. Divide into four pieces, roll these out very thinly, make three incisions in each, and fry them in the sizzling butter until golden. Drain and sprinkle with castor sugar.

If you have no buckwheat flour, take ordinary buckwheat and grind it in the coffee grinder.

The above are similar to Ukrainian fried doughnuts, though more rich as they have more yolks to the amount of flour.

ROBERT SHACOCHIS

The Beauty of Imperfection

Remember during the presidential campaign, how the political ducks quacked nostalgic about the American Family, all those overcooked images from the apple-cheeked icons of Norman Rockwell? Well, sure— it's the business of politicians to manufacture togetherness, stir a big happy pot of ideological taffy out of the culture and its diverse ingredients. On the other hand, isn't it the business of the citizenry—real families and individuals, not media fictions—to survive and strive to transcend this pretense, the inspirational but altogether superficial and much exploited ideals of any society: the perfect bond of blood; the perfect way to live; the perfect mate; the perfect look; the perfect accompaniments to perfect success.

Rhetorical plums, all of them, and more and more the recipe for a nasty neo-puritanical prune stew that I'm being told to eat for my own good.

Last summer, during an animated argument about whether or not folks should be allowed to consume any amount of alcohol whatsoever before they operate a vehicle (no wine with dinner at your favorite restaurant!), I was stunned by a friend's chilly scolding for "liking to make trouble to prove that I'm different than everybody else." I pulled her over at the end of the evening to say, if you're my friend feel free to tell me I'm behaving like a jackass, but don't impugn my motives. No one in the night's gathering of academics, however, would support the cause I was battling for—the freedom to be myself which in this case meant taking a drink, but not being a drunk driver; arguing loudly, but without malice.

The following day I felt darkly comforted by an unlikely ally, Surgeon General C. Everett Koop, one of the few honest leaders we have known in the eighties. Koop was quoted warning that the American people were "traveling the road of retribution" here at the end of the decade, rallying against Utopia's deadbeats: smokers, drunk drivers, teenagers who become pregnant, drug addicts, wife beaters, all the inveterate ne'er-do-wells, and he expressed profound concern for the social fate of those infected with AIDS, that the tragic (Koop's word) national intolerance he observed on the rise was spreading to our most helpless caste of victim—unforgivably imperfect people, dying from a wicked disease.

I clipped the article bearing Koop's bleak prognosis out of the newspaper and, tacked above my desk, let it serve as a daily reminder why lately I have been losing friends left and right. I see myself as a regular fellow, a reluctant iconoclast at best but committed to the autonomy of the good-willed individual. It's true though that I smoke cigarettes, drink booze on weekends, have neither regrets nor recommendations from my younger drug-doing days, permit myself a mild curiosity about pornography, and for the past thirteen years have lived without nuptial contract to a remarkable, intelligent woman who, as a sophomore in high school, was out of it enough to get unwittingly pregnant and be declared mentally unfit to give birth in order to have a legal abortion. My dear girl! So, in the eyes of the pure, I suppose our relationship fattens the list of my shortcomings on at least two counts. Given such an unsavory litany of personal faults, I know this: I am close to being the scourge of the contemporary universe. Only viral-free blood and the fact that I've never smacked my lover or anybody else shields me, it sometimes seems, from tar and feathers.

Whether my erstwhile friends were "good" friends is not at issue; I liked them, for various reasons, and I wish they were still around, though I don't miss their admonitions, their simple well-intentioned (but not best-intentioned) advice on how to grow up. Frankly, these days of aggressive enlightenment are not for me. More and more I feel the awkward compulsion to ask new acquaintances to tell me of something they consider imperfectly beautiful. I don't know really what I'm trying to do with these barometric readings on the weather of their personalities, except the impossible—attempt to forecast the rain or sunshine of friendships.

Everyone has a unique answer. Navajo rugs, purposefully weaved with a hole in them. Japanese pottery, the imperfect asymmetrical forms of the Zen tea ceremony, which express the respect we accord natural beauty, and especially *raku*, with its accidental markings and drips, the pot thrown in contact with flame and water, both uncontrollable elements. The voice of the opera singer Joan Sutherland, its singularities saving her from the anonymity of the chorale, which is where perfect voices belong, herded together. The gap-toothed smile of Lauren Hutton; the ambiguous mouth of Mona Lisa. The paintings of Picasso, the

Baroque poem; Jay Gatsby; for that matter, all of literature.

Intriguing answers, but I wondered why no one was answering, *Laughter, Sadness,* for there is no comedy, just as there is no tragedy, in a world of perfection. What about the awesome beauty of a wild beast eating its kill? A volcanic eruption? Or the disaster of the space shuttle *Challenger,* with its teacher/passenger Christa McCauliffe? McCauliffe was sent into space to educate children; how painfully successful was her final lesson, that life is full of risks we must be prepared to take, that imperfection is not so much a mistake as it is a property of existence. That her mission ended in death, the white contrails forking into devastating silence, does not make the image or the impact of the event less beautiful, only much less pleasant and secure, like the beauty of a storm. And what about quantum physics, which painted a beauty mark—the uncertainty principle—on the smooth face of Einstein's universe?

My desire for fraternal response to the beauty of imperfection was a yearning for an integrated appreciation of the Big Picture, and I suppose I'll have to pose the question differently if I expect the answers to build a bridge between esthetics and ethics, to admit the beauty in the imperfect arts of living. How otherwise shall we admire democracy, the messiest premise of social organization; how else shall we approach love, except with an esthetic passion for its dizzying complexity? "What should I do about love?" a student asked Carl Jung, many years ago in his Zurich classroom. "I cannot tell you what to do," the psychologist answered honestly. "That must be left to the person who always knows what is best for other people."

The ultimate beauty of imperfection is evolution itself, which is the process of mutation, whether we *elect* it consciously for our own benefit, as we do when we stop smoking, or, as with disease, it *selects* us for its own caprice. Yet since natural law glorifies singularity, how did the tyranny of perfection become so ingrained in us, where did it set down its chokehold roots? Easy question. Of course we want to grow as people, be better tomorrow than we were yesterday, but *perfect?* Try this clue, a yeasty aphorism in the dough of western culture:

"The badness of men is better than the goodness of women."

Know your Bible? It's not possible to talk about beauty and imperfection without talking about truth and goodness, two horses that always turn back to the barn of religion. The line above comes from the Old Testament, *Ecclesiastes,* a bullet of wisdom from King Solomon. It took women a paltry few thousand years to recover from the old King's potshots. Might we ask ourselves how much longer before we show a little gratitude for Eve's stupidly maligned decision, how many more millenia before we are at peace with Eve's choice? Which is the real con job—the weaker sex betraying mankind to the devil, beguiled by a phallic serpent; or the myth of Paradise Lost itself?

Eve, created human, made the infinitely sane decision to embrace her condition, human nature, and so entered the house of the world, which already had a rental sign staked in the front yard anyway. *Wanted: Tenants, long term lease available.* Imagine Eve's accomplishment this way: If as beings we were to be fish, she coaxed us from the perfect illusion of the aquarium and led us to the imperfect but greater freedoms—and of course dangers—of the sea. Were it not for Adam's nostalgia, we would have had no alternative but to exculpate Eve; we would never have climbed on her back and spurred her across the centuries like a pretty mule.

Eden's echo, the memory of perfection in Adam's ears, was a dissatisfaction useful only insofar as it resisted becoming an obsession, or a weapon against children. Eve, however, brought to the new neighborhood what was most appropriate, the truth of knowledge, a homemaker's philosophy, that beauty was a reflection of reality; that while not all reality was beautiful, all beauty, including the illusory beauty of Paradise, was imperfect; that beauty, regardless how well it mimicked Adam's memory, must be judged by the temper of its flaws, and valued for the character of its failures in the face of the endless challenge to know God's mind.

Ah, how I would love to see the creation myth turned topsy-turvy to suit the evidence of life; perfectionism rotated into the slot of our consciousness that has harbored the stain of original sin. It would serve perfectionists right, to be shamed for inextricably linking beauty and truth to goodness in our psyches, not at all a bad idea, really, until Adam's disciples suggested that perfect beauty equaled perfect goodness. What a trap that has been for all of us! The more beautiful a thing or person, the higher we were prepared to assume its moral content. Thus we had a formula for breeding fools.

Take feminine beauty, for instance. Throughout mankind's existence it has roamed the scales as well as the anatomy, loving fat, loving bone, swelling the breasts to coconuts and then shrinking them to the size of gumdrops, one era favoring birchpole hips, another era caressing bovine backsides. Beauty's eclectic tastes were, in their whimsy, harmless enough, but in the hands of perfectionists—the courtly knights of the Middle Ages, Romantic poets of the eighteenth century, sentimental

Hollywood directors—feminine beauty was raised upon a pedestal; in order to see how exquisitely formed a woman was on the inside, only examine how perfect she appeared on the outside. But, let's face it, a pedestal is the wrong place for a female unless the idea is to look up her skirts.

You know as well as I do this business of perfection and beauty has gotten wrapped up in the economics of modern life. Place a perfect butt, a perfect face, a perfect family alongside any product and the conclusion is inescapable: Buy one and purchase the means to a better, happier, more fulfilled, more perfect self. Buy one, if you believe in heaven on earth. Buy the Elephant Man's toothpaste and you'll be brushing your teeth in hell. Don't get me wrong: Free enterprise strikes me as a proper response to human nature, but materialism entwined with beauty becomes a moral imperative, and progress—the development of new products and new markets—is made to seem convincingly like headway on the arduous march back to the Garden. Restrain beauty from hyping the illusion of perfection, and materialism relaxes into a more harmonious relationship with need. Suppress beauty altogether and you have something that looks like the Iron Curtain. Institutionalize it, and welcome to Orwell's *1984*. Nationalize it and you're in Nazi Germany.

Perfection has always had an off and on war with the world, mostly on; it's on again here in America, and what's got me vexed is I see too many familiar faces along the line of crusaders. These aren't my traditional conservative foes—as enemies, I trust conservatives and their black and white vision. No, the right hasn't budged an inch in relation to a transgressor such as myself, and it's not blue-collar Reagan-era Democrats I feel breathing down my back. The ones I'm worried about are former colleagues from the counterculture, the untrustworthy but swell-intentioned left who, having stopped a war and clobbered social injustice during the civil rights movement, now seemed ordained to challenge human imperfection—indeed, life's imperfection—to three rounds in a New Age Coliseum of Righteousness.

In a different century, right about now is when I'd head for the frontier, trade with the aborigines until the perfectionists came along and swallowed them. I sometimes tell myself that it's beyond me why such an unusual amount of folks are making it their business not just to keep everybody in a straight line, but to encourage someone like me, by legislative force if necessary, to be a perfect angel. But I know better—it's not beyond me to understand.

I remember in parochial school, the nuns badgered us kids to say the rosary, because, they promised, if *everybody* in the world for just *one* day all said the rosary together, there would never be another war. I thought, back then in third grade, Well gosh, let's do it, and my hands circled the beads with vigorous prayer. I knew in spirit the nuns were right, and though I stopped saying the rosary long ago, I still think they're right today, and so are their secular counterparts. I know man's potential is magnificent, just as I know the faster we're bullied toward perfection, the slower the journey will be.

As long as we remain under the umbrella of reality, the most meaningful art, as well as the most virtuous lives, will carry the signature of imperfection, the growth rings of our failures; and retribution against weakness, vice, or unorthodoxy will always play out as hatred of the diversity of human nature. Religion is a proper response to the notion of God, but brutalizing women who feel they must terminate a pregnancy isn't. Marriage is a proper response to love, but as an institution it is neither better nor worse than other arrangements, and certainly its "perfect state" is a most harmful delusion. MADD and SADD are appropriate responses to grief, to cynical promotion, to drunks behind steering wheels, but not appropriate responses to the existence of alcohol and many people's taste for it. Just saying no to drugs is appropriate propoganda for children; adults, however, are responsible for their own actions until proven otherwise. Wanting to be beautiful in the eyes and hearts of those we care about is a beautiful desire, but, to paraphrase the art critic Eric Gill, if we cultivate a respect for truth—the reality of the imperfection of life—and prove ourselves loyal to goodness, which is the spirit of empathy and compassion, then beauty will take care of itself.

JOSEF ŠKVORECKÝ

How I Learned German, and Later English

When I was a boy, everybody whose aspirations reached beyond becoming a laborer had to learn German. So, at the age of nine, I started going twice a week to the old Jewish school where Mr. Neu, the cantor of the local synagogue, eked out a living by teaching little Jewish boys Hebrew, and little gentile boys the language of the Teutons.

The Jewish school was a dark building in the heart of the old diminutive ghetto of Náchod, my native town, which was founded in the thirteenth century. There Mr. Neu lived in a kitchen. There was another room in the flat, presumably a bedroom, but I was never admitted there. During my lessons, Mrs. Neu, a bulky old lady, sat on a low stool with her back against the kitchen range, and from time to time she would briefly interfere with her husband's instruction by the way of clarifying Mr. Neu's grammatical explanations. Mr. Neu was a gentle old man of a short stature; he had a beautiful tenor voice and his first name was Adolf. He had been born at the end of the nineteenth century when no opprobrium stuck to that name as yet. He gave me a German language textbook that started at the beginning indeed. On the first page, there was a black and white picture of a dirty hen's egg, and underneath it said in hard-to-read *Schwabach: "Das ist ein Ei. Ist das ein Ei? Ja, das ist ein Ei."* My German, in which, later on, I achieved pretty good fluency, was born out of that egg.

I loved Mr. Neu and his lessons. His teaching methods were certainly innocent of any pedagogical sophistication but, strangely enough, they seem to have been effective. I learned declension by repeating aloud, again and again, a set of magic words, until Mr. Neu was satisfied and the words became firmly imprinted on my memory:

> *Der gute alte Wein,*
> *des guten alten Weines,*
> *dem guten alten Weine,*
> *den guten alten Wein.*

At my age, I had never tasted wine, and had no idea that wine, as a rule, has to be old in order to be good. But the words sounded like a beautiful magic formula. I still can see the bald head of the gentle cantor nodding in approval of my recitation, *Der gute alte Wein, des guten alten Weines.* . . . For that matter, I doubt that Mr. Neu ever tasted a really good old wine. On his income, he hardly could have afforded it.

I loved the old cantor, I loved his bulky, motionless but not speechless wife at the kitchen range, I loved the shadows of the old school with a dirty old map of Palestine on the wall in the corridor.

On that same wall there hung also a bulletin board of the Mosaic Church, as the Jewish religion used to be called in my native country. Years went by. I reached the age of fourteen and was still going, twice a week, to the old school. Between the egg and me at fourteen lay a long intellectual distance. By then, under the supervision of Mr. Neu, I was studying *Grossmütterchen*, a German translation of the Czech nineteenth-century classical novel by Božena Němcová. The method consisted in me telling Mr. Neu the contents of the consecutive chapters "in my own words." On my way home one day I noticed a longish list of names on the bulletin board. "The following persons have notified the rabbi of their intention to leave the Mosaic Church in order to be baptized into the Catholic Church." In my mind baptism associated with babies. But that Saturday I saw the venerable Father Meloun pouring Holy Water over the head of old Mr. Stein, annointing old Mrs. Ohrenzug, inserting a few grains of salt into the mouth of pretty Gertie Wotitzky, one of the girls whom I admired, at that age still only from a distance.

Mr. Neu did not leave the Mosaic Church, and in the end evil dealt him its deadly blow just as it did the newly baptized Catholics. He didn't even make it to Auschwitz but died in the halfway house of Terezín. Slowly we abandoned *Grossmütterchen* and my lessons changed into endless conversations, in which, more and more often, Mrs. Neu also took part. The subject was the history of Jewish suffering. At the age of fourteen, fifteen, the impact of historical tragedies had not yet reached my soul. Old sufferings sounded like the *Gebrüder* Grimms' fairy tales, an earlier subject of my linguistic training with Mr. Neu. And neither I, nor Mr. and Mrs. Neu were prepared for what was to come. Nobody was. Slaghterhouse imagery was restricted to the fates of cattle, and nobody ever heard of a gas chamber.

Mr. Neu was a tragic optimist. "*Was wir Juden schon alles mitgemacht haben!*"—that was a new and—in a different way—magical sentence I heard every time I sat down at his kitchen table. "*Aber wir haben alles überlebt!"* he would add reassuringly, and then he would launch into the story of his life in the First World War, blissfully unaware that he had been telling me the story twice a week, week after week, for almost a year. Even in the distant past of World War I he had already been making a living as a cantor and private Hebrew and German instructor. But he wouldn't take money. He asked for bread, flour, *auch ein Stückchen Fleisch*. So he survived. *"Mann kann dir Alles nehmen, Josef,"* he would say in his pedagogical tone, *"nur was du da hast—"* he pointed to his bald head, *"das kann dir* Niemand *nehmen!"* He did not know that, unlike in old Austria-Hungary, in the Third Reich heads could be easily *genommen*.

The idyll of the lazy afternoons with *dem guten alten Weine* changed into what was quickly becoming a nightmare. One day the *Aryan Struggle*, a Czech anti-Semitic weekly modeled on Julius Streicher's *Der Stürmer*, printed a story from its unsigned "Náchod correspondent." It informed its readers—the intention, naturally, was to inform the authorities—that Josef Škvorecký, the *Disponent* of the Dresner Bank, was still sending his son to *German* lessons—"German" was set in italics—to the cantor of the local *Jewish*—italics again—synagogue. My father turned red in the face and for the first time in my life I heard him swear. But my twice-weekly walks to the Jewish school stopped.

About three weeks later the doorbell rang. I opened the door and there was old Mr. Neu in a black overcoat, smiling his gentle smile. *"Was ist mit dir, Josef? Ich dachte du warst krank?"* I blushed, then stuttered: *"Ich—ich darf nicht mehr zu Ihnen kommen." "Du darfst nicht?"* Mr. Neu wondered. *"Warum?" "Ich—"* but at that point my father entered, red in the face again, took Mr. Neu to the living room and closed the door. They stayed long, very long. Finally Mr. Neu emerged, bent, it seemed to me, his beautiful nose sticking out of his face that suddenly became thin. He offered me his hand, I took it. *"Also, auf Wiedersehen, Josef!"* he said. *"Auf Wiedersehen, Herr Lehrer—"* I shook his hand but when his black overcoat disappeared behind the door in the hall, I broke down and cried, although I did not precisely know why. And he was gone. At that moment I did not know that there would be no *Wiedersehen*.

That is why, when I listened to Hitler's speeches on the radio, Hitler sounded like Hinkel, Chaplin's dictator, and like Hinkel's, his language was incomprehensible to me, I did not understand one word. Old Mr. Neu did not equip me with any knowledge of that kind of German.

I must apologize for this lengthy digression that really has nothing to do with my next story, which is purely comical: the story of how I learned English. But, perhaps, it provides a useful background. Critics often wonder about the amalgam of tragedy and comedy they find in the writings of my Czech fellow writers, and in my own books. It's nothing that we would do on purpose, to achieve a special effect. That's how life in Central Europe was when we were young. We cannot help ourselves.

The fact is that, while old Mr. Neu was already preparing himself for death, I, at the age of fourteen, fifteen, was eagerly getting ready for life which seemed to be stretching endlessly before me. And while I was still telling the chapter-contents of *Grossmütterchen* to his gently nodding but already doomed head, I was also clandestinely studying another language from a ridiculous little booklet entitled *Teach Yourself English*. Simultaneously, my private French instructor, *Frau Professor* Hlaváček, was telling my mother: "I am sorry to say this, Mrs. *Disponent*, but it seems to be a waste of money to send Josef to French lessons. I have never met a boy who would be so utterly devoid of talent for languages." "But he learned German so well?" objected my mother. Madame Hlaváček shrugged her shoulders. "All I can say," she said in her nasal Czech, "is that he has absolutely no talent for French."

You mustn't think that the enigma of my excellent German and my French that, after a year of private instruction, was still practically nonexistent, was due to either a lack of pedagogical skill on the part of the French lady, or to some profound dislike that obsessed me toward her. No, she was a nice, probably even a pretty lady, but at the age of fourteen boys do not see the beauty of forty-year-old women—at least they didn't, in those days. And when, at that age, you fall in love, you become blind to the charms of other women—or at least you did, in those days.

Because that's what happened. My father did volunteer work as manager of one of the local movie houses that belonged to the Sokol Gymnastic Association, and I helped out in the projection booth. I was in the cinema literally every day and my father, being something of a ladies' man, did not mind that most of the films were restricted. I saw a lot of American westerns, because imports of American films did not stop until Pearl Harbor. But I never felt any urge to master the incomprehensible language of the cowhands, with no clear vowels, full of strangely blurred sounds, and with nothing like the melodic cadenzas of Isa Miranda and other Italian stars of the day, whose language I did understand a little—not much—due to the dictatorial methods of our Latin teachers at the *gymnasium*. I liked its intonations, the singing qualities of that sunny tongue.

That all changed due to an American film that still makes me scan the lists of the late night movies in the weekly *TV Guide*—with no success so far, for it seems that the film has disappeared. Not even Dr. Joe Medjuck, the celebrated walking film encyclopedia of the University of Toronto and now the successful Hollywood producer of *Ghostbusters* and *Legal Eagles*, knew about it. Sometimes I have the feeling that it was only a figment of my imagination, but that cannot be. Even after forty-seven years its name is still firmly embedded in my memory. It was called *Thoroughbreads Don't Cry*. In it I saw and heard a girl by the name of Judy Garland, I caught fire, and only ashes were left of me, that evening in my father's cinema.

Overnight I developed my gigantic antitalent for French, and purchased the horrible manual *Teach Yourself English*. Of its contents I remember only a poem that advertised alcoholism. Although the cat drinks only water, it explained, it lives only fifteen years, and then listed the average life-spans of other water-drinking animals, to end triumphantly in a punchline that said: "But gin-soaked, rum-soaked, whiskey-smelling man / Survives for three score years and ten!" Many of you probably know that masterpiece of the Irish Muse that should have been banned years ago because it still echos in my mind whenever I make a firm resolution.

At that time I did not mind the pernicious effect on me of that textbook. My intention was to learn English in order to write a letter to Judy. And I managed to do exactly that, about a week before Pearl Harbor, which explains why I never got an answer. In that letter I promised the girl that right after the war I would come to Hollywood and—I can't remember what I promised, but it was certainly something sweet. Boys used to be sweet on girls in those days.

I was in the *quarta* at that time, the fourth grade of the *gymnasium*, when it was announced that, beginning with the *quinta*, the students would have a choice between French and English. That was a radical novelty, almost a revolution in the old Czech school system. Traditionally, Czech students had to learn two foreign languages plus Latin. All were mandatory: first German, in the *prima*, then Latin in the *tertia*, and after that French in the *quinta*. But suddenly we had a choice. Because it was a novelty, and because, after the victorious German *Blitzkrieg* in France, everybody's sympathies were with the British, all students of both *quartas* opted for English. That, however, could not be. The *gymnasium* had to offer both English *and* French; after all, what would become of the French teachers? But since, in spite of the rulers of the land, the old *gymnasium* still had not adopted dictatorial methods, the situation created a problem. The headmaster, Mr. Vávra, solved it in a way that shows his deep knowledge of schools, teachers, and students. It was announced that, the following year, students in the English *quinta* would be taught mathematics by Mr. Bivoj, Latin by Mrs. Sýkorová, history by Mr. Stařec, and German by Mr. Hrušovský, whereas students in the French *quinta* would be entrusted to the care of Mr. Padĕra in mathematics, Mrs. Brožová in Latin, Mrs. Trejtnarová in history, and Miss Althammer in German.

Do I have to explain? Surely you know what sort of pedagogic principle was behind the headmaster's decision. Mr. Bivoj was a monster who, in the span of a fifty-minute class, managed to distribute fifteen Fs among the twenty-one students of the English *quinta*. Mrs. Sýkorová demanded that we learn by heart fifty verses of the *Aeneid* weekly. Mr. Stařec, at examination time, was interested only in exact dates of hundreds of unimportant historical events, and Mr. Hrušovský was that rare bird in Bohemia: a *durch-und-durch* Quisling who demanded the clicking of heels when he called us to the blackboard, and began and ended every lesson with the Aryan salute and the singing of the *Horst Wessel Lied*. That was in store for the anglophiles, whereas the francophiles could look forward to a year of comfortable slumber during the chaotic math lessons of the extremely learned and pedagogically inept Mr. Padĕra; to under-the-desk card games while Mrs. Brožová would neglect the *Aeneid* and indulge in the gossip of Mount Olympus, with the girls in class eagerly listening. The francophiles could also look forward to the engaging descriptions of famous battles by Mrs. Trejtnarová who was a remarkable storyteller; and the boys in the class could dream of the extremely pretty Miss Dr. Althammer who, although a Sudetengerman, was the political opposite of Mr. Hrušovský and started and ended each class with Rainer Maria Rilke, read aloud in her mellow German which I understood; it definitely was not the language of Miss Dr. Althammer's nominal *Führer*. I knew Miss Dr. Althammer from the *prima, secunda, tertia,* and *quarta*. I was so charmed by her that, instead of writing a paper on *Der Herbst* she asked us to write, I composed a poem on that worn-out subject of which I still remember the first stanza:

> *Bald kommen Winterstürme mit dem weissen Schneen,*
> *und langsam wird zum Kot der alte, liebe Pfad.*
> *In meinem Herze kalte Winde wehen . . .*
> *Es ist der Herbst. Er kommt in uns're Stadt.*

In spite of the shaky grammar of the poem, I got an A from pretty Miss Dr. Althammer.

The headmaster's decision also revealed that most students in the two *quartas* were cowards. In the end, the headmaster had to abandon democratic coercion methods and ten scared francophiles were sent to the English *quinta* by decree. I did not become a coward. I stuck to my decision to opt for the English *quinta* in spite of the horrifying Mr. Bivoj and the disgusting Mr. Hrušovský. But, then, love gave me strength.

It did not give me knowledge, though. I metamorphosed from an excellent student to a creature that, year after year, barely made it through regular sups to the *sexta*, to the *septima*, and finally to the *octava*, and then almost failed the matriculation exam.

When I realized that I would not gain much by studying the *Teach Yourself English* booklet, and after the English instructor in the *quinta* had proved a disappointment, I begged my desperate mother to permit me to take lessons with Miss Pokorná, a private English teacher in Náchod. Nobody was like old Mr. Neu but Miss Pokorná was an agreeable, though plain, young woman whose parents must have gone crazy in 1938. Instead of staying in England, where Miss Pokorná's father was the business representative of several Czech firms, they returned to Czechoslovakia after Munich, and after March 15, 1939, they couldn't get back to England anymore. Miss Pokorná went to school in England, from age seven to age seventeen, spoke funny Czech but excellent English, and had a teaching method that was not at all bad: She made me read plays, and so, as soon as I mastered the basics, I was exposed to Oscar Wilde, to G. B. Shaw, and to a number of minor British playwrights. Very soon we spoke only English, which she preferred to Czech anyway, and I was so full of the language that, one morning—by that time I was no longer a student at the *gymnasium*—going to work at the local Messerschmitt factory, I greeted the arrogant *Oberkontrolor Herr* Uippelt with "Good morning!" instead of *"Guten Morgen!"* That led to a scene described in my novel *The Engineer of Human Souls*. The story is practically a transcript from life, except that, at the end of the war, Herr Uippelt was not killed but vanished—my last glimpse of him was a misty morning, he was sitting on a bicycle, pedaling like mad, heading westward.

One piece of advice by Miss Pokorná was that, when I talk to myself, I should do so in English. That developed into a habit, a sort of schizophrenia, and it operates to this very day. In my mind, I have been an English speaker for the past forty-five years or so. I even started saying my daily prayers in the blurred tongue of the cowhands with the result that, when I occasionally attend services in the Czech church of St. Wenceslas in Toronto, I am embarrassed by my inability to recite the Lord's Prayer in Czech.

Another, almost daily source of English instruction were the BBC news broadcasts for listeners in the *Reichsgebiet*—on the continent. The announcers used slow and precise enunciation so that they sounded like robots, but on the other hand, nothing was lost on the continental listener. "Tonight—the—British—Liberator—bombers—were—over—Berlin—again." Good news for us. When the BBC continental news was over I dialed Switzerland where a Swiss gentleman with an absolutely gentlemanly voice impartially enumerated that night's aerial losses, but behind his impartiality I sensed a gentlemanly anti-Nazi bias. Perhaps because that gentleman's German was much more like that of Mr. Neu than that of the German announcers with their "*Aus dem Führerhauptquartier wird gemeldet.*" Perhaps because for some gentlemanly reason, the gentleman from Swiss radio always referred to airplanes as "*Apparate.*" The word had strange, almost poetic connotations, especially when the Swiss gentleman was saying "*Fünfundvierzig deutsche Apparate wurden abgeschossen.*" That was good news, too.

As far as the BBC announcers were concerned, in spite of their clear enunciation, there were a few mysteries. One night the robotlike announcer said that, during a raid on Köln, the Germans, for the first time, used jet fighters. My dictionary identified the word "jet" as the device that sprinkled water in front of the aristocratic mansion of Mr. Bartoň-Dobenín, a big industrialist in Náchod. For a few moments I thought that the Germans, apparently at the end of their tether, were using some sort of water gun to wipe the Flying Fortresses out of the skies. But then I remembered a toy of the ancient Greeks that the horrendous, fifty-lines-by-heart-per-week Latin teacher Mrs. Sýkorová used to demonstrate, called Heron's Wheel. It dawned on me that the new Messerschmitts were driven in the same manner as the ancient device.

I learned quite a lot from the nice robots of the BBC. And soon my stubborn decision to master the language of the cowhands and of Shakespeare was strengthened by another emotional experience whose depth rivaled that of pretty Judy. I bought a record from Mr. Maršík, who sold everything from corkscrews to motorcycles, and when I put it on my gramophone I experienced a revelation of beauty, different from but breathtaking as the beauty of the eyes of Frances Gumm. I heard Chick

Webb's saxophones, and suddenly understood what the phrase about "the music of heavenly spheres" was all about. I also heard a lovely voice over the saxophones that sung in the language of the cowhands.

I listened intently. I could make out the first line: "I've got a guy." The second line was more difficult and there seemed to be a grammatical error in it: "He don't dress me in sable." I looked up "sable" in a dictionary published in 1912—English dictionaries were practically unavailable in the Protectorate and I did not acquire my worn-out pocket Webster until later—and it said that the word meant "mourning attire." That was something of a puzzle. Another enigma met me in the third line: "He looks nothing like Gable." In my boyish naiveté I did not connect "Gable" with the film actor—after all, I was interested only in female stars—and my dictionary gave the meaning as "*štít*", that is, the front upper part of a house. Then came an easy line: "But he's mine," and finally a completely incomprehensible one. I loved the music, I loved the voice—I didn't know then that it was that of Ella Fitzgerald, for in those days singers were unimportant, what counted was the band, identified on the label—but I had mixed feelings about the lyrics. Apparently, the girl got herself a boyfriend who refused to dress her in mourning dresses (meaning, perhaps: he is not a necrophile?) and who did not look like a façade—but, then, who does? The last line indicated that she did not mind her boyfriend's surrealistic qualities. Well, then it went on. Again, the clear first line: "I've got a guy," and then: "When he starts in to—" what? Bet me? Beat me? Bit me? What's that? The meaning of the word "petting" was unknown in Bohemia at that time though the practice of petting was not. Another mystery, followed by yet another utterly incomprehensible line.

I knew the arrangement by heart. Our band, Red Music, even played it. But none of the sidemen were able to solve the enigma of the lyrics either. I struggled with it throughout the war, and finally I played the record to Private Herbert Percy Siddell whom you may know if you read my novel *The Cowards*. He was a British P.O.W. to whom my parents gave shelter during the last days of the war. He, however, did not prove to be of much help. He understood only a little more than I—for instance he solved the mystery of the guy who did not look like a façade—but his British ears did not penetrate the meaning of Ella's incomprehensible black lines either.

There were many such songs, and many titles, that made me wonder. "Walking pompously with a piece of animal carcass roasted whole?" "That's what I call balling the Jack?" Does "balling" mean "throwing a ball"? Throwing the ball at Jack, perhaps? But why the definite article? And so on. What a joy it was when, occasionally, very rarely, I did understand nearly everything. Such joy, over a record of Jimmie Lunceford, led to my initiation into the art of translation:

Hvězdy nad hlavou	Every star above
Ví, že mám jen jedinou . . .	Knows the one I love
Svou Sue, jen Sue . . .	Oh Sue, it's you

Later on in life I translated Faulkner and Henry James. But nothing ever was as sweet as when I sang in the old Port Arthur:

I měsíc to ví,	And the moon on high
Že jsi to jenom ty	Simply knows the reason why
Oh Sue, má Sue . . .	Oh Sue, it's you . . .

GARY SNYDER

On the Path and Off the Trail

This is fine old language, from the days when journeys were on foot or by horse with packstock, when our whole human world was a network of paths. We walked long distances then, hundreds or even thousands of miles. People easily walked village to village, garden plot to garden plot, and with a little preparation would set out to ford rivers and go over lonely passes into the next watershed. Paths everywhere, convenient, worn, clear, sometimes even set with distance posts or stones to measure *li*, or *versts*, or *yojana*. In the forested mountains north of Kyoto I came on mossy stone measuring posts almost lost in the dense bamboo-grass groundcover. They marked (I learned much later) the dried-herring-by-backpack trade route from the Japan Sea to the old capital. There are famous trails, the John Muir trail on the crest of the high Sierra, the old Chisholm trail, the Natchez Trace, the Silk Route.

A path is something that can be followed, it takes you somewhere. "Linear." What would a path stand against? "No path." Off the path, off the trail. So what's *off* the path? In a sense everything *else* is off the path. The relentless complexity of the world is off to the side of the trail. To embrace this imagery one must try to re-imagine an earlier way of life, which was lived on paths going from house to chicken coop to outhouse, to the cucumber plot, the pickle shed, the persimmon trees, the neighbors. Beyond the neighborhood it led on to the road "up" to the capital, or to the nearest large market town.

And prior to the life of gardens, pastures, and villages, there was a world of hunters and herders, and for them trails weren't always that useful. For a forager, the path is *not* where you walk for long. Wild herbs, the huckleberries or camas bulbs, the ducks, elk, mushrooms, fiber or dye plants, are all away from the path. The whole range of items that fulfill our needs are in the vast wild terrain. We must wander through it all to know what's there, and to memorize it all—the field—rolling, crinkled, eroded, gullied, ridged (wrinkled like the brain)—holding the map in mind. This is the economic-visualization-meditation exercise of the people of upper paleolithic times, or the Inupiaq and Athabaskans of Alaska of this very day. For the forager, to just stay on the beaten path is to learn nothing new, to encounter no surprises, and to come home empty-handed.

I do not know of any proverbs from agrarian societies that seem to appreciate the pathless. Perhaps the hunting-and-gathering world was already too remote in time to have left many traces. In that greatest and oldest of agrarian civilizations, China, the path or the road or the way, has been given a particularly strong place. From the earliest days of Chinese civilization spiritual, natural, and practical processes and possibilities have been described in the language of path or trail. Such connections are explicitly employed in the cryptic Chinese text that seems to have gathered the earlier lore and restated it for all of later history, called the *Dao De Jing*, "The Classic of the Way and the Power." The word Dao itself means Way, route, road, trail, or to lead/follow. In this text "way" functions as a subtle and elusive term for the nature of nature. (The terminology of Daoist philosophy was adopted by the early Chinese Buddhist translators. To be a serious Buddhist or Daoist was to be a "person of the Way.") "Dao" had already been long used to mean "a course of action, of life, of art or craft" and for the practice that goes into such. It is a piece of genius and luck that the Chinese should have used the same word for a rigorous course, and also for that which transcends "courses." The later Japanese usage almost blends these two levels. In Japanese "dao" is pronounced *do*, as in *kado*, "the way of flowers" or *bushido*, "way of the warrior." (Nowadays the Japanese half-jokingly speak of the "Way of Money Management.")

So in the Far East the idea of "practice" goes back to the times when boys and girls of thirteen or fourteen were apprenticed to a potter, or a company of carpenters, or weavers, dryers, vernacular pharmacologists, metallurgists, cooks, or such. (In earlier millennia children were taught arts and secrets of hunting, gathering, food-storage, mothering, toolmaking.) The youngsters left the warmth of their tight little homes to go and sleep in the back of the potting shed, and be given the single task of mixing clay for three years, or sharpening chisels for three years for the carpenters. It was often unpleasant. And then the apprentice was gradually inducted into some very precise habits of movement, standards of workmanship, and in-house working secrets. They also began to experience—right then, at the beginning, what it was to be "one with your work." The student hopes not only to learn the mechanics of the trade, but to absorb some of the teacher's power, his or her gift, the *mana*. One must give oneself up to the idiosyncracies, irrationalities, and "meanness" of the teacher, and not go complaining. It is understood that the teacher will not be a perfect human being and will test one's patience and fortitude endlessly. The apprentice must not think of turning back, but just take it, go deep, and have no other interests. For an apprentice there is just this one study, to the limit.

It should then be no surprise that in the Zhuang-zi book, a third-century B.C. witty, radical, pre-postmodern Daoist text, perhaps a century or so younger than the *Dao De Jing*, there are a number of craft and "knack" passages. "The Cook Ting" cut up an ox for Lord Wenhui with dance-like grace and ease. "I go along with the natural makeup, strike in the big hollows, guide the knife through the big openings, and follow things as they are. So I never touch the smallest ligament or tendon, much less a main joint. . . . I've had this knife of mine for nineteen years and I've cut up thousands of oxen with it, and yet the blade is as good as though it had just come from the grindstone. There are spaces between the joints, and the blade of the knife has really no thickness. If you insert what has no thickness into such spaces, then there's plenty of room. . . . That's why after nineteen years the blade of my knife is still as good as when it first came from the grindstone." "Excellent!" said Lord Wenhui. "I have heard the words of Cook Ting and learned how to care for life!" These stories not only bridge between the spiritual and the practical, but also tease us with images of how totally accomplished one might become if one applied oneself far enough.

In practice the "limit" is a realization of accomplishment on the part of dedicated craftspersons that levels out at about age forty. Then they begin to teach in turn, and to pass their skills along. Perhaps they then turn to other interests—take up a little calligraphy on the side, go visit temples, broaden themselves. But even with this expansion of interests, no one ever doubts that the application of yourself wholeheartedly to your calling is what really counts. For a worker who has dedicated him or herself with this spirit to even the humblest craft, there may also be a clear sense of self-discovery, the realization of the connections and interdependences of mind, materials, and energy, and the discovery that one can become a spinning ball of clay, a curl of pure white wood off the edge of a chisel, can be one of the many hands of Kannon the Bodhisattva of Compassion. No matter how humble in theoretical social status, the craftsperson has his or her dignity and pride. This is not to be taken as a defense of feudalism, but an explication of one side of how things worked in medieval Japan. The craft-and-training ethic is also the source of the style of high-culture Japanese arts and crafts, and is at work in the revived folk-arts of Japan. The recent re-emergence, among city and country people alike, of "Taiko" (which are great energetic drum-ensembles—once a village festival pastime) has brought a powerful mix of folk-religion, village communalism, and aesthetic intensity into down-town and university performance halls in both California and Japan. Its practitioners predictably speak of it as a "Way."

These work-lore, craft-lore apprenticeships and the attitudes they have promoted for millennia are what lie behind the style and language of later monasteries and churches and their spiritualized appropriation of "practice." So it is that Zen, the crispest example of the "self-help" (*jiriki*) wing of Mahayana (the big wagon that can take everybody along) Buddhism, has developed its community life and discipline as though it were an apprenticeship program in a traditional craft. A monk at Daitoku-ji once said to me, of the newly installed and relatively youthful Nakamura Roshi, "He's like an old-time carpenter: He won't accept anything that isn't grasped totally and doesn't fit perfectly."

Monastic novices are told to leave their pasts behind—family, friends, dreams—and become one-pointed and unexceptional in all ways except the intention to enter this narrow gate of finely tuned traditional prac-tice. *Hone o oru*, as the saying goes—"break your bones"—a phrase also used (in Japan) by working men, by the martial arts halls, and in modern sports and mountaineering. Zen practice establishments are called *senmon dojo*, which is roughly translated "Place of specialized practice of the Way." A steady schedule of meditation and work is folded into weekly, monthly, and annual cycles of ceremonies and observations that go back to Sung-dynasty China and in part clear back to the India of Shakyamuni's time. Within that effort, one is called on to become mindful, focused, and committed to the welfare of all beings, applying oneself with at least as much purpose to such goals as another youth on a different path might be applying to learning his or her trade or calling. Hours of sleep are short, the food is meager, the rooms spare and unheated, and this is as true in the worker's or farmer's world as it is in the monastery. Such rigor is not always productive. It can make some people nervous, and those with certain weaknesses and shynesses may be thus excluded from these exercises. No doubt that's a loss for both the individuals and the traditions.

And then: There is a point beyond which this kind of training and practice cannot go. In all the arts and crafts there comes a time when further training or practice is not exactly what's called for. If there is a next step (and strictly speaking there need not be one, for the skill of the accomplished craftsperson and the production of impeccable work that reflects the best of the tradition is certainly enough in one lifetime—) it is to "go beyond training" for the final flower, which is not guaranteed by effort alone. After that one can be free, with the craft and from the craft. Seami in his book on the art of *No* drama performance, *The Transmission of the Flower*, speaks of this accomplishment as "surprise." For the person doing it this is the "surprise" of discovering oneself without a self, one with the work, moving in effortless emptiness and grace. For the reader or viewer or hearer, it is the shock of being present at the Creation. (The traditional Singers of Mojave Creation-dream Epics would each argue their own version, saying "I was there.")

The Occidental approach to the arts—since the rise of the bourgeoisie, if we like—is to push everyone to be creative from the first, and to be continually doing something new. This puts a considerable burden on the artists of every generation, a double burden since they think they must dismiss the work of the generation before and then do something supposedly better and different. The emphasis on individual practice and training, on apprenticeship, has become very slight. In a society that follows "ways," creativity is understood as something that comes almost by accident and is unpredictable, a gift to certain individuals that cannot be programmed into the curriculum, and is better in small quantities. It is suggested that one should be grateful for it when it comes along, but we don't count on it, and perhaps we don't need it. When it does appear it's the real thing. It takes a powerful impulse for a student-apprentice who has been told for eight or ten years to "always do what was done before," as in the great production tradition of folk pottery, to turn it a new way. What happens then? The old guys in this tradition look and say, "Ha! you did something new! Good for you!"

Here's the rest of the picture of the life in a Japanese Rinzai Zen *dojo:* cross-legged sitting meditation four or five hours a day. Doing physical work along with everyone else, everyone treated alike—gardening, pickling, firewood cutting, cleaning the baths, taking turns in the kitchen. And then periodic interviews with the teacher-in-residence, the Roshi, "old master," at least twice a day, in which you make a presentation to him or her of your grasp of the meditation assignment that was given. Memorizing certain sutras and learning some rituals that you must conduct or participate in. Learning fine details of an etiquette that is rather archaic and some elder vocabulary that is only used in Zen life now. Learning how to work with lay supporters, often farmers, a downright convivial relationship that reaches from discussions on new seed species to conducting funerals in the main family house. Walking city streets and country lanes begging while chanting, and visiting farther country regions on special begging trips for radishes or rice. And then there are occasional huge gatherings of hundreds of monks of the temple lineage, for a major memorial.

The main practice is sitting in meditation and then visiting the teacher's room over and over again responding to the puzzling meditation themes that in themselves push one over the hump of daily discipline and into the realm of creatively not getting it, and then getting it. It is considered essential that these exercises be done as part of a community that works hard together. When one enters this life one is told, "It will take years, you will not have any sense of making progress, don't have ideas about being original, and "break your bones." I recall—during one of the long meditation retreats called *sesshin*—hearing the Roshi's lecture on the lines "The perfect Way is without difficulty. Strive hard!" This is the fundamental paradox of the Way. One can be called on to break one's bones, but we must also be reminded that the effort of following a path can itself lead one astray, lead one into mere learning, or power, or formal accomplishment. Talents may be nourished by discipline, but discipline alone will not get one beyond "effort" and into the territory of "free and easy wandering" (a Zhuang-zi term). One must take care not to be victimized by one's talent for self-discipline and hard work, it's too easy that way to be a lifetime success in craft or business. One might never get a chance to find out what one's higher—and more playful—talents might have been. "We study the self to forget the self" said Dogen. "When you forget the self, you become one with the ten thousand things." Ten thousand things means all of nature, both natural and supernatural: ephemeral, contingent, ungraspable, subtle, vast, enduring, woven, seamless, wild. When we are open and empty that world can occupy us. Yet we are still called on to wrestle with the curious phenomenon of the complex human self, needed but excessive, that resists letting the world in, and the project given each individual to scrape, soften, tan it. In Zen practice there is a course of action and a curriculum. The intent of the *koan* or meditation theme is merely to provide the student with a brick to knock on the gate, to get through and beyond that first barrier. Then there are many further *koans* that work as flexing, softening, extending, and enacting exercises—enabling one first to be empty, and then let that emptiness embrace all being and reconcile dichotomies.

The *Dao De Jing* itself gives us the most subtle interpretation of what Path might be. It starts out by saying this: "The Way that can be followed ('wayed') is not the constant Way." *Dao ke dao fei chang dao.* The first line, first chapter. Thus it seems to be saying, "A path that can be followed is not a *spiritual* path." Engaging with a spiritual path requires us to recognize that although we can and must work at "following" it, the intention of such engagement can only be accomplished when the "follower" has been forgotten. The Way is without difficulty—it does not of itself propose obstacles to you, it is open in all directions. You probably do, however, suffer from obstacles of your own making—so the Old Teacher said "Strive hard!" It seems most human beings must discover this for themselves.

There are religious schools however that say, "Don't try to prove something hard to yourself, it's a waste of time, your ego and intellect will be getting in your way; let all such fantastic aspirations go, live with a trusting and compassionate heart and you will be strolling in the Pure Land." Such were the the teachings of Ramana Maharshi, Krishnamurti, and the Zen Master Bankei. This was Alan Watts's version of Zen. Such is Jodo-shin, or Pure Land Buddhism, which elegant old Morimoto Roshi (who spoke Osaka dialect) said "is the only school of Buddhism that can scold Zen." It can scold it, he says, for trying too hard, for considering itself too special and for being proud. One must have respect for the nakedness of these teachings, and their ultimate correctness, but they are frustrating for "motivated people," in that no real instruction is offered the hapless seeker. (That indeed is the message.) There are some individuals, to be sure, who seem not to need to go through deliberate spiritual training, but maybe that's only because they have already been ripened in the give-and-take of life. A few are karmic direct-apprehenders.

There are paths that can be followed, and there is also a path that cannot—it is not a path, it is the wildness itself. There is a "going" but no goer, no destination, there is only the wild system. I first stumbled "off the trail" in the mountains of the Pacific Northwest, at twenty-two, while employed on a lookout in the North Cascades. I then determined that I would study Zen in Japan. I had a glimpse of it again in a Japanese monastery, at age thirty, and it helped me realize that I did not wish to live as a monk. I moved to live near the monastery, and participated in the meditation, the ceremonies, and the farmwork as a layperson. When I returned to North America in 1969 with my then wife and firstborn son, I came as a layperson (I'm not even sure what "lay" means, I'm just an ordinary person) and have lived thus since. We moved to the mountains. We live close to nature and land-use politics. This circle of neighbors and friends with whom I work and practice, people who are drawn to Zen and also love the wild, has been gingerly moving in the direction of the deprofessionalization of spiritual leadership: taking note of Ivan Illich's point that there are now numerous "disabling professions" and that we must undertake to recover what is innately our own territory of concern from experts.

This effort has some obvious pitfalls. The entirely dedicated and good-hearted Zen priests of Japan (and real spiritual leaders everywhere) will explain the necessity of having some specialists and experts in these matters by saying that ordinary people cannot get deep enough into the teachings because they cannot give enough time to it. Quite true, the problems for ordinary people are enormous—questions of distraction, money, addictions, child-raising, "car wars," and far worse. If people do gain time to think and look more broadly, they must also concern themselves with corruption of character amongst our leaders, threats of total war, environmental destruction, and so forth. We lead messy, contradictory, partial lives, at the *best*. Many look to the elegance of temples or shrines or churches (and the art museums, libraries, and universities) for models of sane and peaceful order and education. Some yearn for a better social structure. Some find/forget themselves fishing or backpacking or gardening or helping out on the winter bird count. For those who see training, or practice, as essential to what they do (rather than theory, or spectatorship), two questions keep coming up. One is the thorny problem of teachers and their professionalization, the other is how to "get out of your own way."

American groups that do Zen Buddhist practice usually try to make their lives more monastic and emulate the style of a Japanese *dojo*. People who are dedicated to the idea of spiritual practice like to think that the professionals of temple and monastery are indeed the guides and are ultimately more spiritual. It's quite easy to understand why, especially since our own society provides few secular models for cooperative, selfless behavior. But on the matter of the forms in a spiritual training school there is an interesting history to recall: The rules of the Buddhist religious orders were not developed as adversarial to daily life. They are an intensified version of ordinary living—the models for monasteries are old natural societies, the village networks of the neolithic. The very source of the style of the Buddhist organization with its rules of voting and empowerment, established by Shakyamuni the historical Buddha, was the tribal government of the small Shakya ("Oak tree") nation that he was born into. The Shakya nation was a tiny republic much like the League of the Iroquois. Thus the Buddhist sangha is modeled on the political forms of a neolithic-derived democratic community. This is not exceptional; it can be argued that the relatively stable, peaceful, self-governing life of neolithic peoples remains in the memory of most civilizations as nostalgia and ideal and for some groups in history it was the half-remembered model for deliberate utopian social experiments. We sometimes call precivilized societies "natural" because they are self-maintaining, self-governing, taking form from the local regional and biological conditions, largely free of "church and state," and because they often allow great diversity of human behavior and endeavor. In the more sparsely populated world environment of four and more thousand years ago, there was little or no scarcity of space or resources. The economic and spiritual affairs of such societies were entwined on a daily basis with the fabric of nature. The ancient traditions of apprenticeship to craft provided the bones for intentional community discipline. Such societies were not perfect or ideal, but they worked well enough for millennia to leave us with memories of a "golden age."

A lay Zen, or Chan group's approach should not be a matter of seeing how much it can manage to be like a monastery, but how it can be more like a natural community. We can also get some lessons in this way that can't be provided by the "tender junior Buddha"—as Whitman called him, or any of the "world" religious traditions with their dreams of world influence. There are lessons that come from actual life: work and family, love life, the perennially unresolved and utterly essential life of couples living through and in eros, with the subsequent task and delight of nourishing infants, and the life of the spirit in *that*. The instruction of youth, the initiation of adolescents, the councils and discussions that shape policy, are responsibilities that come to all adult men and women. Employers, bankers, mechanics, accountants, doctors, are keepers of despised mysteries we fear to approach, yet must. And there are all the ecological-economical connections of human communities with other living beings, the council of all species, pushing us toward a profound meditation on ultimate identity. We must meditate, it seems, on taxes (and their forms) almost as earnestly as on death. We are inevitably apprenticed to the same teacher that the religious institutions originally apprenticed to: daily reality.

Make *this* into a Way, a Path? it starts with acknowledging one's gender, culture and race, one's context and place, capacities, skills, disabilities, possibilities. And, as apprentice to Being, getting a sense of immediate politics and history, getting control of one's own time, mastering the twenty-four hours. Doing it well, without self-pity. It is as hard to get the children herded into the car pool and down the road to the bus as it is to chant sutras in the Buddha-hall on a cold morning. One move is not better than the other, each can be quite boring, and they each have the quality of repetition. Repetition and ritual and their good results come in many forms. To make this real we must sacramentalize, give mindful regard to, these daily moments. Our messy, contradictory, incomplete lives are all we have. They will do just fine. Changing the filter, wiping noses, going to meetings, picking up around the house, washing dishes, checking the dipstick—just don't let yourself think these are distracting you from your more serious pursuits. This round of duties is not a set of difficulties we hope to escape from so that we may do our "practice," which will put us on a "path"—it *is* our path. It is its own fulfillment too, for who would want to set enlightenment against nonenlightenment, when each is its own full reality, its own complete delusion. We can appreciate whatever condition we find ourselves in. And effectively and unsentimentally change it, too.

Am I saying, then, that we must submit to the demeaning and tedious domesticated world? Press on: It has been said before that "practice is the path." It's easier to understand this when we see that the "perfect way" is not a path that leads somewhere easily defined, some goal that is at the end of a progression. We generally know that we don't want to be helicoptered to the top of the mountain when we *could* hike up it. Being on the summit is the least of the exercise, although the nonmountaineering world insists that we provide a photo of the people standing at the highest point. We do climb peaks because the view is extraordinary, the danger and hardship its own kind of pleasure, the cooperation and comradeship is deep friendship, and that the summit is at one end of the trail. Daily reality, from the victim's standpoint, is impermanent and unsatisfactory and one would wish to escape it. The spiritual hero (or jock) turns it into a challenge to be met and overcome, and declares the view from the top to be superb, just persevere. The real *play* is in the surprising act of leaving the path behind, to go "off trail"—away from this minimal trace of human or animal regularity aimed at some practical or spiritual purpose (most early human trails are simply following the older game paths). We go out onto the "trail that cannot be followed" which leads everywhere and nowhere, a limitless fabric of possibilities, elegant variations a million-fold on the same themes, yet each point unique. Every boulder on a talus slope is different, no two grains of sand on the shore are identical. Would one even want to imagine that one part was more important than another? What is more shapely, the trail, or off the trail? What sustains us? One will never come onto the heaped-up house of a bushy-tailed woodrat, made of twigs and stones and leaves, unless one plunges into the manzanita thickets. Strive hard!

We find some ease and comfort in our house, by the hearth, and on the paths nearby. We find there too the tedium of chores and the staleness of repetitive trivial affairs. But the rule of impermanence means that nothing is repeated for long. Daily reality is transparent and mysterious. Matter itself is utterly amazing. Calming a child's tantrum is like the plunge into the woods that might discover a nest. The ephemerality of all our acts puts us into a kind of wilderness-in-time. We see the frailness of our bits of insight, our energy, of our sense of order. Embracing the whole human realm are the nets of inorganic and biological processes that nourish all entities, flowing with underground rivers or floating as spiderwebs in the sky. Life and matter at play, chilly and rough, hairy and tasty. This ease is of a larger order than the little enclaves of provisional orderliness that we call ways, it *is* the Way.

All our skills and practices are but tiny reflections of the wild world that is innately and loosely orderly, and in the very nature of things wide open. There is nothing like stepping away from the road and heading into a new part of the watershed. Not for the sake of newness, but for the sense of coming home to our whole terrain. "Off the trail" is another name for the Way, and sauntering off the trail is the practice of the wild. But of course we need paths and trails, and we will always be teaching and maintaining them. You first must be on the path, before you can turn and walk into the wild.

WILLIAM TREVOR

On the Way to Suburbia

"Damn!" she said when she was old, on discovering there wasn't another packet of potato crisps. She added a handful of cornflakes to the plate of cold meat she had prepared for her husband, in the hope that he wouldn't be able to tell the difference. She loved the theater, novels and the wireless, breakfast in bed and sitting in the sun. All household matters were tedious.

Photographs taken eighty years ago show a child with long dark hair and solemn eyes. On a Swiss ski slope a slight girl—already beautiful—smiles shyly. More confident, she is elusive on the promenade at Montreux, a movement of her head impatiently blurring the camera's impertinence.

This is an appallingly dull place, she wrote of Wimereux in 1909. She was sixteen then, trailing round the resort hotels of Europe with her mother and her older, more sophisticated sister. Her most intimate friend was her journal, to which she confided a whole adolescent cagmag—as she would say—of secrets, comments, and opinions.

Wimereux, August 6th. Edith was talking to me today about getting married. She says she would do it if she met a man rich enough, but it wasn't worth marrying just for a home etc. unless one did it really well; and then she added that she had never met a really rich eligible man. But she doesn't seem inclined to go the whole hog, as Aunt Matilda did, and marry a person she hated.

They were upper-class Anglo-Indians, displaced by the death of the girls' father. They passed their time reading, writing letters, wondering about the future, and observing their fellow hotel-guests.

Lausanne, September 1st. There is a most amusing trio staying here, a husband, a wife, and a bow-wow. The husband has gray hair and nice absent eyes. The wife has a plain face, what she considers a fascinating giggle, and lovely golden hair (all her own). The bow-wow's hair is dark and barber's blocky. He has a horridly affected way of speaking, and the wife and he are so affectionate. The husband takes it all quite calmly. If he were not married I should say he was on the way to being super.

The slang of the Raj flavors every page. There are doubts and speculations, uncertainty about the future. Should they return to India, or settle for England now? What would living in a suburb be like? Should they simply continue to traipse about the Continent?

Venice, September 13th. Edith was saying the other day how abstract subjects have come back into fashion for conversation between men and girls. In Mother's day, girls had no idea of conversation with a man beyond flirting, and certainly that can hardly rank as an abstract subject. Yet it seems to me that flirting is as much a test of a man's decentness as evening clothes are supposed to be of his appearance.

Letters arrive from Geoffrey and Gordon and Stanley and Wilfrid (*Poor camel, he has failed his exam*). Bicard has been gone on somebody for as long as ten years. Charlie has had bad luck in a briefer romance. Marriage does not seem easy: A stupid wife believes blindly in her husband's virtues, a clever one notices his coarseness and unreasonableness. But there was spirit enough for whatever game of chance had to be played. *I want to grow up as quickly as ever I can. I want to have great fun.*

She intends to enjoy herself a great deal more than her sister did at the same age in India. She sees no reason not to try at least, instead of envying other people. *Emerson says envy is ignorance. He really isn't bad in places, Emerson.*

I met her forty years later, a tiny woman in the English suburb they had wondered about. The wit and perception that were being sharpened in her girlhood journal had mellowed, but the edge of neither was entirely gone. She had come to terms with the suburb and with marriage, with wars and death, and the funless austerity of the England of that time. She no longer kept a journal. She didn't much bother with herself anymore.

An unobtrusive privacy replaced that eagerness to enjoy. A chasm separated the woman from the child and the girl, but I was not aware of it because I did not then know about the other person she had been. The survival kit didn't show. There were no regrets, no words of disappointment, only nicely judged gossip and warmth. The confident anticipation that bubbles through the pages I later read had been transformed into qualities more suited to middle age: Her kindness was extraordinary, her modesty attractive, her sympathy rare. "Amusing" was still her favorite word, and there were traces of the beauty she had once considered not to be a camera's business. Nor had the style of the girl who thought Emerson not bad in places been lost. In the first moment of meeting her I knew she was a singular woman. If she hadn't had great fun herself, she saw no reason to lose faith in it for everyone else. That generosity is not often found.

Blockley, Gloucestershire

When I think of landscape that is special I find myself back in the County Cork of my childhood. But as a child in Youghal and Skibbereen—poor little towns in those days—I wondered about England: There was a Royal Family, Henry Hall on the wireless, important weddings in the Daily Sketch. England spelled elegance, and style, and graciousness. It had a capital city so huge that I was assured it would stretch all the way from Skibbereen to Cork City. Occasionally a G.B. car went by, always gleaming, gray or black. If it stopped by the roadside a picnic would take place, a special little kettle placed on a primus stove, sponge cake brought in a tin box from Surrey. Accents were polished, ladies kindly smiled. One of them gave me a fig-roll once.

There was a board-game we played, long before Monopoly. It had to do with train journeys up and down England, all of them beginning at railway stations that had a magic ring: Paddington, Victoria, Waterloo, King's Cross. "Gloucestershire?" my father said. "It's a county. Like County Cork or County Wexford." If you were lucky with your dice you might hurry away by G.W.R. to Gloucestershire, while others were stuck en route to Huddersfield or Belper. I imagined a leafy place, nice for picnics, threads of gold among the green. It spread itself out like a tapestry in my mind: Nothing was ruined there, no burnt-out houses or smashed castles, no brambles growing through rusty baronial gates as we had in County Cork. The Duke of Gloucester would never have permitted that.

Many years later, when I was in my early twenties but still had not once left Ireland, I came a little closer to Gloucestershire, told about it by the girl I was to marry: about the Slaughters and the Swells, and Adlestrop and Evenlode, in particular about the village of Blockley. That Cotswold world began in marvelous, onion-domed Sezincote, one of Gloucestershire's stately homes which in 1939 briefly became a haven from German bombs. Afterwards there was a cottage in Blockley itself: Little Manor, a bit overgrown these days, opposite the smart new restaurant that has put the village on the gastronomic map.

For being told about this part of England made me want to visit it, and returning now, I find my childhood vision of an orderly dukedom shattered yet again: It's the hard years of war that come rushing back on a warm July afternoon. Cycling to the grammar school in Chipping Campden, taking the wet batteries to be charged, that's where Miss Tavender lived, that's cruel Fish Hill where you pushed your bike for a mile. The three great houses—Northwick Park and Batsford as well as Sezincote—cannot be as once they were, nor is Sleepy Hollow nor Donkey Lane. And Rock Cottage, where that doubtful prophetess Joanna Southcott spent the last ten years of her life, has been burnt down. But leeks still thrive in the garden that was Sergeant Wall's, and Rose of Sharon in old Mrs. Whale's. A peartree still decorates a façade in St. George's Terrace, the house called Rodneys is still the smartest. Irises and lacy delphiniums prosper, valerian sprouts from the cracks in soft brown walls. Old-fashioned roses are everywhere.

In war-time Blockley there were Italian prisoners of war, laughing while they mended the roads. American soldiers eyed the solitary wives and gave a party for their children, real paste in the sandwiches. "Aluminum for the war effort!" these same children cried from door to door, taking it in turn to push the pram. They came away with broken saucepans, and between his dozes on a sunny step the village fat boy watched and was amused. He watched as drowsily when the bull ran madly down the long main street, and again when Mrs. Jones was dragged the length of it by her husband, unexpectedly home on leave. He watched while villagers brought Mr. French a single egg so that he could bake them a cake in Half Crown Cottage. He listened without pleasure while Mr. Lunn consoled himself with Bach, or roused himself to warn against the churchyard in the blackout, his thin voice telling of its restless dead.

Blockley nestles, as Broad Campden does, and Shipston-on-Stour. The wolds encase them: lazy undulations, fields guarded by trim stone walls. Patches of sheep whiten the hilly sward, poppies blaze through a field of rye. In the July sunshine the roadside verges are a yard high, yellowing cow-parsley sprinkled with crane's-bill and campion. Elder fills the hedgerows.

In Stow-on-the-Wold you pass down an ancient passage to the Gents, and the hard black oak of door frames seems tougher than the ubiquitous stone. Above hotels and pubs the wrought-iron signs are motionless on a tranquil afternoon. "The real McCoy!" an American cyclist proclaims, pausing in one town or another, it doesn't matter which. Tea-rooms are full of shortbread and Bendicks' chocolate mint crisps, part of the scenery.

Domestic pastoral: The Cotswold scene is that, the stone of houses is the stone of the wolds, and Cotswold faces are part of nature too. At dusk, old women in summer dresses make the journey through their village to look at someone else's flowers. At dawn, unshaven itinerants move dourly through the fields from one farm to the next. With passing years, these small conventions remain, even if Northwick Park has become a business school and Blockley's silk mills are bijou residences now. The Gloucestershire voice hasn't altered much, either: On market day in Moreton-in-Marsh it's matter-of-fact and firm, without the lilt that sweetens it further west. Like the countryside it speaks for, its tones are undramatic, as if constantly aware that life owes much to sheep, that least theatrical of animals. While landscape and buildings merge, nobody who lives here is likely to forget that the riches and good sense of wool merchants created the Cotswolds.

When I walk in England I walk in Dartmoor or Derbyshire, and I have chosen Devon to live in. I like the English seaside out of season, Budleigh Salterton and Bexhill; it is Somerset I watch playing cricket. But best of all in England there's Gloucestershire to visit and to stroll through, while pheasants rise elegantly from its park lands and rivers modestly make their way. No matter how remote or silent a wood may be there's always a road or a person within reach: I think of Tennyson when I walk in Gloucestershire, the way that runs through the field, two lovers lately wed, an abbot on an ambling pad. I think as well of old Mrs. Whale in her lifetime and Sergeant Wall in his, of Albert the footman at Sezincote, Miss Tavender a schoolmistress, and Joanna Southcott. Blockley Brass Band still performs, weather permitting; there are outings to distant Ramsgate. "Dubious Dog Contest," the sign outside the British Legion hall announces, and I imagine the pink tongues panting on a Saturday afternoon, setters and spaniels that aren't quite the thing, terriers that should have been Dalmatians. The children of the children who ate the American soldiers' paste sandwiches self-consciously tug the leashes. The sun has brought the hollyhocks out.

The countryside is the setting, but people come first: In spite of disturbance and change it is that that continues, and returning now I feel my childhood instinct was not far wrong. In this warm July, or in their war-time years, in snow or sun, the wolds are unique; and their towns and villages perfectly complement them. Crowded with hastening tourists, all three retain their essence: England is unstifled here.

CONTRIBUTORS

JOHN BARTH teaches in the Johns Hopkins University Writing Seminar. His most recent novel is *The Tidewater Tales*.

RICK BASS lives in Montana and has most recently published *The Watch*, a collection of short stories, and *Oil Notes*, a collection of essays. "Notes from Yaak" is excerpted from his next book, *Winter*, to be published by Seymour Lawrence/Houghton Mifflin in February 1990.

ROY BLOUNT, JR.'s most recent books are *Soupsongs/Webster's Ark* and *Now, Where Were We?* He is currently writing a novel.

ANNIE DILLARD is the author of eight books, most recently *The Writing Life*, what she calls a sort of memoir. A few paragraphs from "Luke" appeared in *An American Childhood*.

DENIS DONOGHUE is one of the foremost critics of Irish, English, and American literature. His many books include *The Ordinary Universe*, *The Selected Essays of R. P. Blackmur*, and *William Butler Yeats*.

MICHAEL DORRIS is the author of *The Broken Cord* and a novel, *A Yellow Raft in Blue Water*. He is married to Louise Erdrich and lives in New Hampshire.

GERALD EARLY is the author of *Tuxedo Junction: Essays in American Culture* (The Ecco Press). He is associate professor of English at Washington University in St. Louis.

MONROE ENGEL's most recent novel, *Statutes of Limitations*, was published by Knopf in 1988.

ALMA GUILLERMOPRIETO is a former South American bureau chief for *Newsweek*. Her first book, *Sadness Is Over*, will be published by Knopf in February 1990.

CLAUDIO MAGRIS teaches in the faculty of literature and philosophy at the University of Trieste. *Danube* (translated into English by Patrick Creagh), from which "Castles and Huts" is excerpted, is forthcoming from Farrar, Straus & Giroux (Translation © 1989 by William Collins & Co., Ltd., and Farrar, Straus & Giroux, Inc. All rights reserved).

PETER MATTHIESSEN's *The Tree Where Man Was Born* (nominated for the National Book Award) has been called "*the* Africa book par excellence." A second book on an East African wilderness, *Sand Rivers*, won the John Burroughs Medal. His most recent work is *On the River Styx, and Other Stories*.

HAROLD NORSE's *Memoirs of a Bastard Angel* (from which "A Tangier Episode" is excerpted) will be published in November 1989 by William Morrow. He is the author of twelve books of poetry and a "cut-up" novel, *Beat Hotel*, with a preface by William S. Burroughs.

JOSIP NOVAKOVICH teaches English composition and history at Santee Sioux Community College in Nebraska. His stories have appeared in *Ploughshares*, *NER/BLQ*, *The Paris Review*, and elsewhere.

JEAN REDWOOD lived and worked in the British Embassy in Moscow during the late Stalinist and cold war eras and has traveled throughout the Soviet Union in recent years. She is the author of *Russian Food: All the Peoples, All the Republics*, published by Oldwicks Press (Suffolk, England).

ROBERT SHACOCHIS is the author of *Easy in the Islands* and *The Next New World*. His work has received an American Book Award and the Rome Prize Fellowship from the American Academy of Arts and Letters.

JOSEF ŠKVORECKÝ is a Czech-Canadian writer who was born in 1924 in Náchod, Bohemia, and emigrated to Canada in 1969. He is the author of many novels and short stories and several film scripts, including *The Cowards*, *Dvořák in Love*, *The Engineer of Human Souls*, *Sins for Father Knox* and *The Swell Season*.

GARY SNYDER won a Pulitzer Prize for his 1974 book of poetry, *Turtle Island*. His most recent collection is *Left Out in the Rain*. "On the Path and Off the Trail" is excerpted from "Practice of the Wild," a work in progress.

WILLIAM TREVOR's last novel was *The Silence in the Garden*. He has since edited *The Oxford Book of Irish Short Stories*.

Errata
The editors regret the following omission from *Antæus* 62:

"The Mirror of the Unknown" by Danilo Kiš was translated into English by Michael Henry Heim.

Modern Masters & Classic Collections

MODERN VOICES

Alfred Corn
THE WEST DOOR
"Clearly the result of rigorous craft....No potential has been left buried, no meaning unconsidered"—*Boston Review.*
0-14-058604-0   96 pp. $8.95

Anna Akhmatova
SELECTED POEMS
D. M. Thomas, translator. Nearly 100 selections span Akhmatova's career. "Among the best, the most authoritative, of all recent translations from the Russian"—Martin Seymour-Smith.
0-14-058558-3   160 pp. $7.95

Elizabeth Spires
ANNONCIADE
Pure, mystical, yet elegant poems, "striking and sophisticated....Should win Spires a serious audience"—*The New York Times Book Review.*
0-14-058638-5   80 pp. $8.95

COLLECTIONS

PENGUIN BOOK OF GREEK VERSE
Constantine A. Trypanis, editor. Nearly 350 works trace the historic glory and modern power of Greek poetry from Homer and Hesiod to George Seferis and Odysseus Elytis, in Greek original with English prose translation.
0-14-058595-8   704 pp. $9.95

A BOOK OF ENGLISH POETRY
G. B. Harrison, editor. From the 14th to the 19th centuries, the finest in the English tradition is represented in selections from more than 60 poets.
0-14-058579-6   416 pp. $5.95

THE PENGUIN BOOK OF ENGLISH CHRISTIAN VERSE
Peter Levi, editor. Spanning five centuries, a composite portrait of English religious expression.
0-14-058602-4   480 pp. $7.95

THE PENGUIN BOOK OF GERMAN VERSE
Leonard Forster, editor. More than 300 chronologically arranged works from the heroic *Hildebrandslund* saga to 20th-century expressionism, in German original with plain prose English translation.
0-14-058546-X   512 pp. $6.95

THE PENGUIN BOOK OF MODERN YIDDISH VERSE
Irving Howe, Ruth Wisse, and Khone Shmeruk, editors. A comprehensive bilingual anthology. "A landmark volume"—*The New Yorker.*
0-14-009472-5   752 pp. $14.95

INSIDE BLACK AUSTRALIA
An Anthology of Aboriginal Poetry
Kevin Gilbert, editor. 150 highly charged works rooted in aboriginal life.
0-14-011126-3   240 pp. $7.95

CLASSICS

Sir Thomas Wyatt
THE COMPLETE POEMS
Edited and introduced by R. A. Rebholz.
0-14-042227-7   560 pp. $7.95

William Blake
SELECTED POETRY
Edited and introduced by W. H. Stevenson.
0-14-058596-6   320 pp. $4.95

William Wordsworth
THE PRELUDE: A Parallel Text
Edited and introduced by J. C. Maxwell.
0-14-042214-5   576 pp. $8.95

Ben Jonson
THE COMPLETE POEMS
Edited with preface and notes by George Parfitt.
0-14-042277-3   640 pp. $10.95

PENGUIN USA Academic/Library Marketing, 40 West 23rd Street, New York, N.Y. 10010

DEPARTMENT OF ENGLISH
WASHINGTON UNIVERSITY
THE WRITING PROGRAM

Permanent faculty:

STANLEY ELKIN
DONALD FINKEL
WILLIAM H. GASS
JOHN N. MORRIS
HOWARD NEMEROV
CHARLES NEWMAN

Program director:

ERIC PANKEY

The Writing Program at Washington University is a highly selective Master of Fine Arts program, which involves a demanding curriculum of workshops and traditional academic courses. Seven places in fiction and seven in poetry are offered each year, and generous financial aid is available. Deadline for application and writing sample is December 15, with recommendations and transcripts due no later than January 15. For further information call Eric Pankey (314) 889-5116 or write Washington University, Campus Box 1122, One Brookings Drive, St. Louis, Mo., 63130.

The Poetry Center

of the 92nd Street Y

Calendar of Readings 1989-90

		Single Tickets
September 18	**John le Carré**, master espionage writer	$12
24	**David Hare** and **Michael Weller**, prominent playwrights	$10
25	**William Maxwell** and **Mavis Gallant**, American and Canadian fiction writers	$ 8
October 2	**Margaret Drabble** and **Julian Barnes**, British novelists	$ 8
3	**Harold Pinter** with **Mel Gussow**, British playwright with *NY Times* drama critic	$12
10	**GEOGRAPHIES I: WRITING OF PLACE Writers-at-Work Live Interview:** **Jan Morris** is interviewed by **Leo Lerman**	$ 8
10	**Jan Morris** reads from her work	$ 8
16	**Bharati Mukherjee** and **Mary Gordon**	$ 8
23	**One Art: An Elizabeth Bishop 10th Anniversary Reading** with **Frank Bidart, Mary McCarthy, Sandra McPherson, James Merrill, Octavio Paz, Mark Strand** and **Helen Vendler**	$10
30	**Carolyn Forché** and **Claribel Alegría**	$ 8
November 6	**Umberto Eco**, author of *The Name of the Rose*	$ 8
13	**Alison Lurie** and **Shelby Hearon**	$ 8
20	**John Ashbery** and **James Schuyler**, Pulitzer Prize-winning poets	$ 8
27	Novelists **José Donoso** of Chile and **Luisa Valenzuela** of Argentina	$ 8
December 4	**GEOGRAPHIES II: Annie Dillard**	$ 8
11	**GEOGRAPHIES III: John McPhee** with **Yolanda McPhee**	$ 8
18	**GEOGRAPHIES IV: Writers-at-Work Live Interview:** **Paul Theroux** is interviewed by **George Plimpton**	$ 8
18	**Paul Theroux** and **Peter Matthiessen** read from their work	$10
January 8	**Joyce Carol Oates** and **Richard Ford**	$10
29	**Derek Walcott**, West Indian poet	$ 8
February 5	**Tony Harrison**, British poet and playwright	$ 8
12	**An Evening of Turgenev** with **Irene Worth**	$12
26	**Richard Howard**, Pulitzer Prize-winning poet and translator, reads with poet **Molly Peacock**	$ 8
March 5	**Kurt Vonnegut, Jr.** in a conversation with critic **John Leonard**	$10
12	Czech novelist **Josef Skvorecky** and **Eva Hoffman**, Polish-American author	$ 8
19	**Aharon Appelfeld**, Israeli novelist	$ 8
26	**Robert Pinsky** and **Marilyn Hacker**, poets	$ 8
April 2	**Ann Beattie** and **André Dubus**, American fiction writers	$ 8
8	**Gloria Naylor** and **Josephine Humphreys**	$ 8
23	**John Hollander** and **Edgar Bowers**, poets	$ 8
30	**"Discovery"/** *The Nation* **1990 Poetry Contest Winners**	$ 6
	IRISH LITERATURE FESTIVAL	
May 14	**Seamus Heaney, John Montague, Nuala Ni Dhomhnaill**, Irish poets	$ 8
16	**Paul Durcan, Derek Mahon, Paul Muldoon**, Irish poets	$ 8
21	**William Trevor** and **Edna O'Brien**, Irish fiction writers	$10

For complete information about The Poetry Center's workshops and reading series, please call (212) 415-5760. To charge tickets call (212) 996-1100. The 92nd Street YM-YWHA is an agency of UJA-Federation.

A NIGHT OF MUSIC
Marjorie Sandor

An astounding first collection of stories; a score rich with drama, pathos, tragedy, and the joy that lies beneath the rhythm of lives.

$17.95 (hc), 208 pages, 0-88001-236-6, Fiction, October

GUY DAVENPORT

One of our most exciting and original writers turns his attention to the Balthus masterpieces in a brilliant collection of meditations and musings.

$17.95 (hc), 112 pages, *illustrated*, 0-88001-234-X, Nonfiction, September

TUXEDO JUNCTION: Essays on American Culture
Gerald Early

A report on the seam where black and white cultures meet, it expands the tradition begun with James Baldwin, Richard Wright, and Ralph Ellison.

$19.95 (hc), 320 pages, 0-88001-232-3, Nonfiction, October

FALL 1989

THE ECCO PRESS

ESSENTIAL POETS
Vol. 11
The Essential Burns

Robert Creeley, ed.
$6.00 (pb), 128 pages, 0-88001-194-7, Poetry, October

POEMS 6

Alan Dugan
His first book since the critically acclaimed *New and Collected Poems.*
$17.95 (hc), 80 pages, 0-88001-199-8, *American Poetry Series,* November

ALONG THE ROAD

Aldous Huxley
A literary valise packed with priceless souvenirs from Huxley's many experiences as a traveler.
$8.95 (pb), 272 pages, 0-88001-230-7, *Ecco Travels.* November

THE LIFE OF JESUS

Marcello Craveri
The result of fifteen years of research, it is an authoritative biography of the man called Jesus.
$14.95 (pb), 784 pages, 0-88001-238-2, Nonfiction, November

TALKIN' MOSCOW BLUES

Josef Skvorecky
The first collection in English of his essays, reviews, and interviews.
$12.95 (pb), 384 pages, 0-88001-231-5, Nonfiction. January

THE EDNA LEWIS COOKBOOK

A unique blend of hearty family fare and elegant continental delicacies.
$9.95 (pb), 224 pages, 0-88001-193-9, Cookbook, September

THE GHOSTLY LOVER

Elizabeth Hardwick
"It is mostly Kentucky, as if Henry James had been there, drinking sour mash with William Faulkner."
—*The New York Times*
$8.95 (pb), 288 pages, 0-88001-240-4, Fiction, September

THREE POEMS

John Ashbery
A new paperback edition of one of Ashbery's most idiosyncratic and important works.
$8.95 (pb), 128 pages, 0-88001-227-7, *American Poetry Series.* September

STREAMERS

Sandra McPherson
"Not since Roethke has the life of flowers been so tellingly evoked." —*Poetry*
$7.95 (pb), 112 pages, 0-88001-214-5, *American Poetry Series,* September

BOY ON THE STEP

Stanley Plumly
The poet's power as an observer of the world, of nature and family, is keenly felt in this, his sixth collection of poems.
$17.95 (hc), 72 pages, 0-88001-228-5, *American Poetry Series,* October

THE SOVEREIGN GHOST

Denis Donoghue
One of our foremost literary critics investigates the questions raised by imagination.
$8.95 (pb), 240 pages, 0-88001-239-0, Nonfiction, January

K. S. IN LAKELAND

Michael Hofmann
Britain's most talented young poet in his U.S. literary debut.
$17.95 (hc), 144 pages, 0-88001-197-1, *Modern European Poets,* January

THE ECCO PRESS 26 West 17th Street, New York, N.Y. 10011 (212) 645-2214
Distributed by W. W. Norton & Company, Inc. 500 Fifth Avenue, New York 10110
In Canada: Penguin Books Canada Ltd., 2801 John Street, Markham, Ontario L3R 1B4
In London: W. W. Norton & Company Ltd., 37 Great Russell Street, London WC1B 3NU, ENGLAND